Practical
Investigation
of
Sex Crimes

A Strategic and
Operational Approach

CRC SERIES IN
PRACTICAL ASPECTS OF CRIMINAL AND FORENSIC INVESTIGATIONS

VERNON J. GEBERTH, BBA, MPS, FBINA *Series Editor*

Practical Investigation of Sex Crimes

A Strategic and Operational Approach

Thomas P. Carney

CRC PRESS

Boca Raton London New York Washington, D.C.

Library of Congress Cataloging-in-Publication Data

Carney, Thomas P., 1950-
  Practical investigation of sex crimes : a strategic and operational approach / by Thomas
P. Carney.
    p. cm. — (CRC series in practical aspects of criminal and forensic investigations)
  Includes index.
  ISBN 0-8493-1282-5 (alk. paper)
    1. Rape—Investigation—United States. 2. Sex crimes—Investigation—United States. 3.
Criminal investigation—United States. I. Title. II. Series.

  HV8079.R35C37 2003
  363.25'953—dc22
                                                                              2003055429

Visit the CRC Press Web site at www.crcpress.com

© 2004 by CRC Press LLC

No claim to original U.S. Government works
International Standard Book Number 0-8493-1282-5
Library of Congress Card Number 2003055429
Printed in the United States of America 1 2 3 4 5 6 7 8 9 0
Printed on acid-free paper

Dedication

This book is dedicated to the many men and women who must contend with the horrific crime of sexual assault; to the victims of these horrendous attacks, whose suffering extends way beyond the attacks themselves; to the medical professionals and social workers who are trained to deal with sexual assault victims while collecting vital evidence for the police; to the sensitive men and women of the sex crime units who balance the needs of the victim with those of the prosecutors in order to bring the offender to justice; and, finally, to the prosecutors who persevere through the legal system to bring about just results.

Editor's Note

This textbook is part of the "Practical Aspects of Criminal and Forensic Investigation" series. This series was created by Vernon J. Geberth, New York City Police Department Lieutenant Commander (Retired), who is an author, educator, and consultant on homicide and forensic investigation. This series has been designed to provide contemporary, comprehensive, and pragmatic information to the practitioner involved in criminal and forensic investigation by authors who are nationally recognized experts in their respective fields.

Introduction

Throughout this text the victim is often referred to as female and the perpetrator as male. This is not to suggest that the roles cannot be reversed, nor is it an attempt to discount the seriousness of an attack on a male victim. The terms are merely used for simplicity's sake, as the vast majority of sex crime victims are female and the vast majority of perpetrators are male. By no means does this imply that forcible sex crimes committed against men or same-sex attacks are subordinate in any way. Such attacks are as grave and as appalling as those perpetrated against women by men; they are, however, far fewer in number. The investigative steps outlined in this text can be applied to all types of sex crimes. The same issues arise in each, the same investigative techniques can be employed, and the same need for emotional support is necessary.

The accounts chronicled throughout the text are all true. The names have been changed, but all of the cases are accurate accounts of sexual assault or reported sexual assaults. The purpose of their inclusion is to illustrate relevant points and to generate discussion within an academic setting.

Developing distinctive approaches to deal with the issues that arise from sexual assault investigations is an essential function of all sex crime units. Without these approaches, vital evidence could be lost and the case could not withstand the thorough examination mandated by the court process. This book is designed to give investigators the advantage of not only my years of experience in sex crime investigations but also that of my detectives. Through their ingenuity and their dedication they have taught me a great deal. Together, we have developed successful methods to address the unique issues that have been encountered in sex crime cases over the years. It is hoped that this knowledge and the collective experience will provide readers with the skills they need to develop cases that not only end in an arrest but also withstand the scrutiny of the court process. If we, the investigators, hand prosecutors a faulty product, we cannot blame them or the court system when they fail to convict. The fault for that failure lies solely with us.

It is common knowledge that rape is a highly unreported crime, particularly when it involves an acquaintance or a domestic partner. It is estimated that only one in four attacks is ever reported. Compelling reasons exist for victims not to report these rapes, including the victim's emotional state, her feelings of guilt, her wish not to be victimized again, and her fear that she will not be believed. Understanding the victim and her motivation is necessary as investigators search for the truth. A chapter devoted to the victim has been included to help investigators in this area.

This book outlines various methods that have been developed over the years to obtain corroboration in sexual assault cases. These methods give investigators the tools they need to substantiate the victim's allegation in a manner that will withstand legal challenges, thus preventing the release of sexual predators who will most surely strike again.

The issue of false allegations is also discussed, and an investigative course of action is provided to uncover and deal with these situations. In the end, each investigation is an attempt to uncover the truth. The truth will either convict or exonerate the accused. If uncovering the truth helps convict a sex offender, then the investigator will have done the victim and society a great service. If, on the other hand, the truth exonerates the accused, the investigator will have prevented corruption of the legal system by the accuser and cleared an innocent person.

The purposes of this book are many. It is designed to explain the techniques required to balance the many demands cited, including obtaining the corroboration needed in a legal and proper manner. The discussion provided here should help investigators understand the different types of investigations required for sexual assaults and should prepare investigators to overcome the obstacles they will encounter. If we can console the victim, corroborate her account, and gather all possible evidence, we will have taken an enormous leap toward bringing the offender to justice. Validation of the victim's allegation by a thorough investigation not only facilitates the prosecution's argument against the offender but also gives the victim some of her dignity back by openly proclaiming that she was not at fault — a reaction that is sadly all too common among rape victims.

Ultimately, a great deal of satisfaction can be derived from investigating sex crimes. Experienced sex crime investigators are aware of the gratification that comes from executing their duties successfully. Each investigation leading to an arrest and successful prosecution can be enormously rewarding to those charged with solving the case. The victims are often the most vulnerable in our society, and they deserve the very best from those of us who are charged with the responsibility of investigating their assaults. We owe them the small amount of justice and closure that can come from the legal system.

I recommend reading the entire book and then returning to selected chapters or specific sections that may help enhance an agency's fight against sexual assault. In this way, the reader will gain a better understanding of the many obstacles unique to sex crimes and will be able to then concentrate on improving specific areas that require more attention.

The Author

Tom Carney grew up in the streets of New York City in the Washington Heights area of Manhattan. He spent 30 years in the New York City Police Department (NYPD), and with his wife, Elizabeth raised five children (Brendan, Sean, Kerry, Colleen, and Kieran). His career ended due to an injury sustained while subduing a suspect. That injury forced him to retire, but his passion for finding justice and for ensuring that others understand the unique aspects of sex crime investigations led him to write this book.

During Tom's tenure at NYPD, he received 37 department awards for acts of heroism, including NYPD's second highest award, the Combat Cross. He was assigned to many different areas of law enforcement and commanded several units within the Detective Bureau. He spent the last 5 years of his career as the Commanding Officer of the Manhattan Special Victims Squad, which is responsible for investigating all sex crimes and child abuse cases within Manhattan's 22 police precincts.

Tom started his career in 1970 and worked his way through the ranks to the position of Lieutenant. He spent time within the Patrol Bureau, the Special Operations Division, the Intelligence Division, and the Detective Bureau. Tom commanded a unit of the Intelligence Division and the 32nd Precinct Detective Squad before being tapped to command the Manhattan Special Victims Squad.

Lieutenant Carney holds an undergraduate degree in Criminal Justice from the State University of New York and a graduate degree in Public Administration from Marist College where he received the faculty award for his academic achievements. He has given lectures for NYPD's Sex Crime Course and the Criminal Investigation Course.

During Lieutenant Carney's 5-year tenure at the helm of the Manhattan Special Victims Squads, he handled more than 1500 cases each year. His command consisted of more than 30 detectives and supervisors in one of the most high-profile and media-intense detective squads in New York City. He coordinated the successful investigation of many high-profile sex crime cases, and his expertise in these investigations is beyond question. He has testified numerous times in court and has personally effected and supervised thousands of arrests in his career.

Contents

The Need
for Specialization

1

During my 30 years with the New York Police Department, I found my time as the Commanding Officer of the Manhattan Special Victims Squad to be unique — the most rewarding and the most difficult. My eyes were opened to an aspect of law enforcement that few experience and few understand. When I first took command of this squad, I was unaware of the unique type of investigations for which I was now responsible. Investigating sex crimes and child abuse within Manhattan's 22 precincts (New York City's five Boroughs are comprised of 76 precincts) turned out to be an unparalleled field of the investigative domain for which there were few rules and even fewer experts to consult. Like the typical investigator and the typical police official before me, I had neglected to grasp the distinctive nature of these investigations. The devastating impact to the victim (both emotionally and physically) and the consequences of a substandard investigation are significant.

Anyone new to the field of sex crimes will quickly learn that keeping an open mind to new and creative methods of investigation is vital to success. An effective unit will develop methods to deal with the many extraordinary situations that they face on a daily basis. They will find that the day-to-day routine of handling serious cases is hindered by delays in reporting, lack of evidence, guilt and shame felt by the victims, intoxication of victims, prior victim/perpetrator relationships, and much more. Awareness that these situations are common gives investigators an appreciation for the need to develop new and different approaches that are not required for the investigation of criminal activity that does not involve sexual assaults.

Many of those experienced, as I was, in homicide, robbery, burglary, and wiretap investigations are easily lulled into a false sense of security regarding their knowledge of the investigative field. Although many similarities do exist, conducting a rape investigation requires different skills and a proficiency in areas that are unique to this type of investigation. Unfortunately, however, many investigators have only a limited awareness of the issues that emerge in sex crime investigations and are not prepared to address them when they arise. The general consensus among newly assigned sex crime investigators is that although these investigations are sensitive, they are essentially the same as any other type of investigation; they only differ in the need to console victims in an unusually sympathetic manner. Nothing can be further from the truth. Investigators will soon become aware of the many aspects unique to sex crime investigations and will find that applying normal investigative techniques is a woefully inadequate approach.

Case History 1

This is a true story of two individuals caught in a difficult situation; unfortunately, their predicament is not an uncommon one. I have seen it repeated over and over again in my years of investigating sex crimes, each time with the same outcome. It is a frequent problem that challenges investigators to look beyond the accusations to uncover the truth and to affix responsibility. The names and locations have been changed, but the facts, I assure you, are accurate.

The Crime

John was a 21-year-old college student at a large university. He gained status in the school as a two-time all-American wrestler, and his friendly personality made him well known and liked by a sizeable portion of the student body. He was a good student, and he aspired to dedicate his talents to the political arena after going on to law school. His winning personality and his exceptional grades seemed to equip him superbly for his future aspirations.

One October evening in his senior year, John was out with a group of friends, both male and female, at a local pub. Many students frequented the pub, and on that particular night John and Mary, a 22-year-old senior, were attracted to each other. They had known who each other was during their years at the same college, but on that particular night they decided to seek each other's company. They eventually left the bar together, bought a bottle of wine, and walked arm in arm to Mary's apartment. Once in her apartment, they found that they were not alone. Mary's roommate, Jane, was home but she was asleep in her own bedroom. John poured two glasses of wine, while Mary turned on some music. They sat on the couch, drank the wine, and talked for a while. Mary, however, cannot remember what happened after that. She awoke the next morning naked, lying in her own bed. Lying next to her was John, who was also naked and still asleep. The sensation in her vaginal area was consistent with having had sex, but she could not recall the act itself or anything that happened after she drank the wine the night before.

She was worried about what had occurred and thought that John had somehow taken advantage of her without her consent. (*Note:* If John had sex with Mary while she was incapacitated, then he could be charged with rape.) While John was still asleep, Mary dressed and went to the next room to wake her friend, Jane. Mary asked Jane if she had heard or seen anything that might help her remember what happened the night before. Jane recalled that she heard Mary come in with John, but she did not hear anything unusual, just the music playing and the two of them talking on the couch.

As Jane listened to Mary's account of the previous evening, she became convinced that John had drugged Mary's wine. Both Jane and Mary had heard of the ease with which one can obtain date-rape drugs (Rohypnol and gamma-hydroxybutyrate [GHB] are the most common types; see Chapter 6), and they feared that Mary had become the latest victim. Mary became terribly concerned and went to the hospital with Jane, where they called the police.

Mary told the emergency room staff that she believed a friend may have drugged her and that she may have been raped while she was unconscious. She told them that she could not remember the sex act, but her vaginal sensation was consistent with intercourse. Mary had been sexually active and was confident that intercourse did take place. She suspected that her friend, John, had taken advantage of her while she was incapacitated. The medical personnel in the emergency room prepared a rape kit and took a urine sample to test for the presence of drugs. The attending physician confirmed that there appeared to be semen present in her vagina and that her vaginal wall showed signs of trauma that was consistent with penetration by a penis. The police then responded to the hospital and took Mary's statement. They also interviewed the attending physician, confirming that the medical findings were consistent with intercourse. The physician also informed the police that there were no signs of injury (bruising, trauma) that would indicate the victim was forcibly raped. The investigators then took possession of the rape kit and the urine sample to have them analyzed.

Meanwhile, John had awakened in Mary's bed and was surprised to find that he had been left alone. Not knowing where Mary was, he dressed and went back to his dorm room some five blocks away. Once there, he showered and began to prepare for his next class that afternoon. During that time, the police responded with Mary to her apartment to apprehend John and to retrieve the wine glasses for testing. They recovered the wine glasses and the bottle of wine but discovered that John was no longer there. An hour later, they then found him in his dorm room, and asked him to accompany them to the police station for questioning.

John agreed after hearing that he was suspected of raping Mary and decided that he would willingly talk with the police without an attorney present. He felt that he had not done anything wrong and that his candor would put a quick end to the investigation and any subsequent embarrassment that was sure to come from a charge of rape. At the station house, John's description of the prior evening corresponded exactly with Mary's up to the point that Mary could remember. John, however, was able to fill in the period for which Mary could not. He recounted that after they drank the wine, they began to kiss and that Mary enthusiastically led him to the bedroom where they engaged in consensual sexual intercourse without the use of a condom. John added that both he and Mary had had a considerable amount to drink during the evening and that Mary had become very uninhibited once they arrived at her apartment. In fact, John stated that Mary had been the aggressor and instigated the sexual encounter. He described how their sexual relations lasted for over an hour, with mutual enjoyment for both.

The police arrested John for rape, citing that John had admitted that he had sex with Mary and Mary asserted that she could not remember the events and was therefore incapacitated. They further noted that the wine glasses, the wine bottle, and the victim's urine sample were all at the lab being tested and that when the results were known their case would be proven beyond a reasonable doubt.

The next day, John's picture appeared on the front page of the city's largest paper, and, due to his status as an all-American athlete, his photograph also appeared in the sports section of every paper throughout the country. He was subsequently suspended from both school and the wrestling team pending the outcome of the criminal proceedings. Meanwhile, the local press and the school used this incident to highlight the need to alert young women that the use of date-rape drugs was on the rise. Several articles were published in both the school paper and the local press to expose the dangers of date rape to women. They used this incident as a prime example of the risks that young women take when they visit the college bar scene. John's name soon became synonymous with date-rape drugs, and even his friends began to doubt his innocence.

Two months transpired before the toxicology tests were completed on all of the items. No drugs were found. The wine glasses and the wine bottle contained nothing but wine, and Mary's urine sample only showed elevated levels of alcohol. The charges against John were soon dismissed in court for lack of evidence. His suspension was lifted, and he was allowed to return to his full academic and athletic schedule. Some of the newspapers printed the court dismissal in small articles within their sport sections. Most, however, did not even do that. Mary now realizes that she was too drunk to remember the incident and that John did not rape her. The damage, however, was done. To those who knew all the facts, John was vindicated. To the vast majority who did not, John was still ostracized. His reputation has been seriously damaged. He was a well-known and well-liked student who was looked up to by his peers. He had also been a local hero in his hometown. Younger athletes saw him as someone they wanted to emulate. Parents now discouraged any attempt by their children to replicate John's success on or off the field.

John had spent the previous summer working in the U.S. Senate, and he had aspirations of becoming involved in politics when he finished law school. Those aspirations, however, have changed due to his arrest. He understands that his reputation has been destroyed and that he will never be able to fully recover his good name.

Discussion

The following questions arise from this incident: Was Mary incapacitated during the sex act? If not, was she raped, or was she a willing participant, as John claimed? Could any other investigative steps have been taken to answer these questions? Were the investigators relying merely on the allegation of rape to support their actions and not looking beyond that to build a case that could hold up to prosecutorial scrutiny? Can the investigators be accused of conducting a shoddy investigation?

Although John and Mary have gotten on with their lives, their case presents a common dilemma for those of us investigating sex crimes. When faced with horrendous crimes such as rape, do we give the benefit of the doubt to the victim or to the violator? Do we take the victim's side and believe her, even if the violator's side is more plausible? Or, do we take the suspect's side and believe him, perhaps giving a sexual predator the freedom to attack again?

The answers lie in the investigation. In our scenario, Mary never claimed that she had been raped. She suspected that she was, but was not sure. She merely recounted the events of the prior evening to the police, and in her account she blacked out after drinking the wine. When she awoke the next morning she was naked. She was lying next to John, who was also naked, and she had the sensation that she had had sex. The police made a judgment, albeit a wrong one, that Mary must have been drugged. An argument could also have been made that the police felt that Mary was so incapacitated that she was unable to consent and that her incapacity to consent supported a charge of rape — a difficult hypothesis to prove based on the information they had from both Mary and John.

Because only two people were in the room at the time of the incident, and the only one able to recall the incident (John) states that Mary was the sexual aggressor, the assertion that Mary was raped is virtually impossible to prove through normal investigative methods. The safety of the victim, however, is primary, and any delay that would place her in jeopardy must be measured. The following questions should have been considered first: Is Mary in any further danger from John? Does he have access to her apartment? Is he stalking her? Is he a threat to flee? Do any physical injuries or medical evidence support the suggestion that force was used? Because the only physical evidence that would support the supposition that Mary was drugged are the urine sample and the wine glass, does any other evidence exist that would support an immediate arrest?

In this case, the answer to all of these questions was *no*, even though the analysis of the rape kit will confirm that John and Mary had sexual intercourse. Remember, John contends that the act was consensual. Consequently, the investigatiors should have postponed the arrest until a case could be built to support their rape charge. Such a postponement would have given them adequate time to complete a thorough investigation — an investigation that would gather all evidence possible and one that would build a case against the alleged perpetrator without alerting him to the existence of an investigation. If that investigation were to uncover additional evidence to support an arrest, then one should have been made. If, however, the investigation exonerated the accused, then an arrest would not have been made. In either event, we, as investigators, owe it to society and to those involved to use every means at our disposal to uncover the truth. In our case, Mary was only seeking the truth, not to punish an innocent person. It was the police that carried it to the next step, not Mary. Once the truth is determined, it is that truth that will determine the need for an arrest or the need to exonerate.

Liability

Overlooking this window of opportunity left the police open to civil liability from Mary, John, and the university. The victim and the alleged perpetrator suffered damages. They were both ostracized by their peers — Mary, for allegedly making up an outrages fabrication against a well-liked acquaintance, and John, for the suspicion that an arrest for a hideous crime such as rape brings. Although the charges against John were dropped, his arrest on rape charges had extensive implications. He suffered from the embarrassment brought on by the national publicity associated with his arrest; he suffered social ostracism by his peers, particularly female friends; he endured a highly publicized suspension from school; and he abandoned his future aspirations of a life dedicated to politics. He knows that any attempt to enter public office in the future would be met with suspicion once his past arrest for forcible rape was known. The university's image suffered because of the rape of another student by a scholarship athlete, an image that would hurt its financial standing with supporters. It appears that the police will be kept busy defending their actions in civil court for some time, all because they never attempted to find the truth. They simply made an arrest based on what they perceived was an allegation. Although Mary is sorry for what transpired, she cannot change what happened to John, nor is she to blame for it. She merely told the truth. She informed the police that she thought she may have been drugged and raped, not that she knew she was. The blame falls upon those conducting the faulty investigation and with those who rushed to effect an arrest. Understanding that the victim was not in danger of another attack, the investigators could have postponed the arrest and utilized the investigative techniques outlined in the following chapters to build a case against John.

Impact on Community

Rape Fuels Fear in Rosedale (*New York Daily News*, October 22, 1999)

Fear of Rapist Stalks Upper West Side (*New York Daily News*, February 25, 2001)

Walk to Subway Turns to Terror for Bronx Woman (*New York Daily News*, April 9, 1999)

The fear of sexual assault, particularly when committed by strangers, has had wide implications for our society that extend beyond the physical and emotional trauma of the victim to impacting entire communities. A rapist who attacks a stranger will certainly attack again, and the impact of a serial rapist has consequences that extend throughout all social interaction. The resultant fear can create a climate that affects the collective behavior of an entire community as it adapts to the perceived threat. Heterosexual relationships and individual lifestyles are strained. Changes are mandated to remain safe, and young, active, single women, particularly those who travel alone late at night, are extremely vulnerable. They are not only susceptible to an attack from a stranger but are also vulnerable to acquaintance attacks due to their youth and the frequency of shared social experiences. Their exposure to date rape situations is a real and constant worry that can come from both new and old acquaintances. The frequency with which they have become rape victims attests to this vulnerability. Consequently, no parent alive today does not fear sending a daughter off to college or to live on her own. Parents ask themselves if they have taught their daughters enough to recognize the signs of potential trouble and if they have armed them with enough knowledge to avoid threatening situations. Also, they wonder if their daughters will become victims despite their guidance.

Impact on Police

Police Failed Women During Park Attacks (*New York Amsterdam News*, June 22, 2000)

NYPD Blew It As Media's Wolfpack Converges and Photos Fan Flames of Hate in Central Park Attack (*New York Amsterdam News,* June 22, 2000)

These headlines appeared after a series of sexual assaults occurred in New York's Central Park after an ethnic parade up Fifth Avenue. Accordingly, many police departments, colleges, businesses, and other institutions have felt the pressure of the media and have been forced to take extraordinary steps to address the issue of sexual assault. The fear caused when these crimes occur can undermine the confidence of an entire community, business, or institution and impact the quality of life for all.

Because everyone can feel the effects of this type of crime, unsolved rape cases will erode the public's confidence in its police force faster than any other crime. Not only does such a crime force women to change their habits out of fear of being attacked, but it also forces their male acquaintances to become increasingly protective as the threat continues. Police departments nationwide recognize that unsolved rape investigations have a direct impact upon their public image. They know that as long as the public's demand for results goes unfulfilled, support for the police is sure to plummet. They also know that fundamental changes within the investigating agency itself may be forced upon them if they do not address the public's concerns in some way. An all-out war against the threat, utilizing every available resource, is the only response possible for the police. Likewise, businesses and institutions have the same concerns as the general public and will also need to address the threat. Tactics to be employed in these cases are discussed in Chapter 7.

Prior relationships between suspects and their victims often cause problems that demand a different investigative approach. Although sex crimes have emerged as one of the most difficult to prove, agencies that have established specialized units with trained investigators to address this need have enjoyed much success. Simply dedicating personnel to full and exhaustive investigations, however, is not enough. Various advocate groups have rightfully advanced the need to address the impact of sexual assault upon the victim both physically and emotionally. Their influence has convinced the majority of the public of the need to deal with victims of sexual assault in a more sensitive and caring manner. Such advocates correctly argue that victims will accept the demands of the investigation if their needs are addressed adequately. Also, the public's perception that the needs of victims are not being addressed adequately can offset any gain that may be attained by making an arrest. Accusations of insensitivity can spur a public demand for more responsive police tactics and can generate a media bias against the police that will be difficult to overcome.

Pressure to force the police to take a more responsive stance can come from many sides. When rape victim advocates and community activists portray the police as unqualified, unable, and even unwilling to address a problem that is primarily a women's issue, a larger spectrum of the community will become involved. And, when arrests fail to produce successful prosecutions, media and political attention is sure to follow and force a change in policy. The animosity created by forcing the issue, however, can have a long lasting and deleterious effect upon the police. The public perception of incompetence and arrogance will take time to overcome and their confidence may never be fully restored.

Case History 2

In 1986, a Toronto woman was raped inside her apartment after her masked attacker scaled her balcony window and forcibly subdued her at knifepoint. She had become the fifth victim of the same rapist. The victim was determined to fight back and wanted to alert the other women in the neighborhood about the existence of the rapist. The police advised her that alerting the public would only make matters worse. The female population would become hysterical, and it would be more difficult for the police investigation. The suspect was eventually caught and sentenced to a 20-year jail term, but the victim sued the Toronto Police Department for their failure in this matter. A judge agreed that the police were "grossly negligent" in their investigation of the balcony rapist and in their long-standing treatment of rape victims. A judgment against the police forced them to pay a substantial sum to the victim. Their reputation, however, with the citizens of Toronto will take much longer to recover.

Corroboration

In the past, corroboration of an attack was required before a rape arrest could be made, a requirement that stems from old English law and one that did not change until the early 1970s. These past practices demanded that various levels of corroboration be established in order to prosecute sexual assault cases in court. Fortunately, they have given way to a more enlightened approach. During the 1970s (the 1980s in some states), the archaic prerequisites of corroboration were removed from state penal codes and never considered again. Today, prosecutors can convict solely on the testimony of the victim. Yet, like any other evidence, that testimony can be disputed by the defense. The defense team can attempt to impugn the victim's credibility by offering the jury a reasonable explanation for their client's actions and by establishing that the sexual encounter was consensual and the victim was a willing partner. The suspect's contention leaves the jury no alternative but to weigh the credibility of the victim against that of the violator. At the same time, however, the jury is bound by a legal system that mandates that proof be established beyond a reasonable doubt in order to convict. Consequently, collecting evidence that can substantiate the victim's allegation becomes paramount and can make the difference between a conviction and an acquittal. Establishing expert sex crimes units to deal with the victim and to gather corroborative evidence is essential to any department's success.

The expertise of the sex crimes units in New York has created many successes for which the NYPD can be proud. In all of them, the Special Victims Squad was integral in corroborating the victim's allegations. Their achievements are evident in the many headlines that proclaim their successes:

Suspect Is Arrested in Rape of Girl, 10 (*New York Times*, April 16, 1996)

Man Charged with Raping Date He Met From E-Mail (*New York Times*, February 24, 1997)

Former Teacher's Aide Is Arrested in Rape (*New York Times*, August 1, 1997)

Man Held in Weekend Attacks on Four Women in Brooklyn (*New York Times*, September 4, 2000)

Rape Suspect Nabbed (*New York Post*, April 24, 2000)

Arrest Has Women Feeling Safer (*New York Post*, April 9, 1999)

Cops Nab E. Harlem Slay and Rape Suspect in Fla. (*New York Post*, February 20, 1999)

Cops Honored for Nabbing Rape Suspect (*New York Daily News*, August 18, 1999)

Student Charged with Sex Torture (*New York Daily News*, December 7, 1996)

The arrest of suspects in cases lacking physical or corroborative evidence are extremely difficult to prove in court, but are sometimes unavoidable.

Fortunately, however, investigators often have sufficient time to collect vital evidence before it disappears, even in these cases. The key is to know what evidence is needed and how to gather it. Ignoring the physical evidence or failing to obtain corroboration does a grave disservice to the victim, to society, and to the institutions the police serve, not to mention that it allows rapists to roam freely to strike again.

Experience has shown that the lack of corroboration is generally caused by the reliance of investigators on conventional methods of investigation — methods that fail to take into account the psychological state of the victim, the importance of corroborative evidence, and the various methods that can be used to obtain that corroboration. Understanding that these investigations are dramatically different from any other type of investigation and that they require a profoundly different approach is fundamental to the success of investigators. Utilizing the various tactics discussed in this book can enhance the typical investigation by providing the added proof necessary for a conviction.

Impact of Sexual Assault of Children

Except for murder, sexual assault (predominantly forcible rape and sodomy) is probably the most serious crime that any investigator will encounter. These crimes are even more egregious when they involve children. Not only do they impact the victims physically, but they also leave psychological scars that affect the victims the rest of their lives. Unlike other crimes, sexual assaults are extremely personal and often cause severe emotional stress in its victims that can lead to subsequent emotional problems, particularly posttraumatic stress disorder (PTSD). Children are especially vulnerable to PTSD and may also suffer from myriad problems that go far beyond those of their adult counterparts.

The sexual assault of children is an extremely sensitive aspect of child abuse and mandates a particularly sensitive approach. The interview process and the collection of evidence are only possible when multiple areas of expertise work in tandem to minimize the trauma to the victim. Those areas include the medical field, the social services, the prosecutors, and the police. Each field brings its own level of expertise to the table, and each can make a difficult process effective, supportive, and as tolerable as possible. This multidisciplinary approach has yielded positive results in the past and has become the model for investigation of child molestation.

Dealing with these profound issues and bringing sex offenders to justice is not an easy task for the investigator. It takes a special type of individual to be able to cope with the victim, examine the evidence, and obtain evidence while building a case against the violator. It also requires a unique type of investigation, one that will not only manage the delicate issues involving the victim but will also help support the victim's account.

District Attorney

Just as the need for specialization within a police department is obvious, so is the need for specialization within the District Attorney's office. Cases like the one discussed earlier in this chapter (Case History 1) are not uncommon, and it is imperative to have attorneys who have knowledge of the issues that arise in sex crimes. They will be called upon to evaluate the evidence, assist investigators in obtaining search warrants when necessary, and prosecute the defendant in court when an arrest is made. They, like the investigators, will have to deal with the physical and psychological needs of the victim during the court process, a process that can be devastating to the victim if she is not prepared for what she will face. Clearly, the needs of the victim and the strains that the system puts on the victim mandate specialization in this field.

Hospital Staff, Social Workers, Rape Advocates

Women seeking help at hospital emergency rooms are often confronted with a staff knowledgeable about treating women who have had unprotected sexual relations, but who are not familiar with the psychological needs of sexual assault victims or the forensic needs of the police. During my tenure investigating sex crimes, many of the major hospitals in Manhattan came to realize their deficiency in this area, and they soon began to specialize. They established medical response teams dedicated to treating rape victims and placed them on call 24 hours a day. Each team consists of a trained medical staff to manage the many aspects of rape: They know how to cope with the psychological trauma that the victim is suffering, and they provide the initial counseling she will need. They have access to sources of long-term therapy and can make recommendations to the patient. They are familiar with the needs of the police, and they know how to obtain forensic evidence. Finally, they are willing to testify in court, if necessary.

What Is Sexual Assault?

2

Definitions

Knowing the elements that constitute the different levels of sexual assault is obligatory for those involved in the investigative process, for it is the law that empowers us to act against offenders and to protect the innocent. Each state has defined what constitutes a sexual offense within its penal code, and although they differ in many ways they are very similar in substance. Unwanted sexual contact is a crime in every state. The specific action that constitutes that assault, however, must fall within a legal state statute for the police to take action. What is offensive may be legal, and what is morally wrong may be within the law.

Public Perception

Defining rape is not always easy. Advocates often maintain that unwanted sexual contact is a crime, but their definition of *unwanted* often does not fall within the legal parameters that govern our authority to act. Their outrage is understandable from a moral perspective, but the law does not always limit reprehensible sexual conduct perpetrated against those they are trying to protect. A young woman who is questioning her alcohol impaired judgment the morning after may have clearly been taken advantage of, but the circumstances may or may not constitute rape. Bourque (1989) studied the various definitions given for rape and noted that the belief that a rape has occurred varies widely based upon people's social status, their education, their perceptions of and attitudes toward violence and sexuality, and their attitudes toward and behaviors regarding those around them. Bourque argues that the determination to classify an attack as rape is often based upon the perception of those making the decision, and that those perceptions are influenced by sociological and psychological experiences. Bourque also found that historical information about the victim or the perpetrator could sway one's opinion of whether a rape occurred or not. For example, knowledge that the victim is a nun or that the suspect has a sordid past with arrests for various crimes tends to sway opinion about whether or not a rape did indeed occur.

Experience has shown that the public, particularly those with little knowledge of the law (some highly educated), have a wider definition of what constitutes rape than those of us in law enforcement. Publicized surveys often complicate matters by giving credence to expanded applications of the concept of rape. For example, definitions of rape in a survey may be limited to cases of forced vaginal intercourse or they may include anal or oral penetration, consensual penetration while intoxicated, or attempts to force sex that are stopped (touching that is stopped with a stern *no* by the victim). Clearly, the public's perception may not agree with what the legal community considers rape. This often poses a communication problem that necessitates attention to detail when speaking with victims. Simply asking the question "Were you raped?" can result in many different answers, as well as confusion for both victims and investigators.

The public's perception of what constitutes a sexual assault and the degree of the problem may often be distorted, but that collective perception must be clearly understood, as it can help investigators assess the value of evidence that will be presented to members of a jury. Although determining whether a rape occurred or not will be based upon legal precedent, the decision to proceed will be determined by an evaluation of the evidence, the credibility of that evidence in the eye of a juror (who is an untrained member of the public), and ultimately in the need to prosecute as determined by the District Attorney.

Legal constraints that prohibit the prosecution of cases can also impact public perception. Investigators must address the public's inaccurate conclusions in those cases where the police determine that a rape did not occur even though the perpetrator is known because the legal elements of sexual assault are not met. Then there are those instances in which the elements are present but lack of evidence prohibits any further action. Honest and open discussions with the victims can alleviate many of these false impressions. Those in the community and the media can be educated regarding the legal limitations that guide investigators' actions. Such efforts have prompted communities and legislative leaders to change archaic legal requirements that at one time were the norm in sexual assault cases. Such efforts can also serve to ensure that the public does not undermine the ability to investigate and prosecute cases in the future. Failure to address the needs of the public may result in their assertion that the police are not taking sexual assault cases seriously or that they are avoiding the needs of women. Their proclamations will ultimately impugn the reputation of the department and make it more difficult to establish a rapport with victims and witnesses in the future.

It is the investigator's duty to gather all possible evidence in an effort to expose the truth. A detailed account of the incident (including interviews of witnesses), coupled with a complete forensic examination, will help uncover the truth and provide authorities with the facts they need to make a legal determination that will withstand the scrutiny of the criminal justice system and the public.

Looking beyond the Definitions

Laymen would correctly define rape as forced sexual intercourse, but their definition of force will often be at odds with that of the law. Their definition appears uncomplicated and unambiguous and would seem to leave little room for interpretation; but that is where the trap lies. Consider the following account (with names changed).

Case Study

When Jane, a 22-year-old woman, moved to New York City, she rented an apartment in the affluent Upper East Side of Manhattan. She came from a prosperous and prominent political family and was a shy and reserved young woman who was admittedly very naïve about heterosexual relationships. Jane was also a virgin and wished to remain that way.

The Initial Report

She reported to the police that an acquaintance of hers had raped her the day before. She recounted how she met a new boyfriend, Mark, and that she agreed to engage in sexual activity as long as it did not include intercourse. She states that on the previous day they were lying in bed naked and that he shocked her by placing his penis in her vagina even though she had explicitly told him not to. As soon as he did, however, she screamed and forced him to leave her apartment.

Jane then became concerned about contracting a disease and she went to a women's clinic for an examination and tests. A social worker at the clinic told her that because she did not give Mark permission to do what he did, she was a victim of rape. He had penetrated her vagina with his penis even though they had explicitly set limitations on their activity beforehand. A rape kit was prepared by the clinic's medical staff, and they told Jane that it was up to her to report the rape if she wanted.

Jane then went to the local precinct to report the crime, and my office was contacted immediately. I responded with one of my detectives to the precinct squad, where we spoke with Jane in private. At first she was reluctant to tell us the whole story, but her abbreviated version clearly had many holes. There was obviously something she was not telling us. Eventually, with some discreet prodding, she told us the whole story about how Mark had agreed to teach her about sex.

Beyond the Initial Report

A few weeks after arriving in New York, she met 30-year-old Mark, and they dated a few times. She eventually confided that she was a virgin and that she did not wish to have intercourse until she married. She did, however, wish to learn as much as she could about sex. Her new suitor was all too willing to help. Mark proposed to teach her all about sex: how to satisfy a man and how to be satisfied by a man. To do so, however, she would need to cooperate and engage in sexual activity with him. She agreed but insisted that any sexual activity not include intercourse. She consented to engage in all types of sexual activity with Mark, while reasserting that intercourse was not allowed. She insisted that her new boyfriend understand the limitations before they began. He agreed, and they went to her apartment for their first encounter.

They engaged in digital stimulation on that first night. Both enjoyed their experience together, and they agreed to future sessions. They continued to meet daily, and on each occasion they engaged in more intense sexual activity of longer and longer duration. One day, after about two weeks, they met at her apartment for an afternoon of sex. This time the session lasted well over two hours. They started in the bedroom, went into the shower together, and returned to the bedroom, engaging in continual sexual activity along the way. They each experienced multiple orgasms throughout the afternoon and were satisfied with each other's performance.

Finally, they were both lying in bed when Mark began to stimulate Jane's vaginal area with his fingers. She eagerly accepted his advance, her eyes closed and in a state of ecstasy. Suddenly she realized that it was his penis inside her and not his fingers. She immediately stopped him and told him that she had forbidden him from engaging in intercourse and that they had both agreed to the limitation. She was very upset, and she told him that she did not want to see him again. He told her he was sorry, and she asked him to leave at once. He did, and she has not spoken to him since.

Upon hearing Jane's initial account of the incident, there are unfortunately many who would immediately pursue an arrest of Mark without further inquiry. Some in the social sciences field would argue that, despite the mitigating circumstances, Mark *did* rape Jane, and perhaps from a moral perspective he did. He clearly preplanned his actions and was only waiting for the right opportunity to act on them. Jane had definitely set the limitations on their relationship, and Mark crossed that barrier on purpose, taking full advantage of Jane's naïveté. He engaged in sexual intercourse without her consent.

The Law

The problem lies with what our boundaries are under the law, and in a case like this it is always sensible to consult with a legal expert before making a decision one way or the other. We did not consider this particular case a rape, and when we conferred with the District Attorney's Office they confirmed our opinion. Although Jane did not consent to the sexual intercourse and she had previously set the limitations on their activity, her actions, particularly on the day of the incident, indicated otherwise. She engaged in activity that resulted in multiple orgasms for her and for Mark, and when Mark placed his penis in her vagina she did not resist. It is reasonable to assume that Mark believed that Jane had changed her mind and was now consenting to have intercourse with him. Mark's actions after being told to stop indicate that he had no desire to continue without Jane's consent. He immediately stopped the offending action, dressed, and left as requested by Jane. If he had continued after being told (either verbally or through a physical indication by Jane) to stop he would then have been guilty of rape.

I am fully aware that such a position may run contrary to that of many rape advocates. We, however, have to live within the law. It is the legal opinion that Jane's actions indicated to any reasonable person that she was willing to go further in her sexual activity and that, because Mark stopped immediately when Jane indicated her opposition, he was not guilty of raping Jane.

Explaining these facts to the victim was not easy. I showed her the penal code, and I indicated our discussion with the legal experts, but she had been convinced by the social worker that she had been raped and wanted to proceed. She eventually came to understand that a reasonable person would construe her actions as an indication that she was giving consent to Mark to engage in sexual intercourse, even if that was not the case. To back up our decision, the Sex Crime Unit of the District Attorney's Office offered, as they always do, to interview the victim if she wished.

The challenge of this case is the interpretation of the law and knowledge of how the law has been interpreted in the past: In this case, no force was used, the victim was of age to consent, and the victim was not physically helpless; therefore, the actions of Mark did not constitute rape.

Legal Definitions

Forcible rape: Usually described as the act committed by a male in which he has sexual intercourse with a female in one of three ways (sexual intercourse is defined as penetration by the penis of the vulva, no matter how slight): (1) by forcible compulsion; (2) with a female who is physically helpless (includes drug-induced conditions); or (3) with a female who is unable to consent because she is under a certain age (usually around 11 or 12 years old but the specified age differs from state to state). Another person (even a female) can be criminally liable for rape if he or she is an accomplice, even though he or she did not have intercourse with the victim.

Statutory rape: Described as consensual intercourse in which one of the participants is unable to consent because he or she is under a certain age. Typically, different categories of statutory rape reflect the different ages of the male and female participants. Statutory rape normally involves victims less than 17 years of age. The age of the victim can vary from state to state, as can the age of the offender.

Forcible sodomy: Described as deviate sexual intercourse (no matter how slight) with another person in one of three ways: (1) by forcible compulsion; (2) with a person who is incapable of consent by reason of being physically helpless (includes drug-induced conditions); or (3) with a person who is unable to consent because he or she is under a certain age (usually around 11 or 12 years of age). Note that *deviate sexual intercourse* means sexual contact between the penis and anus, the mouth and penis, or the mouth and vagina.

Statutory sodomy: Defined as consensual deviate sexual intercourse between two persons when one of the participants is unable to consent due to his or her age. The same provisions that apply to statutory rape regarding age differences apply to statutory sodomy.

Sexual contact offenses: A number of other sexual contact offenses are described within each states laws. These laws govern sexual contact or the use of a foreign object by: (1) forcible compulsion; (2) with a person who is incapable of consent by reason of being physically helpless (including drug-induced conditions); or (3) with a person is unable to consent because he or she is under a certain age (usually around 11 or 12 years of age).

Consent: The lack of consent is an element in all sex crimes, even in statutory rape and sodomy cases. In those cases, the lack of consent comes from the victim's inability to consent due to her or his age. The lack of consent can come about in different ways:

- Forcible compulsion (*no* means *no*)
- Incapacity or inability of the victim to consent
- Victim being underage
- Victim being mentally incapacitated or defective
- Victim being physically helpless

Bibliography

Bourque, L. B., *Defining Rape*, Duke University Press, Durham, NC, 1989.
New York State Penal Law, Section 130.

Personnel Criteria

3

Every experienced public and private manager will acknowledge that human resources are the most deciding factor in determining the success or failure of their organization. To that end, great care should be taken when assigning personnel to investigate cases that will almost certainly provoke the public's scrutiny and generate demands for immediate results. Sexual assaults clearly fall within this domain. Incidents of sexual assault are sure to have a lasting impact, not only upon the victim and the community, but upon the public's perception of the effectiveness of investigating agency as well. One has only to read the headlines when rapes occur:

Police Seek Rapist on Upper East Side (*New York Times*, October 3, 1996)

Queens Rape Victims Tell of Broken Lives (*New York Daily News*, July 15, 2000)

East Side Sex Suspect Under Arrest (*New York Post*, August 16, 2000)

Sexual Attacks in City Schools Are Up Sharply (*New York Times*, June 3, 2001)

Armed Rapist Strikes on Lower East Side (*New York Post*, November 9, 1998)

Rape Resists Inroads of City's War on Crime (*New York Daily News*, February 23, 1998)

Victim Relives Her Night of Horror Three Years Ago (*New York Post*, August 31, 1998)

With headlines like these, it is imperative that the investigating agencies assign their best personnel to the task; consequently, the choice of personnel can have an enormous impact, not only upon the successful conclusion of the investigation, but also upon the perceptions that are reached by both the victim and the public, whose view of the dedication and competency of the investigating department can have significant consequence. Adverse reactions can snowball and create public relations nightmares simply because the victims and their supporters felt that the initial responding officers or the investigators were not sensitive enough.

Public relations experts may be able to put an end to an immediate crisis, but the long-term impact of not having the proper personnel in key areas of the organization will certainly create a lasting and deleterious impression of how the organization is perceived. As *The Economist* (July, 1997) noted: "Nothing seems to stir people's passions more than their dealings with [a firm's] employees. Whether it is a selfless flight attendant or a clueless switchboard operator, the caliber of the firm's front-line personnel can have a huge impact on its image." Certainly, those who are in key areas such as sex crime investigators will be scrutinized even more. Their ability to do the job in a professional and competent manner will reflect upon the organization as a whole and can create a long-lasting appreciation for its expertise, or it can attest to its insensitivity and inefficiency. The reaction will depend on the quality of the personnel assigned. Consequently, the selection process should not be taken lightly. Blohowiak (1995) noted that "of all the responsibilities you face as a manager, hiring is your most important, not only for your organization but for you personally."

Sexual assault, particularly forcible rape and sodomy, can be described as one of the most hideous and gruesome acts of cruelty that one person can inflict upon another. Other than homicide, investigators will deal with no more cruel or repugnant a crime. Due to the repulsive and vile nature of these attacks, however, the average investigator, like everyone else in society, finds that the subject material generates passionate feelings that can impede his or her abilities. As with the general population, investigators can easily let their emotions take over and lose their sense of objectivity and professionalism. In doing so, they may overlook vital evidence, fail to exploit opportunities, or neglect to clarify embarrassing issues that conflict with the account given by the victim.

Failing to assign sensitive and emotionally supportive investigators who can examine the evidence objectively will only make a difficult situation impossible to manage. Finding the suitable people for this task is not easy. As Cook (1998) concluded, "Selecting anyone important requires longer, more elaborate selection procedures." Picking personnel to investigate sex crimes necessitates that additional criteria be used in the selection process, specifically in the area of personality. It takes certain personal traits, coupled with training and proficiency in the investigative arena, to be successful in this field. Training can be provided and proficiency instilled in a person, but personality changes cannot.

Impediments

A number of impediments can prevent many investigators from becoming experts in the field of sexual assault.

Aversion to Subject Material

In my experience, I have seen that most investigators struggle with the subject material presented to them in sex crime cases. Although many have a plethora of experience interviewing victims of trauma, the interview of sexual assault victims seems to engender deeper emotions that can inhibit individual interviewing skills. They are uncomfortable speaking with victims and their transparent discomfiture often has a twofold affect. First, it prevents them from asking important questions regarding the details of the attack, thus limiting any knowledge of the attacker, and, second, it conveys to the victim that her ordeal is offensive, causing her to become even more uncomfortable with the interview. She will typically avoid any further embarrassment by withholding facts from the investigator, facts that may be important to the investigation. In either case, the investigation will be inhibited by the personal traits that the investigator brings to the interviewing process. Sex crimes can illicit deep emotional responses in all of us that are not easily overcome. Urquiza and Wyatt (1997) conducted a study of those involved in sexual assault interviews. They found that, "A different perspective about why such interviews may be difficult for interviewers primarily involves the personal characteristics that the interviewer brings to the interview process." They also noted that "an important aspect of developing a team of capable interviewers involves careful selection and hiring of interviewers."

Emotional Support and Control

Sex crime investigators should be able to balance the needs of the victims with the needs of the investigation. The ability to be emotionally compassionate while taking control in a highly sensitive situation is a difficult task. Investigators are required to interview victims while they recount what can probably be described as the worst moments of their life. Getting the necessary information entails more than just sorting through the details of the crime. It involves giving the victim emotional support to help her face the need to recount the attack. The impact of sexual assault can also cause the victim to suffer from posttraumatic stress disorder (PTSD), which can manifest itself in both physical and psychological terms. Medical attention that goes beyond the initial emergency treatment is often necessary and can be complicated by insensitive and indifferent investigators who do not realize the extent of the damage they can cause, not only to the victim but to the investigation, as well.

A Different Type of Investigation

Average investigators are unaware that sex crimes require a different type of investigation. They examine the evidence as if it were a homicide, a robbery, or burglary investigation, and they either fail to take into account the emotional state of the victim or are unable to deal with their own emotions effectively. In either case, they frequently fail to access all of the different investigative avenues that will lead them to the truth. Instead of amassing evidence to corroborate the allegations, they focus most of their resources on the whereabouts of the perpetrator and do not focus on the prosecutorial needs of the case. For example, the typical investigator who is confronted with a complaint of rape is usually inclined to accept the victim's version of the incident without question — a generally acceptable approach while investigating robberies, burglaries, and assaults, but one that has negative consequences for sex crime investigations. A longer look by the investigator will often uncover obvious inconsistencies in the victim's version. Witnesses, physical evidence, and factual contradictions made by the victim will necessitate further examination and analysis. (The many legitimate reasons for these inconsistencies, such as guilt, shame, and revictimization, are discussed in Chapter 5).

Limitations of Training

Although training can generally help most investigators overcome these obstacles, some are not able to come to grips with their own emotions and are simply not psychologically suited for the task. Their abilities and their talent may lie in other areas of the investigative arena. Their talent as skilled investigators and their abilities as interrogators are not in question; rather, it is their personality and their ability to deal with victims in this unique area. They may be some of the best detectives within a department, but they are not suited for this particular task.

Recognizing the different nature of these investigations allows the investigator to utilize a broader method of collecting evidence. Changing the approach used by successful seasoned investigators recently assigned to investigate sex crimes, however, is not an easy task. Their successful methods have served them well over the years, and training them in different methods is often difficult and time consuming, but not impossible. Intense training that combines the support of experienced sex crime personnel with an analysis of actual crime situations will make the difference. Demonstrating how new investigators can incorporate the sound techniques they have used in the past to develop a comprehensive strategy for addressing sex crimes will provide them with a way to integrate their own approaches and apply them to the unique demands that await them. The wealth of experience that they possess should not be tossed aside in an effort to make every investigation identical. Talents and abilities differ from investigator to investigator, and, although basic requirements apply to each investigation, the skills of the individual investigator should be exploited and not abandoned. A wise old detective once told me that criminal investigation is an art, and that investigators are all artists. Use your talents as best you can to make your own tapestry.

The uniqueness of sex crime investigations is that they often require more than just the testimony of the victim, especially a victim who may have had a prior relationship with or grudge against her alleged attacker. If we allow investigators to make arrests without building a case or developing sufficient evidence to prosecute, we do a disservice to the victim and provide the violator with a means to escape prosecution. If, on the other hand, we maintain our professionalism and gather all possible evidence, then we will have developed a case that has prosecutorial merit — a case that, like it or not, will usually require more evidence to prove because the offender will almost certainly contradict the victim's account and blame her in some way.

It can be very disconcerting to observe arrests made by well-intentioned but untrained police officers end in dismissal of the charges. Relying only on the statement of a victim, without any corroboration, often places a needless burden on the prosecution. In doing so, the police have clearly stacked the deck against the victim. Unless the victim can provide extremely credible testimony that can overcome the intense cross-examination that is sure to follow, she will watch her attacker walk free. Defense attorneys will dwell on the discrepancies that are sure to arise. A good investigator, however, knows that a case will always have discrepancies (some minor, some important) and failure to expose them during the investigation will create serious problems for the prosecution. It is the trained investigator who exposes those discrepancies beforehand to uncover the truth and thwart attempts to free the attacker.

Qualities of the Sex Crime Investigator

Frequently, the reluctance of many investigators to engage in sex crimes investigations is a result of their inability to deal with the sensitive subject objectively. They are embarrassed by the topic and find it difficult to speak with a victim about the details of the incident. They also find it difficult to articulate certain facts to others, thus inhibiting any discussion that may help solve the crime. This is not to say that they are not excellent investigators. Quite to the contrary, I have seen many first-rate detectives who possess superior investigative skills but are unable to deal with the emotions and content associated with sexual assault investigations. Experience has shown that it takes a specific breed of investigator to be successful in this field, and it is the duty of commanding officers to find those who fit the task. Barry (1997) commented on the responsibilities of leaders and noted, "Leaders take into consideration the fact that each individual comes to the organization with their own set of values and perceptions. An effective leader attempts to blend the individual value system into the organization." Ignoring those values and perceptions will doom the unit to failure.

Compassion and Professionalism

Effective sex crime investigators must be able to show compassion for the victim while maintaining a professional posture. This is a unique field of investigation that requires more than just skill. It requires personal traits that permit investigators to be empathetic with someone suffering extreme emotional anguish while maintaining the composure necessary to collect vital evidence competently. A nurturing approach coupled with experience and training are critical to being assigned to this type of work. *Warning:* It is possible, during the selection process, for management to put too much emphasis on the trait of compassion while ignoring the individual investigator's professional posture. The resultant danger is that management will find themselves with investigators who, although compassionate, are unable to function in an acceptable manner. These investigators fall into one of two risky categories that can cause a great deal of harm to the unit and to the department. The first is the investigator who becomes emotionally attached to a victim; in this case, the investigator loses all perspective and his or her actions become highly unethical. Such an investigator should be removed from the case immediately, before causing the victim further emotional distress or before creating a scandal for which the department will have to share responsibility. The second category is the investigator who lets his or her compassion extend to the suspect, thus creating a situation in which the investigator is more of a social worker than a police investigator. In these instances, the investigator feels compelled to counsel both the subject and the victim in an attempt to mediate the situation instead of building a case against the subject. Although this type of investigator is not as dangerous as the first, such actions are not appropriate and should not be tolerated. We are the police, and our function is not to talk victims out of pursuing criminal action. Instead, we should be helping the victim by getting to the truth and corroborating her accusations. If we cause charges to be dropped, then we hold some responsibility when the same perpetrator attacks the victim again or attacks another individual. Any investigator engaging in this kind of activity should be removed before any harm can come to a victim or to the department.

Ability to Gain Confidence of Victims

The successful investigator gains the confidence of victims by adopting an empathetic approach and a demeanor that elicits positive responses from victims, thus allowing them to delve into the most intimate aspects of their lives and medical conditions. A confident and positive manner can go a long way in soliciting information. Singer et al. (1983) conducted a study of interviewers and found that, "Interviewers whose attitudes were more optimistic achieved significantly higher response rates than those with less sanguine expectations." Because obtaining information from the victim is both essential and problematic in sex crime cases, everything should be done to obtain and then maintain the victim's complete confidence in the handling of her case. The investigator should always be honest with victims and protect them from those who would try to manipulate them. The investigator should also impress upon victims that their cooperation is vital and that a prosecution cannot proceed without them. Failure to maintain the confidence of the victim can easily result in her wish to remove herself from any further dealings with the police or with prosecutors — an unacceptable and avoidable situation that will allow her assailant to roam free and surely attack again.

Nonjudgmental Approach

We all integrate our own principles and ethical standards into our work. They are part of us, and they are part of what establishes who we are, what our priorities are, and how we approach our work. They can often, however, be at odds with the lifestyles observed in some victims. Sex crimes investigators will find that the lifestyles of victims span the spectrum of modern society. Some you may approve of; others you may abhor. In either case, good sex crimes investigators know that *all victims* deserve the investigator's best efforts. And, in order to supply that effort, a nonjudgmental approach to all victims is necessary. Judging victims by one's own standards can be perceived by the victims and will only prevent them from being open and forthright, thereby creating obstacles that may never be overcome. It has been my experience that taking a nonjudgmental approach has allowed me to establish a rapport with victims that has facilitated open and honest discussion. In keeping with this observation, Miller (1997) noted in a study of violence against street prostitutes that by displaying a nonjudgmental demeanor she also was not perceived as a threat and was able to establish a rapport with the women that enabled her to elicit frank discussions about the lives of prostitutes and their treatment by society. A good approach is to treat victims as a medical professional would be expected to treat them — that is, in a knowledgeable, professional, and nonjudgmental way specifically designed to help victims deal with their current ordeal.

Case History

In 1999, Manhattan experienced a pattern of rapes in which a male attacked women on the street. The first attack occurred in a known prostitution location, and the victim was a prostitute. She reported that a male approached her late at night, forced her below the stairway of a brownstone building, and raped her. A few days later, a woman in another part of Manhattan exited a subway late at night and was accosted by the same male. He incorrectly assumed by her dress that she, too, was a prostitute. He forcibly raped her by a phone booth on the corner. The description of the suspect, the open-air locations of the attacks, and the similarities of the victims caused me to declare that a pattern rapist was roaming through-out midtown Manhattan. In addition to the investigative efforts that were being conducted by my command, eight precincts, two housing authority districts (police commands), and two transit districts (police commands) were targeted for intense patrol activity that was directed at searching for and gaining information about the rapist. Sketches were prepared and distributed to all police in the area; detectives addressed the roll calls of the various precincts, transit districts, and housing areas to give as many details as possible to the officers on patrol and to solicit their help in obtaining information from the communities they served. Two days later, the man attacked again. This time he attacked another prostitute, but in a different part of Manhattan. The attack, however, was the same. She was accosted on the street late at night (just before dawn) and forced to walk with the perpetrator to a location between two trash dumpsters near a construction site. She was then raped in the same manner as the other two victims. She waved down a passing patrol car and reported the rape imme-diately. A search was conducted in vain, and my detectives and I responded immediately.

The latest victim was a recent immigrant from South America and she spoke little English. She was skeptical of the police, and although she appeared to be our best witness (she had seen him before and could defi-nitely identify him again) she was reluctant to cooperate. She feared the police because she was an illegal immigrant, and because she was a prostitute she did not think that we would believe her. It took a great deal of persuasion on my part to get her to work with us and help us find the rapist. I treated her with the utmost respect, not judging her occupation or her status as an immigrant. Instead, I showed consideration for her plight, and I made sure that any police officers who came into contact with her were nonjudgmental and gave her the respect she was due as a victim of a violent crime. Our efforts paid off. Two nights later, she spotted the suspect in an all-night delicatessen and called the police. Lineups were conducted, and the other victims also identified the suspect. The suspect was prosecuted for all three cases, and DNA evidence and eyewitness testimony subsequently sent him to jail for 25 years to life.

Knowledgeable and Skilled Investigators

The significance of sex crimes and the impact they can have on communities mandates that only knowledgeable and skilled investigators be considered for assignment. The consequences of allowing unskilled and untrained investigators to run these sensitive investigations are too serious, not only for the victim but for the police as well. Identifying evidence, acknowledging its forensic potential, and pursuing all leads should not be left to the unqualified. Only those who have proven themselves in the past should be considered for assignment. Additional training regarding the needs of victims, where they can obtain psychological support, and how to help victims through the system is needed to augment investigative skills.

Skilled Interrogators

Sex crimes often rely on the abilities of the investigator to interrogate suspects. Gaining the suspect's confidence to induce him to tell his side of the story requires a specific skill. It takes perseverance, patience, and endurance coupled with the ability to connect with the suspect at his own emotional level, for at times the only corroborative evidence available will be the disclosures made by the suspect. A skilled interrogator knows the importance of these disclosures and encourages suspects to unburden themselves of their shame. Such talents endow investigators with the ability to befriend suspects and encourage them to tell their side of the story, a side that often results in a confession or an account that implicates the suspect in some way. Good investigators are capable of both comforting the victim and befriending the suspect — an uncommon combination that is a must for the successful sex crime investigator. Inbau et al. (1986) documented the many techniques necessary to successfully interrogate suspects in their book, *Criminal Interrogations and Confessions*. The authors found that the emotional offender is more receptive to interrogation techniques that are based primarily upon a sympathetic approach. This requires interrogators to express an understanding of and a compassion for the suspect's dilemma, despite their personal feelings regarding the suspect and no matter how appalling and revolting the crime.

Appearance

The emphasis on a professional appearance stems from the benefit that can be achieved when investigators are perceived as expert and authoritative. Projecting a professional image reassures the victim that her complaint is taken seriously and that competent investigators are handling her case. The neat, business-like, well-groomed appearance of these investigators makes the initial interview more palatable for the victim and relays to her a sense that her case is important. Business-like appearances will also give suspects an idea that they are dealing with knowledgeable professionals, not inexperienced officers. Men should wear suits and refrain from displaying earrings or visible tattoos while on duty. Women should wear pantsuits that will allow them to take enforcement action if necessary (skirts or dresses may be acceptable for court appearances, but not during investigations that may lead to enforcement activity). Both men and women should refrain from wearing shoes that would prevent them from engaging in enforcement (platforms, high heels, etc.). Such a dress code can have a positive impact upon the *esprit de corps* of the unit. When deciding what is acceptable and what is not, the benefits that can be achieved by projecting a professional image to suspects and fellow personnel should always be considered before making a final determination. The squad office appearance should also be considered when interviewing victims. Investigators should ensure that the office area is neat, clean, and conducive to interviewing victims which means that posters, jokes, or drawings should not be displayed where victims can see them. The professional appearance of the office will enhance the image projected by investigators and provide an appropriate atmosphere for victims.

Managerial Support

The quality of the personnel assigned to sex crimes units will ultimately determine whether the units are successful or not. Within the NYPD, the Manhattan Special Victims Squad is charged with investigating all sex crimes and child abuse cases in the Borough of Manhattan (comprised of 22 precincts). As its commanding officer, I held to the policy that personnel were the single most important factor to the success of my command. To that end, I was fortunate. My superiors appreciated the uniqueness of sex crime investigations and quickly learned that it took an exceptional individual to become proficient at investigating sex crimes. Not only do such matters require the expertise of experienced homicide investigators, but they also require a particular demeanor and professionalism — attributes that would allow investigators to interview victims and interrogate suspects under the most psychologically upsetting circumstances.

It has been my experience that executives within police departments, unlike their counterparts in private industry, are often unaware of the need for a separate selection process, particularly for units that have an impact on the public perception of the organization. Once they understand that the traditional standards for assessing the suitability of personnel are significantly different in sex crime investigations than for other areas, they usually become supportive and provide appropriate personnel to address the need. Those inexperienced executives who do not perceive the risks, however, can and should be educated by investigators in the field. Investigators can make them aware of the importance of sex crime investigations to their professional success and to the department's reputation, and how failure can have wide-ranging repercussions for everyone involved. As they gain experience, such executives are sure to temper their opposition to implementing special procedures. Experience brings about an appreciation for the impact of sex crimes on both the public and the department. Before long, even the most intransigent managers become keenly aware that investigations into these matters require the most thorough and professional response an organization can muster. Inevitably they will come to realize that if we refuse to address such serious and heinous crimes as rape, sodomy, and sexual assault, the public will have little confidence in our ability to investigate other crimes, including robbery, burglary, assault, and larceny.

I was fortunate to be given the privilege of selecting personnel who exemplified the best that the Detective Bureau had to offer — a privilege that should be copied by any department wishing to take a comprehensive look at sex crimes. My personnel were selected not only for their talent and their ability to maintain professionalism under the most trying of circumstances, but also for their temperament and compassion. In recent years, more and more employers have discovered that personality traits of their employees can have a significant impact upon the performance level of their organizations. They often require that candidates take personality tests to measure both internal skills (to match personalities with job requirements) and external skills (to measure candidates' people skills). Over the last 50 years, academics have debated the usefulness of personality testing within the workplace to hire and place employees in the appropriate positions. Schmitt and Chan (1998) noted, however, that one of the most important lessons to emerge from these debates is that the personality traits being considered need to be relevant to the function of the job in order to be an appropriate measure of job performance. I can think of no other job within law enforcement where particular personality traits can affect the success of investigations more than in the investigation of sex crimes, a reality that all managers need to consider when reviewing their selection process.

The Gender Issue

Should the selection of sex crime investigators be based upon gender? Should female investigators exclusively interview female victims of sexual assault? The short answers to these questions are *no* and *no*. The selection of investigators should not be based on gender. Too often the assumption is made that only a female can interview another female regarding a sexual assault. Experience has shown that that is not the case. In fact, it is frequently more advantageous to have a male interview a female victim. The same is true for a male victim and a female investigator. Logic would dictate otherwise, but the success of opposite-sex interviews cannot be denied. The degrading acts that the victim was made to endure are often difficult for one woman to describe to another, or one man with another. Instead, they may find it easier to recount the facts to members of the opposite sex, provided the person listening is compassionate and perceptive. These observations are only offered to rebut those who would argue for same-sex interviews in every case. The skills, the abilities, and the emotional support that the investigator can give victims should be the controlling factors in assignments, not gender. In an interesting study, Currie and MacLean (1997) found that women might disclose serious sexual victimization at a higher rate to men, at least under some conditions. Although their research showed that male interviewers were more successful in obtaining disclosures of sexual assault at higher rates than women, the authors do not suggest that interviewers be exclusively male. Rather, they suggest that gender-based modes of interacting are learned behaviors, including interactions between the same sex — that is, male–male interaction and female–female interaction. They found that both male and female interviewers can overcome their learned behaviors by acquiring a manner of interacting that is gender sensitive and characteristic of good interviewing practices. Those who advocate same-sex interviews have failed to take into account the gender relationships that exist among women within our society and among men. Currie and MacLean note that gender dynamics exist not only in male–female interactions, but also in female–female and male–male exchanges.

Staffing a sex crime unit with both men and women has many advantages. Because heterosexual crimes dominate reported sex crimes, having both male and female investigators within any sex crimes investigative unit is a recognized need that comes not only from their ability to complement each other during interviews and interrogations, but also from the different perspectives they bring to the investigation. Men can provide a masculine perspective in regard to the actions of the perpetrator, while women can provide the victim's feminine perspective. In each case, the total viewpoint can help steer the investigation toward a successful conclusion. On the other hand, utilizing only one viewpoint (male or female) limits the investigation and prohibits the pursuit of all possible leads, thereby wasting precious time that could be employed in a constructive manner elsewhere.

Establishing a unit that is not dominated by either sex provides a diverse outlook that can be used to the squad's advantage. I can attest to the many instances in which the combined perspectives facilitated the needs of investigations and enabled us to channel our resources in the appropriate direction. Discussing various aspects of sexual issues with other investigators of the opposite sex would generally be frowned upon within the context of a work environment; however, in a sex crimes unit it is frequently done in an attempt to understand the actions of the victim or the perpetrator and is extremely useful if done in a professional and courteous manner. Such discussions allow the case detective to understand the motivation behind particular acts (both on the part of the victim and on the part of the perpetrator) which can lead to additional evidence that can facilitate an apprehension or help understand and corroborate the victim's allegation. Consequently, the need to include both mature men and women within a successful sex crime unit is not only imperative; it is necessary.

Provisional Status of New Investigators

It is essential that, when detectives have been selected, they receive the appropriate training, both formal and informal, before they are asked to tackle cases on their own. The formal training should emphasize interviewing techniques to be used with sex crime victims and the latest techniques in forensic science, particularly as they relate to sex crimes. The informal training should consist of in-house instruction by seasoned sex crime investigators and supervisors within actual crime settings.

I cannot emphasize enough the importance of selecting personnel who are accomplished detectives and possess the behavioral qualities that can make them successful in this field. To ensure that the correct personnel are selected, investigators should be placed on a 3-month probationary status within the unit. They should be told of their status beforehand, and they should be aware that they will be monitored. I found that this practice gave me time to evaluate their personal traits as they relate to dealing with victims along with their investigative skills. Those that could not make the grade did not remain. Some were exceptionally fine investigators but were simply not suited for this type of assignment. Their investigative skills served them well while interrogating suspects, but they lacked the personal traits that could make them successful sex crime investigators. Others understood their own limitations and concluded on their own that they were not suited for the emotional stress that came with these investigations. They were the first to request a reassignment; others required forcible removal. In either case, policies should be in place to ensure that the careers of those who are transferred out of the unit are not damaged. To do so would only impair future recruitment and would unfairly injure personnel who through no fault of their own do not possess the inherent abilities needed by sex crime investigators. Their talents may lie in different fields, and their rejection from a sex crime unit should not affect their status as expert investigators in other areas.

Unlike their counterparts in other investigative fields, commanding officers of sex crime units must be given more latitude to remove investigators who are unable to perform adequately. Allowing them to remain will only jeopardize important cases and could create public relation problems that will be difficult for the department to overcome. The sensitivity and the importance of these cases demand this latitude.

Conclusion

Technical expertise, education, training, and an ability to communicate are often cited as parameters for selecting personnel. Personality, however, is frequently overlooked. Its importance has often taken a back seat in the selection process, but its significance cannot be understated, particularly for sex crime investigations. Research has shown that, even in the private sector, personality has a significant impact upon job performance. Borman et al. (1997) noted that, "Fit between personal attributes and characteristics of the target organization contributes to important individual and organizational outcomes." These outcomes are magnified by the personality fit or lack thereof within a sex crimes unit. Those in the investigative field of law enforcement know many highly trained and enormously talented investigators who have proven themselves time and again when investigating cases such as homicide and robbery. Their expertise is unquestionable. They can interview victims, interrogate subjects, and gather evidence in a professional and legal manner that results in solid convictions time and again. Their investigative expertise has served them well, and they may be considered the best at what they do. Sex crimes, however, may pose a situation for which they simply are not suited. Their skills are not in question; it is the personality fit that is.

The critical importance of personality to sex crime investigations is significant because of the role that it plays when dealing with the victim. Although many investigators have distinguished themselves throughout their careers, finding one that can deal with the emotional distress of sex crime victims while attending to the needs of the case can be difficult. It takes the previously mentioned personality traits to function effectively in this field.

Those traits will determine the extent to which sex crime investigators will be effective. Although training is imperative and can help overcome many obstacles, it cannot address the issue of personality. The many criteria outlined in this chapter should be considered when assigning personnel in order to minimize the many problems that are unavoidable in this type of investigation. The impact of sex crimes is too broad to trust to untrained and unqualified personnel.

The support of management in the selection process cannot be overemphasized. It is essential that management be educated regarding the different manner by which suitable personnel are assigned to sex crime units and that commanders be given a certain amount of latitude in assigning and transferring investigators whose individual personality traits may or may not be suitable within a sex crimes squad. Managers need only to look at the headlines and the resulting pressure when rapes occur or when they are handled incorrectly to appreciate the need for a skilled and knowledgeable sex crime unit that takes care of the needs of the victim while addressing the needs of the department and the public at the same time.

Bibliography

Barry, T., *The Creative Thinking Organization: Beyond Motivation to Nurturing*, Federal Publications, Salungar Darul Ehsan, Malaysia, 1997, p.15.

Blohowiak, D., *How's All the Work Going to Get Done?*, Career Press, Franklin Lakes, NJ, 1995, p.15.

Borman, W. C., Hanson, M. A., and Hedge, J. W., Personnel selection, *Ann. Rev. Psychol.*, 48, 299–338, 1997.

Cook, M., *Personnel Selection: Adding Value through People*, 3rd ed., John Wiley & Sons, New York, 1998, p. 302.

Currie, D. H. and MacLean, B. D., Measuring violence against women, in *Researching Sexual Violence against Women: Methodological and Personal Perspectives*, Schwartz, M. D., Ed., Sage, Thousand Oaks, CA, 1997, chap. 12.

Inbau, F. E., Reid, J. E., and Buckley, J. P., *Criminal Interrogations and Confessions*, 3rd ed., Williams & Wilkins, Baltimore, MD, 1986, p. 79.

Miller, J., Researching violence against street prostitutes: Issues of epistemology, methodology, and ethics, in *Researching Sexual Violence against Women: Methodological and Personal Perspectives*, Schwartz, M. D., Ed., Sage, Thousand Oaks, CA, 1997, chap. 11.

Schmitt, N. and Chan, D., *Personnel Selection: A Theoretical Approach*, Sage, Thousand Oaks, CA, 1998, p. 117.

Singer, E., Frankel, M. R., and Glassman, M. B., The effect of interviewer characteristics and expectations on response, *Public Opin. Q.*, 47(1), 68–83, 1983.

Urquiza, A. J. and Wyatt, G. E., Clinical interviewing with trauma victims, *J. Interpersonal Violence*, 12(5), 759, 1997.

The Two Crime Scenes

4

In any investigation into sexual assault, investigators must recognize that two distinct crime scenes have to be processed. The first is the location of occurrence, a location that must be secured and processed in a professional manner similar to that of a homicide. The second location is that of the victim herself. She will frequently retain critical forensic evidence on her body, within her body, or on her clothing. Trained personnel must process the first location in the same painstaking and meticulous manner as they would any serious crime scene. The second, however, requires more finesse, more specialization, and additional training. It entails a cooperative effort that utilizes a team approach consisting of medical personnel, counselors, and sex crime investigators. This combined effort is designed to take into account the needs of the victim while collecting the vital evidence needed for prosecution before it is destroyed. If we fail to take care of the victim's needs (both emotionally and physically), we will not succeed in securing her cooperation for collecting evidence, nor are we likely to gain her cooperation in the future.

Both crime scenes are crucial to the investigation and great care is needed to preserve the evidence in each. Modern science can decode forensic evidence not only to help identify suspects but also to substantiate the victim's account in a legal setting. Gilbert (1998) noted that the importance of physical evidence has grown over the years, and he maintains that court decisions will continue to place more and more emphasis on scientific evidence in the future.

Ordinarily, investigators have only one shot at securing this evidence, and great care should be taken to ensure that all corroborative evidence is preserved for forensic examination. Identifying and preserving evidence at a crime scene, however, are not the sole responsibilities of the investigator. Geberth (1996) noted that, in his investigations of homicides, he found that the success of his investigations often depended on the actions of the first officer, who is aided by such support personnel as dispatchers, who alertly transmit crucial information to help identify evidence and witnesses before they are lost. Clearly, the preservation and collection of evidence are collaborative efforts that begin with the first officer on the scene, are reinforced by the first officer's superiors, and utilize the expertise of forensic technicians combined with input from investigators.

The First Officer and the Location-of-Occurrence Crime Scene

It is imperative that the crime scene in a sexual assault be treated the same as for a homicide and secured as soon as possible. The first officer on the scene will be the first law enforcement official to speak with the victim, and his or her manner will set the tone for future interaction with the victim. A compassionate and professional manner is crucial at this stage. Although the first officer may feel unqualified in this area, it is the officer's duty to ascertain the facts and determine if a crime has indeed occurred. It is essential that the first officer maintain a polite and nonjudgmental demeanor in order to make the victim as comfortable as possible and to prevent her from becoming agitated and uncommunicative. The first officer will obtain preliminary information from the victim to help determine the size of the crime scene. It will be necessary to ascertain the sequence of events that led to the attack in order to make such a determination. The first officer will also secure the crime scene and limit access to prevent contamination, in addition to calling for medical personnel to treat the victim and for sex crime investigators to respond immediately.

Determining the crime scene location may not be as straightforward and uncomplicated as one may think. For example, I can recall many cases where the victim had walked to her apartment building alone and observed the attacker leaning on an object (car, railing, etc.) near the entrance to the building. When the victim had unlocked the lobby door, the suspect attacked from behind, forcing her into a stairwell or into her apartment, where she was sexually assaulted. The responding officer might determine that only the stairwell or apartment should be considered the crime scene and limit access to those areas only; however, the circumstances depicted here dictate that the lobby door and the outside object (car, railing, etc.) on which the suspect was seen leaning be secured as well.

The standard of creating the largest possible crime scene should be maintained until investigators can elicit more particulars from the victim that will allow them to evaluate the scene and expand or reduce it as needed. Crime scenes that are inordinately large can be scaled back to a smaller confined area without contaminating evidence. Those that are too small, however, create significant problems. As they are expanded, the likelihood that evidence has been contaminated increases in proportion to the amount of traffic the area has sustained. Nevertheless, the fear that an area has been contaminated should not prohibit expansion of a crime scene. Fingerprints and footprints of officers and witnesses, along with other types of evidence, can always be collected to eliminate them from those of the perpetrator. If agencies consider these crimes noteworthy, then the inconveniences of collecting elimination fingerprints or any other eliminating evidence should not deter their efforts nor should it inhibit their investigations.

When the first officer responds and finds that the location of occurrence is a residence other than the victim's (or any locked structure) and no one is in danger, the officer should secure the location and inform investigators immediately. A search warrant may be necessary to process the crime scene. Investigators can confer with the District Attorney's Office regarding the need for a search warrant. Collecting vital evidence without the appropriate authorization will only reduce its admissibility in court.

Steps for the First Officer to Take

- Ensure the safety of the victim and render medical assistance; the first priority is always the safety of civilian personnel.
- Be alert to persons and vehicles leaving the area.
- Make an apprehension, if possible.
- Offer assistance to arriving medical crews and investigators.
- Notify the investigative unit that will be responsible for the investigation.
- Advise victim not to bathe, douche, brush her teeth or rinse her mouth, or wash clothing or bedding.
- Make notation regarding the victim's physical condition (e.g., bruises, lacerations, torn clothing).

It is crucial that the first officers on the scene secure the site and not contaminate the crime scene, if possible. Be aware that semen from the perpetrator may be found in many areas other than on or in the victim. Clothing worn by the victim may contain traces of semen and should be secured. If the attack occurred on a bed, the sheets should be seized for examination. The floor may also contain droppings of semen from the assailant. Officers should be aware that it is not uncommon for rapists to wipe their penis with a tissue, which they then discard nearby after an attack.

Determine the facts and expand the crime scene to the location where the victim first observed the suspect. Remember that the suspect's fingerprints and other evidence might be found not only at the location where the victim was assaulted, but also in other areas such as a parked car where the suspect hid from the victim prior to the attack, a lobby door or an elevator used by the suspect as he followed the victim, or anything else that the suspect may have come in contact with prior to, during, or after the attack. The first officer must also:

- Detain potential witnesses and keep them separated.
- Identify potential physical evidence and instruct arriving medical and police personnel of its existence to minimize contact.
- Obtain a detailed description of the perpetrator and transmit it.
- If the crime is recent (within the last half an hour) and the victim is able, have her canvass the area for the suspect.
- Search the area for items that may have been stolen and discarded (purse, weapon, etc.).
- If a condom was used, conduct a search to see if it was discarded nearby.
- Determine the extent of the crime scene based on the evidence gathered so far and cordon off the area.
- Establish control of the crime scene.

Care should be taken to isolate the area and prevent the curious from contaminating evidence or removing important traces of the crime. Generally the public will appreciate the investigators' concerns and realize that the inconvenience is temporary and essential to a professional investigation. Quite often, in fact, the greatest problems that we encounter come not from the public but from our superiors. Limiting their enthusiasm is difficult, and it requires tact to subtly suggest that they not enter the cordoned area. Permit only those involved in the investigation to enter the enclosed area.

- Make detailed notations regarding the condition of the crime scene, the lighting, windows (opened/closed), weather conditions, and positions of various items within the crime scene, including items such as footprints that may disappear as they dry. Make notations regarding any smells (e.g., marijuana, perfume, urine, gas).
- Document any statements by the victim and witnesses, and give this information to the detective in charge of the investigation.
- Step away from the crime scene to place telephone calls or discuss strategy.
- Maintain a log of the time and date of all persons entering the crime scene, and give this information to the detective in charge of the investigation.
- Document the response to the crime scene, the conditions upon arrival, and all statements made by the victim, the witnesses, and the

suspect, if present; failure to document can be problematic at future court proceedings.

- Upon the arrival of investigators, advise them of all conditions.

Remember, the response by the first officer on the scene often can determine the extent to which forensic evidence can be collected; this evidence is often the only link to identifying the perpetrator and bringing a sexual predator to justice.

Obstacles for the First Officer to Overcome

The first officer will encounter many obstacles at the crime scene; for example:

- Weather conditions (rain, snow) may cause vital evidence to be washed away. To counter a condition like this, have objects removed to a dry area and secured. If removal is not possible and evidence, particularly serological evidence (blood, semen, saliva, etc.) is about to be washed away, the officer can use whatever is available to soak up the evidence (clean cotton swabs are best). I have seen one quick-thinking officer use paper bags to soak up blood that was being washed away in the rain. His actions preserved valuable DNA evidence that was used to identify the suspects.
- Civilians may have already contaminated the scene.
- The crime scene may limit access to buildings, elevators, stairwells, etc., so temporary arrangements must be made to reroute civilians.
- Responding police may contaminate the scene. This type of contamination is common, particularly among energetic and inexperienced superiors. Limit access as much as possible and document the names of any individuals entering the crime scene, also noting the time they did so.

Case History

Let me recount a true story of the type of interference I have run into. One November evening, a young tourist and her friend were out at a famous restaurant/bar in Manhattan. It was late (after 1:00 A.M.), and they had planned to leave the bar soon. When they finished their last drinks, the young woman asked her friend to wait while she used the ladies' room. The bathroom was on a balcony floor in the rear of the bar, and it had small, individual rooms for the toilets, instead of stalls. The inside was empty. When she entered, she was pushed from behind and led to one of the toilet rooms by her attacker. He beat her and forced her to undress before he anally sodomized her and raped her. He removed his penis before ejaculating and ejaculated on her buttocks. He then wiped her clean with toilet paper, and threatened to kill her if she did not stay put for five minutes.

The victim exited the bathroom minutes later and told her friend who immediately called the police. The responding patrol captain decided to ignore the established protocol in such cases and began to conduct his own investigation. He interviewed the victim, the patrons, and workers in the bar. He had the victim transported to the hospital, but he never told her not to wash the area where the perpetrator had ejaculated. Unfortunately, while she was waiting to see a doctor, she went to the bathroom and cleaned herself.

Meanwhile, the captain instructed the local precinct evidence unit to process the bathroom for fingerprints and nothing more. Although these units are excellent, they are trained to process robbery and burglary scenes but are not trained to collect serological evidence; consequently, none was collected. The janitor was then allowed to clean the bathroom, destroying any semen that was left behind on the floor. He also emptied a trash can that could have contained the tissue from the suspect. Upon completion of his investigation, the captain let all of the witnesses and the workers leave without recording their names and addresses for the detectives.

Needless to say that when I arrived on the scene I was furious. The bathroom had been mopped by the janitor, and a sanitation truck had already picked up the trash that was removed by him. Potential evidence had been destroyed through carelessness. The witnesses were allowed to go home, and their names and addresses were never recorded for future investigative purposes. Finally, the victim had not been properly instructed to refrain from washing the area where the perpetrator had ejaculated. In short, the captain let his enthusiasm take over and he lost all professionalism. In doing so, he compromised the investigation and created significant problems for the investigation.

Through the hard work and dedication of my detectives, however, the case was solved, and the suspect was later identified in a lineup. Because no DNA evidence was available, the case was difficult to prove, but thanks to the tenacity of the Manhattan District Attorney's Office and the courage of the victim the suspect was convicted and sentenced to jail.

Because no serological evidence was collected at the crime scene or from the victim, a court order to have the suspect's blood drawn for comparison with other cases was not possible until he was convicted. Once he was convicted, however, his blood was drawn for a DNA profile (a new law in most states including New York State) and entered into the database. The DNA profile of the suspect turned out to be identical to a suspect wanted in a series of unrelated subway attacks. The *modus operandi* (M.O.) in those attacks was completely different. The rapist had stopped his attacks, and the case had gone unsolved for over a year. Had the patrol captain not destroyed vital DNA evidence in the bar case, the apprehension of a serial rapist would have occurred without delay. Because he allowed the evidence to be destroyed, however, the span of time from apprehension to conviction to testing was approximately one year, during which a climate of fear still permeated the subway system while the case of the serial subway rapist went unsolved, not to mention the added expenditure of manpower that was dedicated to patrol the subways searching for the rapist.

The Investigative Team

Forensic Techniques

Although forensic technicians are typically well versed in their field, investigators will need frequent updates regarding the latest forensic advances. Those who are not familiar with these advances are likely to overlook vital evidence or will fail to alert technicians regarding its importance. Untrained investigators will routinely neglect to ask victims the appropriate questions regarding the location of all types of evidence that can be recovered using the latest technology, particularly DNA evidence. Investigators need not know the details of DNA collection; it is sufficient that they have a good working knowledge of where to find it and how to secure it properly when it is found. Forensic biology has opened up a whole new world to the investigator, but the cost of that analysis has limited forensic testing to only the most serious of crimes. Fortunately, sex crimes are high on that list, and the prevalence of DNA evidence in sex crimes make it a suitable area for utilizing the latest advances in forensic biology.

Case History

I recall a case in which the suspect had worn rough work gloves as he pushed his victim into her apartment. Once inside, he removed his gloves and placed them in his pocket before raping the victim. As he fled the scene, he dropped one of the gloves on the street outside the building. Because he had used a condom during the rape, no semen was available to provide the DNA that could identify him; however, skin cells were found on the inside of the glove. Technicians at the Medical Examiner's Office (the DNA experts in New York City) were able to remove those cells and provide a DNA profile of the suspect. An astute detective had recognized the potential value of the glove and submitted it for DNA testing. It is these aspects of an investigation that today's investigators must be aware of. By utilizing an analytical approach to crime scenes, their likelihood of capturing vital evidence at crime scenes is greatly enhanced.

Responsibilities of the Investigative Team

In addition to taking an analytical approach, investigators should:

- Get details from the first officer on scene.
- Assess the crime scene (expanding it, if necessary).
- Determine if a search warrant is needed.
- Conduct a preliminary interview of the victim at the hospital or at the scene, with a detailed interview to be conducted the next day or as soon as the victim is capable (see Chapter 5).
- Determine if any adjustments are needed in the size of the crime scene.
- Determine what evidence may be obtained from the victim's body (e.g., possible semen in the victim's vagina, anus, mouth, or on her body; possible saliva on part of the body that the perpetrator licked or kissed; possible skin cells of the perpetrator under the fingernails of the victim).
- Confer with medical personnel at the hospital to ensure that all evidence is properly obtained (see The Victim and Residual Evidence section on following pages).
- Confer with the forensic team to discuss the crime scene.
- Ensure that witnesses are separated and begin taking statements.
- Determine if additional investigators are needed.
- Canvass the area for additional witnesses.
- Canvass the area to record all parked vehicles.
- Conduct a search of the area for articles missing from the crime scene (include search of garbage and sewers).
- Confer with the forensic team when they have completed their processing; walk through the crime scene to determine what evidence was recovered (prints, blood, semen, etc.) and where each piece of evidence was found.

See Chapters 7 and 8 regarding particular actions to be taken in stranger cases and serial cases.

The Forensic Team: Evidence Response Team

The crime scene should not be processed until the sex crime investigators have spoken with the victim and determined the extent of the crime scene itself. Their preliminary interview will allow them to determine what objects the suspect may have touched and where they may find both serological evidence and other items such as hair, fibers, and fingerprints. They can then give the forensic technicians an accurate description of the attack and direct them where to look for evidence.

The forensic team consists of highly trained experts who are well versed in the latest techniques of forensic science and will minimize contamination while supplying forensic evidence to the investigators. Their field of expertise requires a meticulous approach coupled with information supplied by the case detective to process the scene appropriately. They cannot process a sexual assault crime scene properly without the detailed information that can only be supplied from the victim and/or witnesses. The forensic team will:

- Walk through the crime scene with the case detective to determine where and what to process.
- Measure and diagram the scene.
- Photograph and/or videotape the scene.
- Use ultraviolet light to detect the presence of semen on the floor, clothing, bedding, etc.
- Collect body fluids from scene, taking the proper precautions when collecting body fluids.
- Be alert for evidence where DNA might exist: cigarette butts, tooth-brush, bed sheets, tissues, napkins, etc.
- Process scene for fingerprints.
- Collect hair and fibers.
- Collect ballistic evidence, if necessary.
- Determine trajectory of ballistics, if needed.
- Obtain fingernail scrapings, if not done by hospital personnel.
- Maintain the chain of custody for all evidence.
- Confer with case detective upon completion of processing to discuss what evidence was recovered and where. They will then process any additional areas if requested.
- Photograph the victim and her injuries as required, if not done by hospital staff.
- Provide documentation, documentation, and documentation, as the largest failure of police at crime scenes is their failure to document properly; it is important to document all details fully.

Investigative Search of Crime Scene

Once the forensic specialists have processed the crime scene, investigators may need to conduct a further search for evidence, particularly when the location is the suspect's residence. In that case, a search warrant should have been obtained before the crime scene was processed. If any questions arise regarding the need for a search warrant, investigators should confer with their District Attorney's Office beforehand. Investigators will then look for additional items of evidence that can corroborate the victim's account. Searches should be conducted for:

- e-Mail messages
- Drugs used to incapacitate victim
- Pictures of victim or other victims (undeveloped film)
- Written documents indicative of the suspect's behavior
- Sex objects
- Pornography
- Any item that will corroborate the victim's allegation

Note: If a search warrant is necessary and an item is not listed on the warrant, the warrant must be amended in order to seize the evidence.

The Search

It is essential to maintain control over the area to be searched to ensure that every piece of evidence is recovered and that all evidence is properly recorded and secured. Maintain a log of names of everyone who enters the location, and control the search by investigators by limiting the people involved to a supervisor and two investigators. Designate one investigator as the recording officer, whose job will be to draw a diagram of the location, to record all of the evidence that is recovered, and to label and secure the evidence properly. This person should not get involved in the actual search; a second investigator will be responsible for conducting the search. The supervisor should not get involved in the search except to help when a heavy object needs to be moved. The second investigator should also be the assigned case investigator. This will limit testimony in court when recovered items are entered into evidence, as this investigator's testimony should be sufficient regarding the recovery of evidence. In regard to the search itself:

- Draw a diagram of location before beginning the search, and be sure that large items such as beds, couches, dressers, and closets are depicted.
- Search one room at a time; do not allow investigators to roam from one room to another.
- Select the room farthest from the entrance and begin there.
- In each room, begin with the ceiling; remove panels from suspended ceilings and search the area above.
- Pick a corner farthest away from the entrance to the room and search there before proceeding further.

- If searching for small items such as papers, conduct a thorough search under, over, and inside every object; look inside pockets of clothes, inside books, inside notepads, etc.
- Move to the rest of the room, and move items into the previously searched corner to expose wall and floor area.
- Document, seal, and properly secure all items that are removed; record the exact location where the item was found, and note the exact time of entry and departure.

To avoid the often-intrusive temperament of some superiors, investigators can overtly document the superior's presence, listing the exact time of his or her arrival and departure. Such an action politely sends a strong message that this person's presence has been documented and that he or she may be called upon to testify in the future. This simple action usually has the desired effect of limiting such interference and allows investigators to conduct their search unimpeded. I know; it worked for me. On one occasion a high department official attempted to "assist" us search an apartment in a highly publicized case. When he observed me writing his name and noting the time, he decided to take a cursory look around and then left me to conduct the search unimpeded.

Automated Fingerprint Identification System

Automated fingerprint identification systems (AFISs) have revolutionized the way police departments search for fingerprint matches. In the past, fingerprint technicians conducted manual searches through prints on file, and their success in finding matches was limited. With the advent of AFIS, fingerprints found at crime scenes can be plotted and entered into a database that contains the fingerprints of all criminals and of other crime scenes. Results can be obtained within minutes, and the success of this technology has led to the apprehension and conviction of countless felons. The only limitation to this system appears to be the incompatibility of the several AFIS technologies in use today. The AFIS technology in use by one state or city may not be the same as that in use in another. Consequently, when different systems are used, data entered in one system cannot be read by another system. Re-plotting fingerprints and inputting them into is necessary for each different system.

The Victim and Residual Evidence

Semen is the primary bodily fluid left behind by rapists. It can be found wherever the violator ejaculated, and an interview of the victim will be necessary to discover where that is. If he raped the victim, semen should be present in her vagina (assuming a condom was not used). He may have removed his penis and ejaculated on the victim, in her anus, or in her mouth. If a condom was used, locating the condom becomes a priority. He may have dripped semen on bedding, the floor, or clothing during and after the attack. He may have wiped his penis with something and discarded it (tissue, piece of cloth, etc.). Whatever the circumstances, obtaining this information is vital in order to ascertain the location of the evidence.

In the moments after an attack, however, rape victims often have a difficult time recounting the incident accurately. In their emotionally distraught state, they may leave out vital information that will help the police identify the evidence — evidence that may soon be destroyed if not recognized. Questions regarding specific actions of the perpetrator are necessary and must be asked before requesting the hospital staff or the crime scene technicians to collect forensic evidence. Although they are trained to collect all evidence, forensic teams need to know where to look specifically in order to avoid losing or overlooking items that may prove vital to the investigation.

In order to collect the bodily fluids that can lead to identification of a suspect, anyone advising the victim must instruct her *not* to:

- Bathe
- Douche
- Brush teeth or rinse mouth
- Wash clothing or bedding

As with any crime scene location, investigators may witness the imminent destruction of evidence; for example, the victim may refuse to cooperate, particularly in the case of oral sex, and insist upon rinsing her mouth and brushing her teeth. If that is the case, police officers should be aware that this evidence is crucial and should try to preserve it as best as possible. If a victim of oral sodomy insists upon rinsing her mouth, it is suggested that an oral swab of the interior of her mouth be prepared before she rinses. A vigorous rubbing with a cotton swab, clean napkin, etc. could capture the semen that is still present before it is destroyed. Such evidence should be allowed to dry and then preserved in a paper envelope or bag to prevent decomposition and contamination. These procedures do not preclude the need for a medical exam that will document and collect additional evidence.

Case History

A suspect was attacking young women as they entered their apartment buildings in a section of Manhattan. In one case, he forced the victim behind a stairwell and forced her to orally sodomize him. He ejaculated in her mouth and then fled without injuring the victim any further. The victim immediately called the police, and two of my detectives arrived within minutes. She was aware of the sexual assault pattern because we had alerted the public to the presences of a serial attacker. The detectives transmitted a description of the suspect immediately, and personnel on patrol conducted a canvass of the neighborhood. While the detectives spoke with the victim, she stated that she was not going to wait until she arrived at the hospital to wash her mouth. She insisted upon washing her mouth immediately. Realizing that vital evidence was about to be destroyed, the detectives quickly obtained two clean paper napkins from the victim and asked her to swab the inside of her mouth thoroughly before she washed. These napkins were then sent to the lab where semen was retrieved for DNA analysis and future identification. The alertness of these detectives prevented the destruction of vital evidence.

At the Hospital

When the victim arrives at the hospital, medical personnel will examine her in private. Some advanced hospitals have established rape teams (doctors, nurses, psychologists, and rape counselors) who are trained to deal with the victims of rape and to take into account the needs of the police. Unfortunately, however, most hospitals throughout the country do not have such teams, and it may be necessary for the investigator to instruct the doctor on the collection of evidence. In either event, the treating physician will always be consulted with prior to the exam. During that consultation, the police will give the physician all the information he needs to know to collect evidence. Advising the doctor of whether oral, anal, or vaginal penetration occurred will provide the information required to collect smears from any or all three of the areas. If the perpetrator ejaculated on the victim, the doctor will take a scraping of the area where he ejaculated to collect the semen. Likewise, if the perpetrator licked the victim or spit on her, swabs can be taken of those areas for analysis.

Case History

A young woman was walking home from work late at night. The perpetrator approached her from behind, pointed a gun in her back, and forced her into a dark alley. Once in the alley, he forced her to remove her pants and panties. He then anally sodomized and raped the victim. When he was about to ejaculate, however, he removed his penis and ejaculated on the victim's abdomen. In an effort to destroy the evidence, he then wiped the area clean with the victim's panties, which he then took with him. When we arrived at the hospital, we interviewed the victim and she recounted the above facts. We then asked the medical staff to take a scraping from the victim's abdomen and secure it with the rape kit, in addition to the usual vaginal and anal swabs. The lab processed the vaginal and anal swabs first. The anal swab was negative, but signs of semen were present in her vaginal swab. That semen, however, had come from her husband, with whom she had sexual intercourse the night before. The abdominal skin scraping was the key. It showed minute signs of semen, and sperms cells from the perpetrator were found in that semen. A DNA profile was then prepared and entered into the databank to identify the suspect positively. Such an identification was necessary because darkness prevented the victim from observing the facial features of the perpetrator and she would not have been able to recognize him in a lineup. Because the victim bore no visible signs of semen, an untrained investigator might have been satisfied to let the medical personnel limit their exams to the anal and vaginal cavities and would not have collected scrapings from the abdomen. To one knowledgeable in recovering evidence from sex crime victims, however, taking this extra step is routine. Knowing what to ask and how to seize evidence before it is destroyed were a vital part of this investigation, as it is in all investigations involving sex crimes.

A real-life example such as this illustrates the importance of collecting the residual evidence left on victims and the need for police to be attentive to the details as the victim communicates them. Such attention to detail leads to positive identifications and provides prosecutors with the evidence necessary for success in court. The perpetrator was eventually identified through his DNA after a conviction for robbery. As per state law, his DNA was analyzed and put into the DNA database. The database made the connection and the perpetrator is now doing an additional 20 years as a guest of New York State in an upstate jail.

The Rape Kit

Medical personnel at the hospital will prepare the rape kit after discussing the attack with the police. The victim will *always* be given the utmost privacy while this exam is being done. The fact that an investigator and the victim are the same gender does not allow this rule to be broken. The police do not need to be present during the exam. The doctor or nurse will document the collection of evidence and release the completed rape kit to the police. All attempts to preserve the victim's dignity at the hospital will help when it comes time to ask the embarrassing and pointed questions that must be asked.

The rape kit should consist of the following:

- Sheet of examination table paper; the victim should disrobe over this sheet to allow retrieval of any trace evidence that might fall from the victim's clothing
- Vial of the victim's blood
- Oral, anal, and/or vaginal swabs (penile swab with a male victim) to test for the presence of semen and/or lubricants
- Smears or scrapings from other areas on the victim's body where the violator may have ejaculated sperm, licked with his tongue, bit, spit, urinated, or defecated, with documentation of the exact locations from which the smears or scrapings were taken
- Fingernail scrapings
- Envelope containing the results of combing the victim's pubic hairs (the perpetrator's hair may be mixed with the victim's, and semen may be present)
- Trace evidence

The victim should be examined for any trace evidence that has adhered to her body. Dried semen, dried blood, dried saliva, hair, debris, grass stains, etc. can lead to an identification through DNA or at least can substantiate the victims allegations. The rape kit should also include:

- Victim's clothing, particularly panties, as seepage of semen from her vagina or anus may have occurred, depending on where the perpetrator ejaculated, and pubic hair or other trace evidence from the violator may be present
- Paper bag containing any debris found on the victim's body
- Detailed documentation of vaginal and anal exam (e.g., vaginal and/or anal tears will help confirm victim's account)

To further assist the case, forensic technicians may also need the following:

- Photographs of injuries, measured to scale (SANE professionals can perform this task which, depending on the location of injuries, may be more acceptable to the victim) (see section on SANE)
- Photographs of bite marks, measured to scale (utilizing SANE professionals as necessary)
- Vial of blood from anyone with whom the victim had sexual relations in the last 72 hours

Deliver the blood samples and the rape kit to the forensic laboratory for DNA
testing. Maintain custody of the photographs for court purposes, and use the
bite marks to compare with those of the suspect when he is arrested. Obtain
the medical record of the examination and the documentation of injuries
from the medical staff.

Sexual Assault Nurse Examiner (SANE)

In order to alleviate much of the trauma that is associated with collecting
the above evidence in an emergency room setting, a program called SANE
(Sexual Assault Nurse Examiner) was developed back in 1976. It did not gain
momentum, however, until the late 1980s and early 1990s. Today, it is in
place at most major hospitals and has been responsible for aiding the collection of sexual assault evidence in a professional manner while supporting
the victim through her ordeal. This program trains teams of hospital staff to
respond to emergency rooms when sexual assault victims enter. They are well
versed in handling evidence, and they are willing to testify in court should
the need arise. The typical staff of a hospital emergency room, however, does
not possess the expertise required in these situations. They are unfamiliar
with legal requirements surrounding the chain of evidence and the storage
of evidence, and generally they are inexperienced regarding the needs of the
police. The SANE staff, however, not only addresses these needs but also adds
a multidisciplinary approach that is designed to treat all of the medical and
emotional needs of the victim, including treatment for sexually transmitted
diseases, pregnancy prevention, and counseling to assist the victim as she
copes with the trauma of the attack. Investigators should keep in mind that
the emotional well-being of victims is of vital importance to the investigation
(see Chapter 5). Victims who cannot cope with the trauma will not be able
to assist in the investigation. Their emotional state can leave investigators
with no recourse but to close cases where suspects have been identified but
no other evidence exists to convict. Whatever can be done to support the
victim's emotional recovery should be done, not only because it is the right
thing to do for the victim, but because it will also help in the investigation
and prosecution of her case.

DNA

Retrieving information from evidence collected at crime scenes and from
victims and suspects has been revolutionized by DNA (deoxyribonucleic
acid). DNA contains the genetic code for all living cells and with the exception
of identical twins is different for all individuals. The use of DNA has allowed

law enforcement to positively identify suspects, often without the need for eyewitness identification, and has led to a whole new way of collecting evidence. Identifications made by eyewitnesses can sometimes be questionable, but an identification based upon DNA evidence is indisputable. The recent developments in DNA technology have helped investigators and prosecutors prevent convictions of innocent people due to false accusations and mistaken identifications. Not only has DNA technology proven to be a benefit to investigators, but it has also proven to be a godsend to those who are falsely accused and those who may have been wrongly convicted in the past.

Case History

A pattern of rapes had plagued the upper east side of Manhattan for a number of years. Sixteen attacks had occurred over a 5-year period. Press conferences were held to alert the public and to obtain their cooperation, sketches were distributed, thousands of tips were investigated, psychological and geographical profiles were developed (see Chapter 9), and a plan was instituted that utilized a task force of uniformed and plainclothes personnel. Many suspects were named, but all were eliminated because of their physical description, DNA, or confirmed alibis (e.g., being incarcerated during the attacks). Then, one suspect became the target of our investigation. He had grown up and worked in the area targeted by the rapist but had since moved to another area of Manhattan. Attacks had occurred outside of the target area, and the suspect had relatives living in those same areas. He looked very much like the sketch that we had distributed, and his racial makeup (black father, white mother) fit the description we had received from all of the victims. From the suspect's psychological profile, we knew that he would have trouble holding down a job and that he would have difficulty speaking with women. We found that the suspect had gone through a number of jobs and had been discharged from the Army for failing to pass his training program.

We began surveillance on the suspect, who would regularly walk from his neighborhood to the target neighborhood, apparently to reconnoiter the area for future victims. At one point, one of my female investigators bumped into him and asked him for directions to the subway. His response was blunt in that he grunted he did not know. Again, this was consistent with what we knew about the rapist (that he had trouble speaking with women). He then began to follow her, but stopped when he was confronted by a homeless man on the street. As we followed the suspect, we were able to obtain two samples of his body fluids for analysis. The first came when one of my detectives observed him spit on the street and then walk on. The detective, who was armed with clean cotton swabs and envelopes, retrieved the spit for analysis. The second opportunity came when the suspect was observed drinking a container of coffee which he discarded into a trash can when he had finished it. The cup was retrieved and the skin cells in the saliva matched that of the spit that was recovered. His DNA was then compared to that of the rapist and the analysis showed that he was not the rapist. Because some time had passed for some of the victims, and because the suspect did look extremely similar to the suspect, identification based on a lineup could have yielded tragic results. The circumstantial evidence implicated him, but the DNA evidence positively removed him as a suspect.

Combined DNA Index System

The Combined DNA Index System (CODIS) is a system sponsored by the FBI to collect and identify DNA in databases on a national basis. The theory is that the more DNA profiles that exist, the more likely it is that a match will be found. Each state and some municipalities maintain their own databases. DNA samples of arrested and convicted felons are entered into their respective state's system for analysis and comparison. Each state, however, has different standards for collecting DNA from convicted individuals. Some collect DNA samples from all felons, and others limit the collection to specified crimes. Differences in standards for collecting DNA have not limited implementation of CODIS, but different analysis standards and different database configurations have. To date, the many jurisdictions throughout the country utilize their own analysis standards and their own database structures, most of which are not compatible with each other. The current lack of a standard analysis system and a standard database system has limited the success of CODIS. CODIS can, however, distribute DNA profiles throughout the nation for entry into the various databases for possible identification.

Identical Twins and Identification

Every living organism contains a unique genetic code that is specific to that living being. The only exceptions are identical twins and cloned organisms. Identical twins can still be distinguished, however. Their genetic codes may be the same, but their fingerprints, like every person's, are unique to the individual and are therefore different. Fingerprints are formed after conception and after the genetic code has been determined. The many environmental factors that exist *in utero*, such as positions within the womb and the differences in the flow of amniotic fluid, influence the formation of fingerprints. Because these factors are different for everyone, all individuals possess a unique fingerprint profile, even identical twins.

Collecting Samples for DNA Analysis from Suspects

In the past, I ran into a number of roadblocks when attempting to collect samples from suspects for DNA analysis. At the time, the only acceptable method was to obtain a vial of the suspect's blood. To take the suspect's blood, however, required that he first agree to the procedure, then sign a form, and then be transported to a local hospital to have his blood taken. This delay, coupled with a medical staff that frequently counseled the suspect not to succumb to the procedure, often caused the suspect to change his mind about the procedure. When this happened, a court order was the only way to obtain his blood; however, we frequently did not have enough evidence against a suspect to establish the reasonable cause for a court order. In those cases we were left with a suspect and no way to obtain his DNA for analysis.

I brought this problem to the forensic biology unit for the New York City Medical Examiner's Office. They are charged with analyzing and documenting all DNA evidence in New York City. They probably conduct more DNA testing than any other laboratory in the country. They had a simple and acceptable solution. Take a buccal swab (described below) from the suspect while you have him in custody. At a meeting of Special Victim Commanders, I instructed them to teach all of their investigators how to obtain buccal swabs, and I subsequently instituted a procedure for collecting DNA samples from suspects in Manhattan. In lieu of obtaining blood, buccal swabs can be used to obtain evidence that can either exonerate or convict suspects. Several other methods of obtaining DNA evidence can be used by investigators to legally collect evidence against suspects that can definitively link them to particular crimes through their DNA or can exonerate those who are under suspicion.

Legal Criteria

In order to obtain voluntary DNA evidence from a suspect, a signed authorization should be obtained. Suspects and others whose DNA evidence is needed in an investigation have a legal right against self-incrimination and cannot be forced to give DNA samples for analysis. The below form was used by my office after consultation with the Manhattan District Attorney's Office for those suspects who voluntarily provided a DNA sample for analysis.

Buccal Swab

The skin cells on the inside of the mouth continually break up and fall into the saliva, which is normally swallowed or spit out. These skin cells provide a perfect opportunity for the collection of DNA. The unique genetic code that is associated with particular skin cells is exclusive to one individual and

DATE _____

TIME _____

By signing below, I am consenting to have an oral swab and/or a blood
sample taken from me for the purposes of identification and DNA testing.
This sample will be used by the New York City Police Department and
the New York City Medical Examiner's Office for investigative purposes.

_____   _____
             Full name   *Address*

                                                _____
                                                            City, State

_____
             Signature

             -

_____   _____
      Witness – Rank, Name   *Signature*

_____
             Command

is the same genetic code that appears throughout that person's body (blood,
organs, semen, hair, etc.). Items required for a buccal swab include:

- Two sterile cotton swabs in their original wrappers (medical swabs
  generally come in packages of two sealed in a paper wrapper)
- Paper envelope
- Latex gloves
- Wet paper towel

The procedure is as follows:

- Explain the process to the suspect to ensure that DNA is collected
  correctly the first time.
- Put on latex gloves to prevent contamination of items with your own
  DNA, sweat, etc.
- Remove cotton swabs from the wrapper and give them to the suspect.

- Have the suspect vigorously rub the inside of his mouth (cheek area) for 30 seconds.
- Place the swabs in the envelope and leave it open to allow the swabs to dry. Moisture can contaminate cells.
- When the swabs are dry, seal the envelope with the wet paper towel. *Do not lick the envelope.*
- Sign, date, and place the time on the envelope; also, put pertinent information about the suspect and the case number on the envelope.
- Hand deliver the envelope to the laboratory for testing.

Surreptitious Collection of DNA from Suspects during Questioning

The simplest and easiest way to obtain DNA samples is from saliva, but they can also be obtained from blood, semen, skin scrapings, etc. A discarded coffee cup, used napkin or tissue, half-eaten piece of food, or spit can all be used to obtain DNA evidence. In each of these cases, the evidence is something that was discarded by a suspect and can therefore be legally seized, provided of course that it was discarded in a public place or a facility to which the police have access. If it is discarded in a place for which the police do not have access, permission or a search warrant is required for its removal. If any questions regarding the legality of seizing items for DNA analysis arise, consult with the prosecutor for guidance. If a suspect is at a police facility, the investigator can offer him a cigarette (forgetting for a moment about the no-smoking ban in the building), a cup of coffee, a soda, a sandwich, etc. The investigator must be sure not to touch the items; the suspect is the only one who can handle these items. (Remember, the legality of an interrogation could be in jeopardy if the subject is not fed anyway.) Skin cells from the inside of the mouth fall out onto the lip and are then recoverable from cigarette butts, coffee containers, soda cans, napkins, etc. Be sure that an ashtray and a wastebasket are available to the suspect and that they are both empty and clean. When the object is discarded, collect it for analysis, but be careful to wear latex gloves while handling such objects to prevent contamination.

Collecting DNA Samples from Suspects under Surveillance

In a similar manner, evidence can be collected from suspects under surveillance. My squad and I have spent many hours tailing suspects and collecting DNA samples from suspects for whom we had no other evidence. In each case, investigators were armed with sterile cotton swabs, envelopes, and latex gloves. As we followed suspects, we waited for them to discard items that had touched their mouths or observed them spit on the street. Investigators then seized the evidence, sealed it in paper envelopes, labeled the envelopes (see buccal swab labeling procedure above), and hand delivered the envelopes to the laboratory for analysis. In those cases where the subject was a suspect in a stranger case or a series of rapes, he was kept under constant surveillance until results could be obtained. Although it usually requires 2 months to receive results of DNA analysis, procedures set up by the Medical Examiner's Office could cut that time to 48 hours. This has proven especially helpful in those cases where manpower was being overextended on surveillance or when there has been a threat to the public safety. Of course, each time a rush is placed on evidence, a backlog is created that delays the processing of other evidence from crime scenes, victims, etc., which extends their processing time beyond the 2 months. Consequently, a rush for DNA analysis should only be requested when absolutely necessary.

Seizing a Suspect's Clothing for DNA Evidence

Clothing may contain evidence that can be connected back to the victim. If a suspect is under arrest, his clothing can be seized as evidence, provided of course that he is arrested wearing the same clothing and that he hasn't washed them. In a hospital setting, the staff can be helpful by providing medical scrubs for a suspect to wear if his clothing is seized. If a suspect is not in custody, however, and evidence is not visible, a search warrant will probably be required to seize his clothing. In either event, confer with the local prosecutor about the legality of seizing clothing before proceeding; do not make the mistake of seizing evidence that will not be permissible in court.

Searching for DNA Evidence under Court Order: The Search Warrant

If a search warrant is obtained and evidence for DNA analysis is sought, the warrant/order should request the seizure of any item on which DNA might be found. Under some circumstances, judges may feel that this definition of possible evidence is too broad. In those cases, specific items suspected of containing the suspect's DNA should be listed on the warrant for seizure. Bloodstains, bedsheets (where semen stains might exist), cigarette butts, the suspect's toothbrush (if appropriate), and the suspect's comb (if appropriate) are typical items that would appear on a search warrant. Any additional items that are found that may contain DNA will require that the warrant be amended before seizure. Amending a warrant is a fairly simple procedure and must be done before leaving the premise. It merely explains the importance of the potential evidence to the magistrate who issued the original search warrant and whose written permission must be obtained.

Media at the Crime Scene

The presence of the media at crime scenes is often troublesome. Although the public has a right to know, investigators also have an obligation to ensure that the confidentiality of the victim is maintained at all times. The press can unwittingly reveal facts that ought to remain confidential and can thereby compromise the trust that victims both expect and deserve from the police. Crime scenes are particularly problematic as they are often located at the victim's residence or entrance to her residence. Divulging the exact location of occurrence may be tantamount to divulging the victim's identity. Great care and sensitivity are needed when revealing anything to do with the victim. For example, advising the press that the victim is a college student may not disclose her identity if the location is a dorm or a building occupied by a number of college students; however, if she is the only college student at that address, the press should be requested not to divulge the exact location. Each case must be judged on its own merits using a common sense evaluation to ensure confidentiality.

Large news organizations have been severely criticized in the past for revealing the identities of rape victims and have become more receptive to the victim's needs over the years. Generally, they maintain policies that prohibit journalists from revealing the identity of rape victims, but they are often not attuned to the subtle ways in which a victim can be identified. Overaggressive and enthusiastic reporters often fail to see the significance of divulging specific information that, regrettably, will disclose the victim's identity. Simply reminding them that they have been responsible in the past and requesting that they continue to be discrete are generally enough to obtain their cooperation. Failing to point out the need for discretion regarding seemingly obscure facts, however, is a fault of the investigator and his superiors, not the fault of the media. We have an obligation to the victim to advise the media of what they should and should not reveal. Allowing them to report an incident without that directive could jeopardize the investigation when certain facts are revealed that could cause greater emotional stress for the victim. This situation could result in her decision not to proceed with the investigation. Decisions such as these prevent cases from moving forward and allow assailants to attack again.

On the other hand, the press can be an effective tool for the police. I have used them to alert the public of threats to their safety to prevent similar attacks from occurring in the future. I have also used them frequently to request assistance from the public when it is needed. They can display artists' sketches derived from the victim's recollection or video stills from security cameras that captured the suspect on film. They can help alert the public to the need for their support in identifying the suspect, or they can be used as a means to advertise rewards effectively. The press is an invaluable tool, if used correctly.

Obtaining their cooperation, however, often comes at a price. They want the inside story; we want to solve the case in a manner that is prosecutable. I found that both objectives are not necessarily mutually exclusive and can be achieved through a cooperative approach that benefits both. I have often made it a point to remind members of the press that the relationship cultivated through this cooperation benefits them more often than it does the police. This understanding ensured their continued cooperation and limited their aggressive nature. Instructing them to film a block or a neighborhood, instead of a particular building, is often a reasonable compromise that satisfies their needs while maintaining the confidentiality of the victim. Similarly, identifying the victim by race and age may be sufficient to meet the needs of the press without placing the victim in jeopardy.

I have found that maintaining a cordial and professional relationship with the press can foster a spirit of cooperation that may be of use to the investigator. Film footage of crowds and vehicles in the area of the crime scene may be of use. The publicity surrounding an arrest of a sex offender may motivate other victims to come forward and report their attacks, as well. The ability of the media to warn the public to a dangerous situation is unparalleled and can prevent further attacks against otherwise unsuspecting women. The media can also facilitate the search for clues by publicizing police contact telephone numbers while requesting the public's assistance. I have seen many cases solved on the basis of anonymous tips that were generated when the press publicized crimes and requested the assistance of the public to help solve them. Clearly, this can be a two-way street. If we both acknowledge each other's needs and agree to act in a respectful and responsible manner, the media will have their story and the police will have gained an important ally.

Conclusion

The crime scene offers investigators a one-time chance to collect evidence and gather information that will make or break a case. Often plenty of evidence is available; we only need to know where to look and how to identify it. Evidence may help identify a suspect (as in the case of fingerprints or DNA of persons whose information is already on file) or it may only lead to a future identification when the suspect is apprehended (as in the case of those who have never had their information on file). It may also help clear falsely accused innocent people. In all cases, however, evidence gathered at a crime scene is an attempt to unveil the truth.

Advances in science, particularly with respect to DNA have been of great help to investigators and prevented many innocent people from being falsely accused. Modern investigators, however, have their work cut out for them. A concrete understanding of the capabilities of forensic technology is essential for every investigator, particularly with regard to DNA. Those who are knowledgeable have a clear advantage when it comes to identifying and collecting evidence. Their appreciation for the resources available to them through the latest technological advances gives them a distinct advantage as they seek the truth and search for suspects. They understand that they do not need to know the finer points of such technology. They only need to keep abreast of its limitations, to know how to preserve evidence for experts, and ultimately to be able to identify evidence that would be missed by the untrained eye.

The need for corroboration is unique within sex crime investigations and poses a major problem that sex crime investigators must overcome. The emotional attachment of many victims with their assailants and prior consensual sexual relations that they enjoyed can fly in the face of the victim's assertion that she was raped. Corroboration can be obtained through the physical evidence; torn clothing, bruising on the victim, pulled-out hair, fingernail scrapings, vaginal examination, and rape kit preparation can all be used to verify the victim's assertion that she was forcibly raped. The lack of such evidence does not negate the victim's assertions, but it does force the investigator to look elsewhere for corroboration.

This chapter was designed to help investigators familiarize themselves with the many unique aspects of crime scenes, particularly sex crime scenes, and to develop a mindset that is insightful and receptive to the collection of evidence.

Bibliography

Almiral, J. R. et al., *Crime Scene Investigation*, U.S. Department of Justice, Office of Justice Programs, National Institute of Justice, Washington, D.C., 2000.

Fisher, B. A. J., *Techniques of Crime Scene Investigation*, 6th ed., CRC Press, Boca Raton, FL, 2000.

Geberth, V. J., *Practical Homicide Investigation: Tactics, Procedures, and Forensic Techniques*, 3rd ed., CRC Press, Boca Raton, FL, 1996, p. 1.

Gerber, S. M. and Saferstein, R., Eds., *More Chemistry and Crime: From Marsh Arsenic Test to DNA Profile*, American Chemical Society, Washington, D.C., 1997.

Gilbert, J. N., *Criminal Investigation*, 4th ed., Prentice Hall, Saddle River, NJ, 1998, p. 88.

Ladray, L. E., *Sexual Assault Nurse Examiner (SANE): Development and Operational Guide*, U.S. Department of Justice, Office of Justice Programs, Office for Victims of Crime, Washington, D.C., 1999.

The Victim
and the Interview

5

The difficulties that investigators encounter while investigating sex crimes are quite different from those involved with any other criminal investigation. Sexual assault victims suffer from a unique array of problems and are often in a fragile state when they encounter the police. It is imperative that investigators be educated to understand the emotional trauma that victims suffer in order to adjust their investigation to meet the needs of victims effectively and create a productive atmosphere — an atmosphere that not only helps the healing process of the victim but produces positive investigative results.

In view of the fact that the vast majority of sex crime victims are female and the vast majority of perpetrators are male, the victim is referred to here as female and the perpetrator as male. Investigators, however, should be aware that the psychological and sociological impact upon male victims might be even more profound than that of their female counterparts, thus requiring additional sensitivity. Mezey and King (2000) noted that male sexual assault victims, unlike their female counterparts, have more trouble accessing the psychological help they need after an attack. The sociological conditioning of men has made it less likely that they will acknowledge feelings of distress and vulnerability. They will not seek help because to do so would be an affront to their masculinity. The issues that do arise when conducting interviews of male victims, however, are often the same as those that involve female victims. The techniques and the strategies to address those issues are outlined in this chapter and can be employed whether the victim is male or female.

Thankfully, most of us have never experienced the pain, embarrassment, or emotional distress that investigators see in sexual assault victims. That deficiency means that investigators must seek a keener understanding of the problem and then adjust the investigation to deal with the unique, albeit unfamiliar, issues that arise with sexual assault victims. Without this modification, the investigation is certain to be deficient in several important ways: it will alienate the victim, it will prolong her emotional recovery, it will limit the information that the investigators will be able to obtain from the victim, and, if the victim decides not to cooperate further, it is almost certainly the basis for her decision.

The emotional responses of rape victims can run the gamut from rage to fear to feelings of worthlessness. Understanding these responses allows investigators to adjust their interviewing techniques appropriately. It also helps them recognize the legitimacy of some of the emotional responses the victim is exhibiting — responses that we may view as being inadequate or even peculiar at the time. Keep in mind that victims will not exhibit a set response. There is no such thing as a typical or an acceptable reaction that investigators can expect to see in sexual assault victims. Instead, it is important to understand that many types of responses are possible. Each victim is an individual with different emotional needs, and the range of reactions can run the gamut from uncontrolled hysteria to calm, or a jocular retort.

Case History

It was the Christmas season in New York, and the stores were filled with shoppers. Tourists crowded the streets and restaurants well into the night. A 26-year-old professional woman was working late in her office, which was located on a crowded street, and the six-block walk to her residence was lined with stores, hotels, and restaurants, as well as hundreds of holiday revelers. About 11:00 at night she left her office and began to walk home. After she had walked one block on the crowded Manhattan street, a male approached her from behind, pointed a hard object in her back, and ordered her to walk with him. He told her that he would kill her if she did not do what he said. They walked about two blocks, passing hundreds of people and motorists along the way. He took her to an isolated area between two buildings and began to undress her. He noticed, however, that motorists stuck in traffic could see what they were doing, so he decided to take her somewhere more secluded. Holding the gun to her back, he forced her to walk another two blocks, where he found a darkened stairwell of a parking garage. Along the way, again they passed hundreds of additional pedestrians and motorists in the crowded streets. When they arrived at this second location, he forcibly raped her. After the rape, the assailant decided to rob the victim and forced her to walk with him to a bank ATM, one block from the rape scene. After she withdrew the maximum amount of cash from the machine, he fled on foot.

In total, the victim had been with the perpetrator for 45 minutes. Together, they had passed hundreds of people on the street and hundreds more in cars that were stuck in traffic. The logical question that comes to mind for anyone questioning the victim would be "Why didn't you try to summon assistance from someone on the street? Surely, someone would have helped." The skeptic among us might even ask, "How is a rape possible under such circumstances — did it really happen?" The victim said that her attacker told her that the object in her back was a gun. She understandably believed him, and she feared that he was going to kill her if she made any sudden moves. She asserts that she tried to get the attention of people on the street by staring at them and rolling her eyes, but no one seemed to understand her motions. She felt that she had no choice but to act the way she did.

After the initial shock of the first 24 hours, the victim displayed what some may consider unusual coping strategies. When she was brought in to the Detective Squad office, she was asked to help in the investigation by viewing photos, by looking at surveillence tapes from commercial establishments along the route of the attack, and by assisting a police artist in preparing a sketch of the assailant. She was very friendly and almost giddy. She joked with detectives about everyday matters (she never joked about the attack) and seemed to be having a good time in the company of my detectives. The trained eye, however, could clearly see that she was trying to avoid the pain that came when she was forced to think about her assailant and her near-death experience. Her reaction after the attack was merely her way of coping.

Discussion

The victim in this case displayed two interesting responses. The first was during the attack; the second was afterward during the investigation.

A number of studies have dealt with the subject of how victims cope in the aftermath of an attack. Frazier and Burnett (1994) noted many coping strategies employed by victims and studied their short- and long-term effectiveness in the recovery process. Their study reveals that victims employ many different coping strategies (their study lists 20), with varying degrees of success. For the investigator, it is sufficient to understand that victims will utilize various and assorted coping mechanisms to help them manage the ordeal.

As for the victim's responses, or lack of responses, I recall that in this case she was an innocent young woman who knew little about how to stay safe in a large city environment. She was a kind and trusting woman who came from a rural area of the country and never had occasion to think through what to do in the case of an attack. Her trusting character and her innocence are desirable attributes, but they are also obstacles when it comes to recognizing danger. Unlike most lifelong city residents, she never thought through what to do if she was accosted on the street.

Instead, she acted on her instinct to survive. Her mind was racing once her attacker confronted her. She believed that her life was in danger and that if she made a mistake she would be dead. Because her life was being threatened, her reactions during the ordeal were controlled by her instinct to survive. She decided to comply with her attacker's demands and fortunately she did survive to tell about it.

Her comment that she tried to get the attention of others with her eyes while she was walking with her assailant sounds almost ludicrous to those of us in law enforcement, but it is not an uncommon response. I have heard several rape victims relay the same response: "I tried to get the attention of people by staring at them and rolling my eyes" or "I stared into the eyes of people passing and then moved my eyes from side to side." Some were on crowded trains, some were on crowded streets, and others were at events with large crowds.

We need to recognize that our skepticism comes from judging rape victims by our standards and our experiences as law enforcement officers. We spend a great deal of time in training. We are taught to plan ahead and be prepared for every dangerous situation that can be imagined. We constantly evaluate and revise our tactics to incorporate new scenarios that may arise. Our tactics become second nature, and we execute them intuitively. Rape victims, on the other hand, are not law enforcement officers. They do not plan to be in dangerous situations; they often do not think through what they would do in a dangerous situation and are unprepared when one comes along.

Counseling

Access to rape counseling is necessary in order to deal with the range and the depth of the emotional trauma victims have suffered. The Cohen and Miller (1998) study found that 20 to 25% of mental health clientele are crime victims and that sexual assault is by far the single most common reason that victims seek mental health providers. A Los Angeles study by Golding et al. (1988) looked at the usage of mental health care by victims of sexual assault. They found that 17.8% of the women who were sexually assaulted at some point in their lives sought mental health care, while that number decreased to 9% for those without such a history. Their study revealed an increased likelihood for sexual assault victims to suffer from mental health problems. Professional counselors are clearly effective at helping victims get through their ordeal and can also be of enormous help to the well-informed investigator. Not only will counseling facilitate the victim's recovery, but it will also help the victim come to terms with the investigation. Therapists understand that the healing process and the investigation need not be mutually exclusive. The treatment of the victim frequently supports police intervention and the ensuing investigation.

Psychologists have long recognized that reporting the crime and helping the police can have a positive impact upon their patient's recovery. Doing so verifies the woman's status as a victim in a meaningful way and serves to demonstrate that her attacker is at fault, not her.

In their study, Creamer et al. (1992) noted that high levels of intrusion (events that stimulate the memory of traumatic events), although stressful, are associated with reduced symptom levels in the long run. Simply stated, the recounting of events by a rape victim may be extremely stressful and does have a positive therapeutic impact upon the long-term psychological state of the victim. Their study showed that the initial deleterious effect of intrusion (which occurs when investigators question victims) is outweighed by the long-term positive results.

Gilboa-Schectman and Foa (2001) conducted an analysis of two studies and found an even stronger relationship. They established that emotional engagement of traumatic events is necessary in order to process trauma successfully. In fact, their study showed that when delays in confronting emotions are encountered recovery is impeded.

In her book *Shattered Assumptions*, Janoff-Bulman (1992) described trauma (similar to that suffered by rape victims) as the abrupt disintegration of one's inner world. Overwhelming life experiences (such as rape) split open the interior world of victims and shatter their most fundamental psychological assumptions. Janoff-Bulman also noted that, although victims are affected by a number of conditions that will impact their ability to cope with being a victim of rape, the use of the term *recovery* is overused and inaccurate. She explains, as anyone who has suffered through a severe traumatic experience knows, that victims will forever be changed by the event. As she states: "Trauma victims go back to a state of health; they do not, however, go back to where they began."

Investigators will occasionally run into roadblocks erected by well-intentioned friends and relatives of victims. Those individuals often believe that the investigative process will have long-term detrimental psychological consequences for the victim. They believe that the investigation will deepen the psychological scars of their loved ones, thereby prolonging their suffering. In fact, the opposite is true. Investigators should be aware that studies have shown that victims who confront their emotions are more likely to achieve some form of recovery than those that do not. Everyone concerned with the victim, however, should also understand that the event has changed her forever. Counseling can help her confront the psychological impact of the attack and help her grow, but the victim will always retain permanent emotional scars. Counseling can help her deal with those scars, but they cannot make them go away.

Initial Response of Victims

Rage

Those victims who feel rage at being attacked are generally more helpful in the beginning stages of an investigation because they want to do whatever they can to strike back at their attacker. Controlling this rage can become an issue if the woman is left untreated. She may become angry at anything that she associates with the attack. She may become belligerent toward all men, including a male investigator. She may become angry with all men who are of the same race as the attacker, particularly if that race is different from hers. She may become angry with all men who are approximately the same age as her attacker. Rage is frequently mixed with the feelings of fear and low self-esteem that churn within the victim as she fights to balance her emotions. She should be encouraged to seek professional counseling for these problems.

Fear

Rape victims may have to confront several different types of fear:

- *Fear of dying* — During the attack, many rapists will threaten to kill their victims if they do not comply. Most who cooperated fully with their attacker have reported that they sincerely felt that they were going to die if they did not comply. Some thought that they were going to die even after complying. Such beliefs make most rapes a near-death experience for its victims.
- *Fear of seeing the rapist again* — The woman becomes hyper-vigilant and worries constantly that she will become a victim again.
- *Fear that the rapist will return if she tells the police* — The woman fears that the police will not be able to protect her.
- *Fear that a particular act or location will stimulate memories of the attack* — This fear must be confronted for long-term emotional stability.
- *Fear of no longer being in control of her own safety* — This fear is compounded exponentially when the attack takes place in a location that was considered safe, such as her home, place of work, or well-traveled public place (crowded street, school, etc.).
- *Fear of being re-victimized by the criminal justice system* — What will the victim endure if she goes through with a prosecution and possible trial?
- *Fear of not being believed* — This fear is especially common in domestic and date-rape situations.
- *Fear of shame* — The victim's perceptions of what her family and friends will think can create additional emotional stress.

The victim described previously was raped after leaving work and walking on a crowded street. She still lives and works in the same area, passing the location of her attack daily — an attack in which she was convinced she would be killed. Surely her fears have been compounded by the constant reminders she faces each day and concern that she may encounter her attacker again. Although some of those fears most likely diminished when the assailant was eventually arrested and jailed, the victim still lives with the daily reminder of what happened to her. She has been changed forever by the event.

Worthlessness

Loss of self-esteem can result from an attack. The victim may want to withdraw from society. This can be an effective way for the victim to cope with her emotions temporarily but can be dangerous if it continues for an extended period.

Guilt/Blame

To those of us who have never suffered the indignity or the terror of a sexual assault, it may seem odd that the victim would blame herself for the attack. After all, we know that she is the victim and that the fault clearly lies with her attacker. Why should she feel guilty? Why should she shift the blame for the attack to herself? The answers lie in how we, as individuals, deal with traumatic events and how others express their feelings to the victim upon hearing of the attack. In the aftermath of an attack, the victim is in a struggle to take back control of her life. Her own sense of guilt, however, is a cruel complication that often impedes her recovery, especially when it is compounded by feelings of personal responsibility. She begins to look within for answers to her questions but that is not where the answers are to be found. She begins to ask questions such as the following. These questions, however, can only result in attributing culpability to herself, not to her attacker:

- Didn't my family tell me not to be out alone at night?
- Didn't my boyfriend say that if you can't defend yourself you shouldn't be out alone?
- Wasn't I taught to be aware of my surroundings? Why wasn't I looking when I entered the parking lot/my apartment/etc.?
- Why did I go to that bar?
- Why did I trust him when I only just met him?
- Why did I let him into my car/apartment, etc.?
- Why did I dress so provocatively?
- Were my remarks too provocative?

All of these questions place blame on the victim, not on the rapist, who is unquestionably the responsible party. Compounding the problem may be the reactions of family, friends, coworkers, and the police, who ask many of the same questions. Sensitivity to the issues is one thing; addressing them is another. Investigators need to ensure that blame is not placed on the victim by anyone coming in contact with her. Reminding those who come in contact with the victim to be vigilant about their reactions to her situation takes only a few minutes and can be extremely beneficial to both the victim and the investigation.

Reporting Delays: Attacks by Strangers

Conventional crimes (robbery, burglary, larceny, etc.) are normally reported immediately when they happen or as soon as they are discovered. The impact of a sexual assault on the victim, however, will almost always cause a delay that can give the suspect the time he needs to escape. It can also impede the investigation in several ways: As time passes, critical forensic evidence can be destroyed before it can be identified, witnesses who can verify the victim's account can be lost because they are unidentified and are no longer present, medical evidence that can support the victim's claim may be gone, and forensic evidence may be destroyed. Unfortunately, there are some who feel that the delay in and of itself is cause to disbelieve the victim. They reason that if the attack really happened then it would have been reported immediately. Such opinions generally come from those not familiar with sex crimes and cannot be further from the truth. As we have seen, sex crimes have an enormous impact upon the psyche of the victim. The initial feelings of shock and disbelief are followed by bewilderment, fright, rage, and despair. Victims need time to sort through their emotions before they can come to grips with reporting an incident to the police. Even with heightened awareness in the midst of highly publicized serial rapes, a delay in reporting often occurs.

Case History

The East Side Rapist terrorized women in an affluent section of Manhattan over a 4-year period from 1994 through 1998. On 16 occasions, he attacked young women as they entered their apartment buildings late at night. Within weeks of my arrival as the commanding officer of the Manhattan Special Victims Squad, we identified the pattern and expanded our investigation. We intensified our search for the suspect by augmenting our resources with increased personnel and enlisting the public's help. Press conferences, community meetings, and increases in police patrols generated a great deal of publicity. A sketch of the suspect was plastered over the front page of every New York paper. Posters were displayed in the lobby of every building, in every storefront window, and on streetlight and traffic poles throughout the community. Literally, thousands of posters were distributed.

It is safe to say that the entire community was well aware of the threat and were on the alert for the suspect. An added benefit to the publicity surrounding this case was that the victims knew that they were not alone. The normal feelings of isolation and the fear of not being believed were eliminated as factors for not reporting an attack. Despite this, in every attack (except one that was called in by a neighbor as the victim screamed) the victim did not call the police immediately. After each assault, the victim would typically go to her apartment and call a girlfriend or boyfriend to seek emotional support before calling the police. As a matter of fact, it was typically the friend who had to convince the victim to go to the police. Unfortunately, this often prevented us from isolating the crime scene and gave the suspect ample time to flee the neighborhood, but the responses of the victims were normal and consistent with what we know about rape victims.

Delayed Reporting and Acquaintance Rapes

It is indisputable that such delays are typical in all rapes, even under the best of circumstances. The gap from the time of occurrence to the actual report to the police is even more severe in non-stranger rapes. Acquaintance rapes may take days, weeks, or even months to report, while domestic and particularly child rapes may go for many years or decades before being reported. Threatening the victim to keep the acts secret are typical when the rapes involve children, and the rapes may not surface until the child is no longer living in the household.

Luckily, some states have recognized the conflict created by delayed reports and the restrictions placed on prosecutions by the statute of limitations. They have taken steps to rectify the situation to some degree by extending the statute of limitations in cases that involve juvenile victims. These victims are now given a longer period that extends into adulthood to report sexual assault cases. Although medical and forensic evidence may no longer exist, cases can still be prosecuted if a case can be put together against the suspect (see Chapter 6).

As discussed earlier, acquaintance rapes, including date-rape situations, tend to generate more feelings of guilt than stranger assaults. Working through those feelings often takes time. It is not uncommon for a victim to seek professional help before telling anyone, and it is often the psychotherapist who encourages the victim to report the incident to the police. Such delays may impact upon the collection of evidence, but they should not be construed to indicate that the victim lacks credibility. In fact, the victim is acting in a typical manner for one who has been the victim of sexual assault. Her need for psychological help may indeed add to her credibility.

Although the delay is a serious impediment for investigators and can jeopardize the collection of forensic evidence, perhaps eliminating it as a supporting element of the crime, it does not preclude the use of the methods that will be discussed in the following chapter to build a case against the suspect.

Domestic rapes, particularly those involving children, have an even deeper impact on the emotional instability of the victim. Imagine the trauma of being raped by someone you trusted and loved or the trauma of no longer feeling safe in your own home. These are the disturbing dynamics that increase the severity of the impact domestic rapes have upon its victims. Women assaulted by husbands or ex-husbands are told that no one would believe them and that they will have to live with it. Remember, it was not too long ago that it was generally accepted that a husband could not rape his wife. In fact, up until the 1970s it was impossible for a husband to be convicted of rape in some states. Methods for investigating these cases are similar to those in acquaintance cases and are also discussed in the following chapter.

The Interview

Ordinarily, at least two interviews of rape victims will be conducted. The first is typically conducted at the scene, or more likely at the hospital where the victim has been taken. The second is a more thorough interview that is conducted at the squad office. In either case, it is imperative that the investigators ask the victim not to bathe, douche, brush teeth (if oral sex was involved), wash her clothes, etc. to prevent the loss of evidence before a medical exam can be conducted. Although it is legitimate and necessary to seek answers to many questions, how they are asked will impact immeasurably on the future cooperation of the victim. If the questions are perceived as demeaning and offensive, a rapport based upon trust and respect cannot develop between the investigators and the victim. She will certainly feel offended and shamed if she is not treated in a dignified manner. She will simply seek to end her pain by refusing to cooperate further with your inquiries. In order to establish a rapport that fosters trust and respect, the following guidelines are recommended.

Length of Interview

At the hospital, the investigator may not have much time to speak with the victim before her exam and before evidence is destroyed. Concentrate on the physical description of the perpetrator and his actions to determine the location of possible evidence (fingerprints, semen, blood, etc.). Ensure that the medical staff are fully briefed on the locations where evidence may be found (vagina, anus, mouth, other location where the suspect ejaculated). Do not interfere with their examination but do ensure that they are aware of your needs. Be aware that the victim may be on medication and may require some sleep before a thorough interview can commence. The interview at the squad office should take place as soon as possible after the attack to ensure that the victim does not forget any details that may aid in the investigation. The length of the interview will depend on the extent to which she can recall information and her psychological state. It may last anywhere from one hour to several hours. Reconstructing the events that led up to the attack may take a great deal of time, and the victim may not understand the significance of your questions. Explain to her your reasons for asking them and assure her that the answers are essential to the investigation.

Privacy

When a hospital interview is conducted, it is imperative that the victim be given absolute privacy during any medical exam. Whether the investigators are male or female, they should reassure the victim that they intend to leave the room when the doctor enters for her exam. This will alleviate any fear that she may have regarding her privacy. The interview should take place prior to the medical exam to ensure that you have documented all the possible locations of forensic evidence, some of which will be collected by the hospital staff. Conduct the interview in private, not within earshot of anyone else. Provide the medical staff with the information they need to collect evidence (e.g., location of semen in or on the vagina, anus, leg, back). It is not uncommon to uncover information from the victim that will aid in the recovery of crucial evidence before a medical exam is completed. The rapist may have ejaculated on the victim's stomach, back, or chest. The investigator can then inform the medical staff of the location of vital evidence and can request that they take swabs of the area for placement in the sexual assault evidence kit and future forensic analysis. Without a preliminary interview by investigators, the medical staff would most likely conduct only an ordinary pelvic exam and crucial evidence may very well be lost.

Setting

The interview at the squad office should take place as soon as possible afterwards to ensure that the victim does not forget important details. This interview should also be done in private. Speaking with a victim in the middle of a busy office, much as you might with a robbery victim, is not only inappropriate but it is also foolish. The victim cannot open up to reveal key elements of the crime in such a setting, nor can you give her your full attention. It is recommended that you set a room aside for this purpose and place an "Interview in Progress" sign on the door to prevent interruptions. Some locales have actually mandated privacy during rape interviews through legislation. Clearly, instances of imprudence on the part of investigators were the reasons for enacting such laws.

Investigators should avoid using rooms that are generally used for interrogations. These cold, depressing rooms that are the norm in most police facilities are generally not conducive to interviewing rape victims. Their windowless design, security bars to which prisoners are handcuffed, and stark metal or wooden furniture are necessary safety features for the interrogation of prisoners but are not conducive to the interviewing process of sexual assault victims. Zulawski and Wicklander (1993), experts in interviewing and interrogation, noted that a comfortable office that provides few distractions is more conducive to an effective interview than the typical interrogation room found at police facilities. They suggest that interviewers try to look at the interview process from the victim's point of view, and I most assuredly agree. I have found that investigators who do everything they can to ease the interview process for victims are more likely to obtain the victim's cooperation and future assistance. Placing the victim in a comfortable office or room set aside for this purpose is without a doubt more conducive to obtaining her cooperation and easing the pain that she is obviously undergoing. Experience has shown that victims who are more comfortable with the interview process will be more candid and will tend to continue their cooperation as their case progresses.

Investigator Gender

As discussed in Chapter 3, past experience has shown that the gender of the investigator is not as important as his or her demeanor with the victim or ability to communicate compassionately with the victim. The ability to recognize the plight of the victim and to adjust the interview to accommodate her emotional state has more to do with the skills of an interviewer than with the gender.

Have a Second Investigator Present at the Interview

It is always suggested to have a second investigator present during the interview process. Victims are so distraught that they often misinterpret questions and can easily become offended. This can happen even when investigators have spent time explaining the reasons for their questions. A second investigator can serve to keep the victim composed and can clarify any misunderstandings that the victim may have during the interview process. Together, the two investigators can provide a collaborative analysis of both the victim and the perpetrator. The second investigator can also serve to protect the department from embarrassment by validating the appropriateness of the interview process should the victim make unwarranted accusations. Remember, she will be in a highly emotional state and can easily misinterpret questions, comments, etc. that will arise.

Discourage the Presence of a Support Person during the Interview

It is not uncommon for a friend, relative, spouse, or parent to be present at the hospital or to accompany the victim to the squad office after an attack is reported. The emotional support that can be given by this person is essential to the psychological recovery of the victim, but it can be counterproductive during the interview process. The victim will have to disclose minute details of the attack, which may include degrading acts that she was forced to endure. The interview will also include a detailed account of the events leading up the attack, including any prior sexual activity. The presence of a support person at this juncture could hinder the investigation by prohibiting the victim from being totally truthful about these facts. Frequently, it will be necessary to explain the reasons for taking this position to the victim and the support person in order to obtain their cooperation. I have found that victims will routinely agree, but the support person often fails to see the logic, particularly when a juvenile victim is involved. Sometimes it is necessary to involve superiors who can use their status as the ultimate authority to reason with and pressure the support person to acquiesce. My detectives frequently asked me to intervene with protective parents who wanted to be present during the interview of their child. I used my position of authority to ensure parents that the investigator was doing what was best for the victim and for the investigation. Parents had a much easier time agreeing with the process when they were given the opportunity to vent their concerns to a person in a position of authority, and when that person reinforced the investigator's insistence on conducting the interview without the parents.

Ease Tension

Begin the interview by introducing yourself and your partner. Briefly explain to the victim your experience in handling sex crime investigations and be sure to explain the questions that you will ask. It will be necessary for you to obtain detailed information about the victim. This affords you a perfect opportunity to ease the tension. Encourage her to expand on her school activities, work, friends, family, hobbies, and activities. A conversation of this nature will often establish a rapport with the victim that will alleviate some of her anxiety. Lead the interview toward the events leading up to the attack, and let the victim speak freely about the incident. Remember, do not be judgmental, or even appear to be judgmental, about her lifestyle, her actions on the night in question, or about any of the details of the attack. Frequently assure her that the perpetrator is to blame for what happened, not her. Allow the victim as much time as she needs to get through each aspect of the interview. Lend emotional support, but make sure that you obtain all of the clinical details of the attack. These details are necessary for prosecutorial purposes and will help the investigator clarify some inconsistencies that are sure to arise.

Expect the Victim to be Untruthful

Once investigators come to understand the emotional trauma that victims suffer, they will be better equipped to deal with the investigation from a professional point of view. Untrained investigators, on the other hand, often conclude that victims are fabricating attacks when they uncover inconsistencies and outright lies. Their conclusions and their deductive reasoning have served them well over the years, and when inconsistencies and lies are exposed in non-sex crimes they normally indicate that victims are lying, usually for some financial or emotional gain. Where a sexual assault is concerned, however, those suppositions are often wrong and can be hazardous to the career of those involved, particularly if they certify that a case is false, decline to investigate further, and another victim is attacked by the same perpetrator.

Victims are often embarrassed by their actions prior to the sexual assault, or they have done something that they consider immoral that they do not wish to admit. Consider the case of a nice young girl who is talked into going to a rowdy bar where many people are involved in drinking games, and she soon partakes in the festivities. She may even expose her breasts to a crowd (we have all seen this happen on television at Mardi Gras). Later she is attacked by one of her male companions, and she denies drinking or exposing herself. Meanwhile, the investigator has a videotape of her doing both. Does this mean that she is lying about the sexual assault? *Absolutely not!* Does it mean that she is embarrassed and horrified about her own actions? Probably. Do her prior actions make it more difficult for investigators to prove her case? Yes, but that does not mean that the victim was not attacked. Her actions may make it more difficult to prove, but that is not an excuse for disregarding a sexual assault.

Question the Reporting Delay

Although legitimate reasons may exist for delaying the reporting of a rape, investigators should not shy away from finding out what they are. Explain to the victim that defense attorneys will focus their interest anywhere they can to avoid the real issue of the guilt of their client. It is important that you resolve this issue. Once it is cleared up, you can then move forward in a positive manner into the interview.

Explain Each Question That You Ask

The victim will be extremely apprehensive about speaking to anyone concerning the attack. She is suffering through what may be the most traumatic period in her life, and she needs to be assured that she is in the hands of professionals. The first step in this process is to assure her that her case is important and that you will do everything possible to apprehend and convict the perpetrator. Next, explain to her that you need her help to gather all the evidence available. Finally, let her know that you will need to discuss all of the events surrounding the attack and that you will ask her to describe the clinical details of the attack itself. For example, you will need to know:

- What the rapist did with his penis — where he put it (in her anus, vagina, mouth, etc.) and where he ejaculated.
- What he did with his mouth — where he put it and whether or not he licked the victim (remember that DNA can be recovered from saliva on the body).
- What he made the victim do.
- What the victim's prior sexual activity was (medical evidence may uncover prior sexual activity or the presence of semen from a consensual partner).

Explain why you need to know all of these details and make certain that she understands before going forward. Clarify any misconceptions that she may have by frequently asking if she understands why you need to know everything. Remember to always be sympathetic to her needs, both emotionally and physically, and use terminology that shows that you genuinely care for her well-being. Act in a professional and courteous manner at all times, much as you would expect a caring and sympathetic medical staff member to act with a child of yours.

If you fail to explain what you are about to ask, the victim will not have time to adapt to the embarrassing questions you are seeking answers to. She may become insulted and rebellious when you ask her direct questions because she does not understand the motivation behind asking the question. She may get agitated and decide not to cooperate any further. Remember that the questions you will ask are difficult enough for the victim under the best of circumstances. She will need your help to see her through this ordeal. Keep in mind that the victim is in a fragile state and that your decisions may have a lasting effect not only on her recovery but on future cooperation as well.

Maintain a Nonjudgmental Attitude

It is generally necessary for the victim to chronicle many things about her personal life during the interview. She may engage in a lifestyle that makes her more vulnerable to such an attack. She may have been intoxicated or on drugs at the time of the attack. She may have acted promiscuously, in the investigator's eyes, or she may have flirted with her assailant before the attack. None of these actions justifies what happened to her, and investigators should not let their personal feelings about such lifestyles interfere with their duty to conduct a complete and thorough investigation. To do so would only engender a reluctant attitude in the victim. If you convey any negative opinion to the victim regarding her actions, it can only have a negative impact upon the interview. She may become more self-conscious, and she will hesitate to talk about things that will again produce the negative response by the interviewer that she has already witnessed. It may even become impossible for the investigator to continue. The victim will set up a defensive wall to prevent any further embarrassment, and she will refuse to cooperate any further. She will consider herself a victim once again. This time, however, she will consider the investigator to be the perpetrator of her latest assault. As mentioned earlier, the presence of a second investigator in the interview process is always a good idea. This investigator can deflect any criticisms the victim may have and take over the interview from that point forward. Repeated negative reactions, however, will only trigger an entirely uncooperative attitude on the part of the victim, thus causing the loss of your primary witness. Miller (1997) conducted a study of violence against street prostitutes. She documented the extent to which a nonjudgmental demeanor during interviews can elicit more information and cooperation. Her study showed that interviewers who were perceived to be nonthreatening were able to establish a rapport with those being interviewed. That rapport enabled them to elicit more information and more details during the interview process.

In the case discussed at the beginning of this chapter, the victim was accosted on a busy street and forced to go with her attacker. She states that she tried to get the attention of people by staring at them and rolling her eyes. Even though this approach might seem slightly absurd to a seasoned investigator, any display of criticism on the part of the interviewing detective would have had a negative impact. The victim would sense that she was being judged and would be less than forthright in order to prevent embarrassment.

Likewise, intoxicated victims who let passing acquaintances take them home and are then raped should not be judged for what can be perceived as stupidity. Stupidity is not a crime. The male took advantage of her intoxicated state and had sex with her against her will. He is the one who has committed a crime. He is the one we should focus our rebuke upon. Remember, we all do stupid things, but luckily we all do not become rape victims.

Be Respectful

The demeaning actions that the victim was made to endure can have a devastating effect on her self-esteem. Using the appropriate titles of Miss, Mrs., or Ms. will express your desire to treat her with utmost respect and professionalism. She is in desperate need of such respect and will interpret your attitude in a positive way. The mutual respect that is generated is more conducive to obtaining all of the facts and will facilitate future interactions as the case progresses.

Case History

A tourist visiting a large Manhattan museum went to the ladies' bathroom on the main floor. A rapist followed her into the bathroom and attacked her in one of the stalls. After the rape, she walked around the museum and then decided to call the police. Detectives from the local precinct interviewed her but failed to notify any sex crimes investigators. They took her back to the museum to identify the exact location. After arriving at the scene of the attack, one investigator had the victim show him exactly how the attack occurred. He placed her in the stall and asked her to stand in the same position that her attacker made her stand in while he assumed the position of the rapist. These detectives may have been trying to ascertain the exact facts as accurately as possible, but they clearly did not treat the victim with any respect. They failed to see the trauma that they were placing her in, and they jeopardized her future cooperation. It took some time and an apology by my detectives to gain the victim's cooperation.

Do Not Touch

Understandably, well-intentioned investigators often feel the strain of the emotional distress they witness in victims. If a similar situation were to happen within their private lives, they would undoubtedly become very protective and consoling. A sexual assault against a friend or family member would naturally arouse intense feelings of sympathy. The natural inclination is to reach out and hug or hold that person to try to console her. In a professional setting, however, investigators must refrain from such contact with the victim. Although it may be natural to put your arm around a victim who is clearly suffering emotionally, your actions can be easily misinterpreted. The perpetrator of this crime has touched her intimately and has violated her in the most vile and atrocious manner imaginable. She does not need another stranger, particularly a male, touching her again. In her emotional state, she may even interpret it as sexually aggressive act. *Note:* The need to comfort and make sexually abused children feel safe and reaffirm their innocence, however, is different. They usually need both emotional and physical contact to feel secure.

Questions to Ask during the Interview

The information sought during most interviews that do not involve sex crimes generally includes a description of the perpetrator, the method of entry, the direction of flight, and a description of the property taken, all of which are vital to the investigation. For sex crimes, however, additional matters require attention. The nature of the attack offers a unique insight into the intimate physical characteristics of the perpetrator and his sexual preferences — information that can be of enormous help in many ways. It can facilitate the identification or elimination of suspects, help identify serial rapists, and corroborate the victim's account.

Physical Characteristics of Suspect

Due to the nature of the attack, victims will observe areas of the suspect's body that are not normally exposed. Scars, tattoos, and birthmarks are all features that can help identify suspects. The victim's observation of them on unexposed areas of the suspect's body will not only help identify or eliminate a suspect but also enhance the victim's credibility considerably for prosecutorial purposes in court. The victim's knowledge of whether the suspect is circumcised or not will also go a long way toward eliminating suspects and connecting cases and is an important question to ask. One should be careful, however, to ensure that the victim is aware of the difference in appearance between a circumcised and an uncircumcised penis. It is not unusual for some women (particularly young girls) not to know the difference or not want to admit that they do not know. In either event, the investigators should be sure that they and the victim understand exactly what is meant by the term (a rule that should hold true throughout the interview). Using a drawing for clarification can be helpful, as long as the emotional state of the victim is up to dealing with it. Rape pattern investigations tend to generate a great deal of publicity, and justifiably so. The publicity, however, is a double-edged sword. It serves the purpose of forewarning the public regarding what to look for and what to avoid and it generates calls that may lead to the identity and apprehension of the suspect. Conversely, it can also waste valuable resources tracking down leads that have no value. Any information that can give investigators an edge in managing resources, such as specific identifying marks or characteristics of a suspect's genitals that are not made public, should be welcomed without reservation.

Case History

A serial rapist terrorized one of the most affluent areas of the city for a number of years. A great deal of publicity was attached to each attack, and it was exceptionally helpful in alerting the public and generating awareness, which surely prevented some from becoming victims. Literally thousands of calls were made regarding the identity of the rapist. Some came from former girlfriends, some from women who saw a male expose himself on the street, and some from officers who arrested men who also looked and acted like the suspect. In each case, prior knowledge of specific details regarding the rapist's genitals either eliminated or confirmed the individual as a possible suspect. Earlier interviews of the victims had established a certain characteristic about the perpetrator's genitals that was not publicized (such information should not be given to anyone not directly involved in the case). The elimination of suspects saved an enormous amount of time and prevented the squandering of valuable resources. If any doubt did exist, however, a DNA sample was taken for comparison with the evidence in the case.

Detailed Account of Attack

A detailed account of the attack, including meticulous attention to the clinical details of the sex act, is necessary in order to make some determinations regarding the *modus operandi* (M.O.) and the signature of the suspect. Geberth (1996) described *modus operandi* as the "mode of operation or way of doing things. The *modus operandi* is a learned behavior that changes as offenders gain experience, build confidence, or become involved with the criminal justice system." Geberth further states, "The signature aspect of a violent criminal offender is a unique and integral part of the offender's behavior. The signature component refers to the psychodynamics, which are the mental and emotional processes underlying human behavior and its motivations."

Studying the *modus operandi* will help us link cases and increase our evidence pool as we seek to solve our cases. Perpetrators may change their sexual preferences from time to time, but generally their actions are similar from one case to the other. Gathering the clinical details of the attack is essential when linking cases and is necessary to ensure that no one is surprised by unspecified facts during the prosecution of the case. Studying the perpetrator's signature can give us a better understanding of his motivations. As Geberth notes, "The *modus operandi* involves actions necessary to accomplish the activity while the signature aspect represents the underlying emotional needs of the offender." In order to determine both the *modus operandi* and the signature of a sex offender, inquiries should be made about the following:

- How did he approach his victim?
- Did the perpetrator's demeanor (e.g., calm, agitated, or demeaning) change during the course of the attack?
- What details can be provided about the perpetrator's physical appearance (e.g., tattoos, scars, genitals, circumcised or not)?
- Was the perpetrator's clothing neat, sloppy, etc.?
- What was the hygiene of the perpetrator (e.g., unshaven, clean or dirty, presence of body odor, use of after-shave or cologne, soap scent, sloppy, neat, etc.)?
- What statements and demands did the perpetrator make prior to the rape, during the rape, and after the rape? Often the exact phrases are repeated from one attack to another.
- What type of sexual activity occurred and what was the order of that sexual activity (e.g., oral sex followed by vaginal and anal sex)?
- What was the positioning of both the victim and the perpetrator during the sexual assault?
- What was the perpetrator's ability to maintain an erection; for example, did he require the victim to masturbate him first or he did he become flaccid during the attack?
- Did the perpetrator use a condom?
- Did the perpetrator ejaculate into the victim's vagina, anus, or mouth or remove his penis and ejaculate on specific parts of her body or on the floor?
- Did the perpetrator wipe himself, and what did he use to wipe himself with?
- Did the perpetrator wipe the victim to remove DNA evidence? What did he use to wipe her with? Frequently, her panties will be used, which the rapist will then take with him.
- Did the perpetrator attempt to conceal his identity?
- Did the perpetrator take items of clothing from the victim (e.g., panties)?
- Did the perpetrator steal any of the victim's property (cash, jewelry, credit cards)?
- Did the perpetrator remove only items that are not of significant value (identification, pictures, etc.) as trophies of the attack?

Case History

In the year 2000, a woman in her 30s entered her apartment building on the upper west side of Manhattan. As she opened the lobby door, the perpetrator accosted her from behind and tried to force her into her apartment.

She informed her attacker that her boyfriend was inside (which was a lie, as she lived alone), so he decided to rape her on the stairwell instead. Despite the fact that she had clearly seen his face, he tied a scarf over her face as he forced her to undress. He then raped her on the stairwell from behind without a condom. Once he ejaculated, he pulled up his pants and forced her to remain on the stairs face down. He then rummaged through her pocketbook and stole her cash and jewelry, leaving behind her credit cards, keys, and identification. He ordered her to remain on the stairs and count to five hundred while he fled.

A week later I received a call to an Upper East Side location where a woman in her 50s had been raped. As she entered her building, she was accosted from behind, and the perpetrator forced her into her second-floor apartment. Although she had seen his face clearly, the perpetrator still tied a scarf over her face and raped her from behind on her bed without using a condom. After the rape, he ordered her to remain face down on the bed while he stole cash and jewelry from her apartment. He tore out the telephone wires and ordered her to count to a thousand while he fled.

Clearly we were dealing with the same individual. The peculiarities of the rape, which included the positioning of the victims, the use of a scarf, the lack of a condom, and his demand that they count while he fled had become the suspect's *modus operandi* and allowed us to make the connection immediately. Fortunately, a fingerprint from the lobby door was recovered during the second case that helped us identify the suspect. Subsequent lineups and DNA tests confirmed his guilt. He has since been sentenced to a 25-year to life prison term.

Note: Keep in mind, that it is not uncommon to see a rapist graduate from misdemeanor sexual abuse to rape over a period of time. In those cases, because the crimes are different, the *modus operandi* of the attacker changes as he adapts his tactics to fit the intensity of his crimes. A close examination, however, will reveal the several significant similarities in each succeeding crime.

Prior Sexual Activity

It is important to know if the victim has had consensual sex within 72 hours of the rape. The semen of the perpetrator and the semen of her consensual partner could be commingled in her vagina. It may also be commingled on her clothing (particularly on her underwear where seepage from her vagina may have occurred) or on her bedding (if the rape occurred on her bed). It will be necessary to identify her consensual partner and obtain a vial of his blood or buccal swab (see Chapter 4) to identify his DNA for purposes of distinguishing his semen from that of the perpetrator's. A proper DNA analysis will not be possible without one of them and will prevent investigators from positively connecting cases or identifying suspects.

In cases of date rape and domestic rape, it will be necessary to inquire about the victim's prior relationship and any sexual activity that took place with the perpetrator in the past. He, of course, will allege that all the sexual activity was consensual and that they engaged in consensual sex every so often. A thorough investigation will uncover these facts beforehand and will allow the investigator to adjust his tactics accordingly (see Chapter 6).

Inquiring if the victim is sexually active and how frequently she engages in consensual sex is necessary in order to adjust the investigation as needed. Remember to remain nonjudgmental when making such inquiries. If allegations of promiscuity surface from witnesses, friends, and other acquaintances, it is imperative that the issue be discussed in order to make the appropriate tactical decisions and to avoid being blindsided by a defense attorney after the arrest.

Previous Reports

A thorough investigation will uncover any past crime complaints made by the victim. Those that involve sex crimes should be scrutinized thoroughly. She may have had several unfounded cases in the past, or she may have been arrested for falsifying crimes. In either case, her present allegation should get investigated in a comprehensive manner even though her credibility issues will pose significant difficulties for prosecutors. Then again, her prior complaints may show that she was being stalked or harassed by a specific individual and that she tried to use the legal system to protect herself. In those cases, the prior complaints may help establish her credibility. This is a common situation involving ex-husbands and ex-boyfriends.

Allegations against the Victim and Prior Criminal Activity

Establishing the credibility of the victim is essential in all rape cases. The defendant's attorney will exercise due diligence and complete a thorough background check of the victim. It is essential to ask the victim about any prior criminal activity or allegations that may be used to impugn her integrity in court. Explain to her the necessity of her honesty. She may feel embarrassed by some past indiscretions and may not wish them to be known. The investigator, on the other hand, needs to know about her past in order to preclude its use against her. In cases where the victim's credibility is in question, her candidness in this area will help the investigator evaluate her honesty while weighing the expenditure of resources.

File Photographs

Be sure that the victim has an opportunity to view photographs of all possible suspects as soon as possible. The most appropriate time is generally after her interview at the squad office while her memory is still fresh. A file of sexual offenders should be maintained and updated constantly. Do not limit the search to sexual offenders, however, but expand it as needed to include suspects with similar descriptions who are not necessarily sex offenders. Many large departments have computerized their criminal photograph files. This has proven to be the most effective and efficient way for victims to view photographs. It has many positive advantages in that it provides the most current photographs of criminals, it generally allows victims and witnesses to view as many as six photographs at a time, witnesses and victims can view the same photographs at different terminals simultaneously, it provides the investigator with documentation of how many and which photographs were viewed, and it prevents the victim from viewing the same photograph multiple times which can cause difficulty in court if an identification is made.

Do Not Wait

Do not put off the interview of the victim, witnesses, or any investigative steps that involve the victim. Waiting often exacerbates the problem by discouraging the victim. She will begin to feel that her case is not being given the attention it deserves. Add this reaction to her desire to put this terrible incident behind her, and the investigator will find that the victim has become overwhelmed with the need to move on. She may have already decided not to go forward with the case and only wants to get on with her life.

Keep Victim Informed

Getting the victim involved immediately and keeping her informed commits her to the investigation. As she sees how complex and intense the investigation is, she will become progressively more committed. Her commitment may come from an honest desire to help catch and convict the suspect, or it may come from her sense of obligation to those who have committed their time and effort to her case. Although the former is preferred, the latter will do. Without the cooperation and help of victims, investigations will grind to a halt. Every investigator should realize that the cooperation of victims is always tenuous at best, and its status can easily change. Keeping victims involved and informed helps their emotional state and goes a long way toward securing their continued cooperation. Investigators will find that nothing is more frustrating than conducting a long investigation that comes to an abrupt halt when the victim decides not to cooperate. Sex crime investigators should always remember that one of their main functions is to maintain the delicate balance of keeping the victim both informed and involved while aggressively pursuing the perpetrator.

Prepare Victim for Legal Proceedings

As investigators, we are familiar with the internal procedures that the victim will undergo in court. We tend sometimes to take for granted our knowledge of the system and treat it as common knowledge. The vast majority of victims, however, have no idea of what to expect in court. Once an arrest is made, investigators and prosecutors should work together to ensure that the victim is well prepared for the distress that criminal proceedings are sure to inflict upon her. Explain to her that the defense attorney will do everything he or she can to discredit her and that she should be prepared. Discuss inconsistencies and clear them up beforehand. Discuss any prior relationships with the suspect in detail to prevent surprises in court.

Conclusion

A sex crime investigation is probably the only type of case where the victim can easily be re-victimized if not handled correctly. Although the needs of the investigation will force victims to divulge intimate details, properly trained investigators can minimize her trauma. An understanding of the psychological distress and the physical pain that victims experience will go a long way toward helping investigators deal with victims. This is a unique field of investigation, and many distinctive problems can arise. These problems, to the untrained eye, can raise doubts in the credibility of the victims. Victims will frequently hide details or even lie about embarrassing details to keep them private. The trained investigator, however, sees and understands the unique problems that arise and sorts through them systematically with the victim to expose the total truth. This chapter has been designed to help investigators understand those problems and in doing so provide them with a framework for handling victims in a professional and courteous manner.

Bibliography

Cohen, M. A. and Miller, T. R., The cost of mental health care for victims of crime, *J. Interpers. Violence*, 13(1), 93, 1998.

Creamer, M., Burgess, P., and Pattison, P., Reaction to trauma: a cognitive processing model, *J. Abnorm. Psychol.*, 101(3), 452–459, 1992.

Frazier, P. A. and Burnett, J. W., Immediate coping strategies among rape victims, *J. Counsel. Develop.*, 72(6), 633–639, 1994.

Geberth, V., *Practical Homicide Investigation: Tactics, Procedures, and Forensic Techniques*, 3rd ed., CRC Press, Boca Raton, FL, 1996.

Gilboa-Schechtman, E. and Foa, E. B., Patterns of recovery from trauma: the use of intraindividual analysis, *J. Abnorm. Psychol.*, 110(3), 392–400, 2001.

Golding, J. M., Stein, J. A., Siegel, J. M., Burnam, M. A., and Sorenson, S. B., Sexual assault history and the use of health and mental health services, *Am. J. Community Psychol.*, 16(5), 625–644, 1988.

Janoff-Bulman, R., *Shattered Assumptions: Towards a New Psychology of Trauma*, The Free Press, New York, 1992, pp. 63 and 169.

Mezey, G. C. and King, M. B., *Male Victims of Sexual Assault*, 2nd ed., Oxford University Press, London, 2000, p. 142.

Miller, J., Researching violence against street prostitutes: Issues of epistemology, methodology, and ethics, in *Researching Sexual Violence against Women: Methodological and Personal Perspectives*, Schwartz, M. D., Ed., Sage, Thousand Oaks, CA, 1997, p. 147.

Zulawski, D. E. and Wicklander, D. E., *Practical Aspects of Interview and Interrogation*, CRC Press, Boca Raton, FL, 1993.

Acquaintance Rape and Domestic Rape: Investigative Strategies for Known Rapists

6

Sex crimes are generally classified into three different categories: stranger, domestic, and acquaintance. The difference is significant for investigators because distinct strategies are needed to cope with each type of investigation. The strategies employed in acquaintance rapes are different than those involving domestic situations. They in turn are significantly different from those that involve stranger and serial rapes. Although the strategies employed in the different types of sex crime investigations have some core similarities, the differences are substantial and they compel investigators to adjust their methods accordingly to deal with the distinct demands of each. For example, the investigation into a boyfriend or a husband who forcibly rapes is clearly quite different from that of a stranger who attacks women at random and terrorizes entire communities.

Unique issues arise when investigating sex crimes that are generally not seen in other types of investigations. Although the forensic and evidence-gathering techniques are often very similar to those of most serious crimes, additional obstacles are encountered due to the distinctive nature of sexual assault investigations. The intimacy of the attack, the actions of the victim prior to the attack, the victim's relationship with her attacker, and the victim's need to hide embarrassing issues make the investigation far more sensitive and complex than other types of investigations. These obstacles often appear daunting and insurmountable to untrained and the inexperienced investigators, but to the seasoned investigator they are complications that can be overcome by adjusting the investigation to address the individual needs of the victim as they address the needs of the case.

Burden of Proof

As investigators, we know all too well that the criminal justice system places many hurdles in the path of successful prosecutions of sex crimes. Although the system is justified in placing the burden of proof on the accuser, it does provoke an examination into areas that are rarely contemplated with non-sex crime investigations. Rape shield laws may prevent past sexual conduct from being exploited in the courtroom, but many other areas can be examined by defense attorneys; for example, the victim's prior relationship with the suspect, her flirtatious conduct, her manner of dress, her perceived promiscuity, her emotional state at the time of the attack, her alcohol consumption, and her willingness to be alone with the suspect can all be used against her to show that she was a willing participant in the sexual act. Because the victim is often the sole witness to the attack and her testimony may be the only evidence presented against the accused, such factors as those just mentioned may carry unmerited weight as jurors attempt to weigh the credibility of the victim.

The criminal justice system is designed to protect the rights of the accused and in doing so it appropriately places the burden of proof on the accuser and forces prosecutors to prove guilt beyond a reasonable doubt. Credibility issues are common with sexual assault investigations because of the many additional factors that come into play. Although the credibility of robbery and burglary victims is generally not an insurmountable issue for the prosecution, it is often the primary concern in sex crime cases. The usual duties of most criminal investigations are frequently expanded to establish that a crime actually occurred and that no ulterior motives lie behind the allegations. Most investigations are limited to collecting evidence, identifying the perpetrator, and making the apprehension, but sex crimes investigators are forced to substantiate much more.

Establishing that a crime even happened, particularly in domestic and acquaintance cases, often means corroborating the victim's account through a third party or by amassing evidence that supports her accusation. Unfortunately, I have found that the victim's account of the attack without any form of corroboration is generally not enough to obtain a conviction.

Many people, particularly feminists, may feel that this obstacle is sexist and has no place within our modern legal system. To some extent they are right; but questioning the credibility of victims and witnesses is a just and reasonable mandate that is placed upon all criminal prosecutions by our criminal justice system. Rapes often involve failed relationships, resentment for past wrongs, emotional attachment, uncertainty regarding the intensity of the relationship, perception differences between the two parties, and sometimes economic rewards that can be realized through civil proceedings (as in domestic and employee situations). It is clear that the overabundance of emotional baggage that is attached to rape creates credibility and corroboration problems that need to be addressed by both the investigator and the prosecutor in order to refute the type of denials that will certainly come from the defense.

To overcome these hurdles, investigators first must recognize that they exist. That recognition will expose the vulnerability of individual cases, thus unveiling the vital need to develop effective strategies that will corroborate the victim's allegations, for without any corroboration they are relying solely on the individual credibility of their star witness, the victim, who will certainly undergo an intense cross-examination by the defense. That questioning is sure to expose the victim to scrutiny concerning her motivations (both real and imagined) for making the allegation and for her actions prior to and after the alleged attack. In each case, the defense will assert that the alleged victim was a willing participant, or nothing actually transpired, or, if a crime did happen, the offender was not involved. The defense will further suggest the existence of ulterior motives behind the victim's allegation. Without any form of corroboration, not only is it difficult to overcome the burden of proof mandated in criminal proceedings, but it is frequently impossible. With corroboration, however, that legal hurdle can be conquered and the allegations sustained to the satisfaction of the jurors.

This chapter delves into methods that I have found effective in corroborating allegations of sexual assault victims, particularly those who have no physical evidence or witnesses to substantiate their claims. It will also help investigators uncover false allegations (which will be covered in depth in Chapter 10) by helping them get to the truth.

Statistical Overview and the Problem with Sexual Assault Statistics

In view of the fact that more sexual assaults go unreported than any other serious crime in America, rape statistics can often be misleading. This is especially true of domestic and acquaintance rapes, where the victim's guilt and shame (see Chapter 5) can frequently cause delays. Victims blame themselves for being naïve, for being too trusting, or for not following the advise of others. They fear that they will not be believed and they worry that the criminal justice system will treat them like criminals. Their blame may be misplaced, but it is real, it does exist, and there is good reason for it. Although the police, the prosecutors, and even the media have improved the methods they use to deal with the victims of sex crimes, there is always room for improvement. The lack of progress within the criminal court system, which allows defense attorneys to attack the victims themselves, only adds to the trepidation felt by victims. The court system is focused on protecting the rights of the accused, not the victim. This standard places the burden of proof on the prosecution, albeit justifiably so, but at the same time it makes a difficult situation even more demanding and complex for the prosecution. Victims are forced to describe more than the details of the attack. They are forced to elaborate about prior relationships with their assailants in the open courtroom. Those relationships may or may not have been sexual, but any suggestion that a victim perhaps is not an innocent party can leave enough doubt in the mind of jurors to acquit. Defense attorneys will impose rigorous cross-examinations in which they will portray the victims as promiscuous and conniving women with ulterior motives. They will suggest that the victims are liars motivated by jealousy, greed, revenge, or any other rationale that can be fabricated. This is especially true in domestic and acquaintance rapes, which account for the overwhelming majority of unreported sex crimes.

Statistics from the National Institute of Justice show that for rape and sexual assault the relationship of victim and perpetrator is as follows: acquaintance, 43%; domestic, 19%; and stranger, 38%. These percentages represent the national mean and may vary from community to community. I found that in my command (Manhattan) the rape statistics showed the following relationship: acquaintance, 45%; domestic, 15%, and stranger, 40%. These figures have, of course, varied from year to year, but their proportional relationship has remained relatively constant and in line with the national statistics.

The statistical data regarding the classification of rapes (domestic, acquaintance, and stranger), however, can be very misleading to those who do not have a full understanding of the depth of the problem. Although the data show that the combined domestic and acquaintance categories account for 62% of the national rape figure, it has long been my contention that the percentage of these categories is much higher than indicated by the statistical data and that stranger rapes represent a smaller percentage of the overall problem.

In the previous chapter, we discussed the various motives attributed to victims for not immediately reporting assaults and for declining to report attacks. It has been my experience that these motivations are amplified significantly when they involve domestic and acquaintance rape situations and are not as acute when they involve stranger cases. The self-blame, the shame, and the declining sense of self-worth that often overcome victims and prevent them from reporting attacks to the police are more prevalent in domestic and acquaintance cases than those involving a stranger. McGregor et al. (2000) confirmed this premise in their study and found that women who have been raped by an assailant who is not a stranger are more reluctant to involve the police.

Stranger cases, meanwhile, are not hampered by the same degree of self-analysis that acquaintance and domestic cases are. The emotional strain generated by the feelings of self-blame, although present, is not as severe. Victims of stranger attacks have a much clearer sense that they are not to blame for the attack. The usual reaction of the public to an incident of stranger rape is usually shock and rage. The victim, upon observing this reaction, is often reassured, as it conveys support for her plight as a victim. It validates her understanding that she is indeed the victim and that she should not feel responsible in any way for the attack. Consequently, victims report stranger rapes at a significantly higher rate than they do domestic or acquaintance rapes.

A look at the rape statistics reported by social scientists reveals a different picture than do those reported by criminal justice experts. Epidemiological studies have shown that law enforcement often misjudges the depth of the problem by relying on reported cases alone. Acierno and Resnick (1997) report that several social scientists have conducted studies that indicate the prevalence of rape is much higher than what is reported to the police. Their findings indicate that rape and sexual assault, particularly in domestic (spouse, ex-spouse, and guardian) and acquaintance settings is much higher. This is noteworthy because these studies document that both domestic and acquaintance rapes are seriously underreported.

Another factor impacting rape statistics is the issue of false allegations (see Chapter 10). Those who make these allegations usually do so for personal reasons. Some alleged victims may wish to attract attention because they feel neglected, while others will use a false rape allegation to divert attention away from something they have done wrong (staying out past curfew, associating with prohibited individuals, or other forbidden conduct). In any event, they almost always report that a stranger attacked them. Stranger cases allow such women to blame an unknown person without involving a real third party in their deception. Because the police cannot solve a crime that never happened, the alleged victims can rely upon the inability of the police to make an arrest, thus maintaining their victimization while furthering their deceptive objectives. The failure of many investigative agencies to thoroughly investigate these cases and uncover the truth often results in an artificial inflation of the documented stranger rape reports, making the stranger assault problem appear more severe than it actually is.

False accusations involving domestic and acquaintance situations, however, certainly do occur, but their ratio of false reports is far less than that of stranger allegations. The strategies for dealing with these allegations are discussed in this chapter. They are designed to help investigators establish the credibility of allegations involving known perpetrators and to expose the truth. That truth can establish the victim's credibility or uncover her deception.

Outside influences can also affect the statistical data of reported sexual assault cases. For example, a heightened sense of awareness of such crimes can temporarily increase the reporting of sexual assaults within a particular population. This intensified awareness can be due to the media attention that often follows high-profile cases, greater availability of school counseling on the subject, school policy decisions that ensure that all cases are reported, and community groups and outreach programs (particularly those that operate within college settings) that educate women regarding the extent of the problem and encourage them to report all assaults. Each of these factors can trigger reports to the police of cases that would have otherwise gone undocumented and not investigated. I witnessed many statistical fluctuations that were brought about by just these types of factors; unfortunately, however, these influences are usually temporary and are not sustained by those initiating them. Media attention wanes, school policies are not reinforced, and community groups lose their funding, lose interest, or find more compelling projects. Without a consistent effort to maintain an awareness of the problem within the affected population, the statistical fluctuations based on these influences will most likely continue.

The inconsistent manner in which groups raise a heightened sense of awareness, the false allegations that inflate the number of stranger cases, and the severe underreporting in domestic and acquaintance cases all play havoc with the statistical data used by criminal justice experts and social scientists to analyze the depth of the sexual assault problem. Compounding this issue is the fact that most rapists should be considered serial rapists. Those who commit date rape have almost certainly attacked others in the past. In fact, their proficiency at the crime and their ability to keep victims quiet often suggests that they have perfected their methods over time. They prey on the weak, and they employ psychological mind games to threaten victims if they report the attack.

If the truth were known, both acquaintance and domestic rapes are epidemic within our society and represent the vast majority of unreported cases. In order to combat this predicament, the investigative agency ought to commit itself to treating them in a manner that suggests that they recognize their repetitive nature. The expenditure of resources and the quality and thoroughness of the investigations will testify to that commitment.

Although investigators can only deal with those cases that are reported to them, they should be keenly aware of the factors that impact the reporting process for sex crimes. Of course, resources must be allocated based upon documented incidents, not upon the conjecture of social scientists, and the number of investigators assigned to a given task is determined by the case load they can manage; however, an awareness of the statistical problem can alert investigators that it is possible that multiple victims or multiple crimes committed against the same victim could surface during any individual investigation. Overhead commands should allocate resources to permit investigative units to pursue other possible victims of the same offender or to uncover evidence of multiple attacks. The result may be a temporary increase in reported cases, but the overall impact will decrease the future number of sexual assaults as convictions and incarcerations increase.

Case History

Prostitutes often have a difficult time communicating that they have become victims, especially those who are addicted to drugs; consequently, they rarely report attacks unless they are assured that they will be believed. In one case, a young Asian woman was lost and found herself in an area of Manhattan frequented by drug-addicted prostitutes. She spoke little English and, when a man in a Mercedes came by to offer her a ride, she accepted. He was driving a Mercedes-Benz and he appeared to be legitimately concerned about her safety. He drove a short distance to his apartment on the pretext of needing something inside.

He said he did not want to leave her in the car, so they both went inside. Once inside, he forcibly raped her and then tied her up on the bed. He repeatedly raped her during the next several days while she was tied to the bed. When she was not tied to the bed, he kept her handcuffed, and he locked her in his closet when he left the apartment for any reason. He took numerous pictures of her naked during her imprisonment and he continually threatened to kill her if she did not comply with his sexual wishes. After a week, an acquaintance of the suspect accidentally discovered that the suspect was holding a sex slave in his apartment. He convinced the suspect to leave him alone with the victim on the ruse of having sex with her when he left. He immediately freed the victim and brought her to the police.

The subject was arrested a short time later. A search warrant was conducted, and we recovered at least 60 photographs of women who appeared to be held against their will in the same manner. They were all naked and tied to the same bed. Some appeared to be on drugs, and others were tied in such a manner (with wire hangers) that they were clearly in a great deal of pain. An investigation into the identity of the victims uncovered that they were all prostitutes. Some had agreed to pose for the pictures and willingly consented to sexual acts for a fee. Others, however, had been forcibly tied and held in a manner similar to that of the victim. The subject had relied upon the lack of credibility given to prostitutes and their reluctance to report incidents to the police. Over time, he had perfected his ability to hold victims by selecting those who were most unlikely to report sexual assaults. He learned to select victims who were illegal immigrants, appeared to be prostitutes, and were addicted to drugs. He supplied more drugs during their captivity, and he convinced them that they would be killed if they ever informed on him. The subject was subsequently charged with eight additional counts of unlawful imprisonment, rape, and sexual assault. He is now serving the rest of his life in jail for his crimes.

Drug-Induced Rape

Alcohol

By far, the most prevalent drug that is used to overpower sexual assault victims is alcohol. It is readily available, legally taken (assuming the victim in not underage), and consumed willingly by the victim. Social gatherings often include the use of alcohol and when consumed in moderation these gatherings can be enjoyable. When social gatherings include members of both sexes and alcohol consumption is excessive, however, many things can go wrong. Playful banter between members of the opposite sex can escalate into misunderstandings about relationships and desires for sexual relations. Introverted victims may lose their inhibitions and engage in playful conduct that they would never think of doing if they were sober. Male friends may interpret their playfulness as promiscuousness and an invitation to engage in sexual activity. Potential victims may even become uninhibited and agree to sexual activity that they would normally never consider, activity that they may regret afterwards. Such a regret does not, however, justify accusations of rape. Her perceived attacker may have taken advantage of her reduced resistance while she was in an intoxicated state and his actions may be morally reprehensible, but they do not constitute force nor do they constitute rape.

In my experience, I have found that it is not unusual for young women, particularly those of college age, to experience blackout periods when they overindulge and abuse alcohol. Investigations often reveal facts that the victim cannot recall. Witnesses are sometimes found who observed the victim in an intoxicated state and acting in a promiscuous manner (for example, grinding her body against his or even grabbing his crotch as they danced in full view of everyone). Further investigation is definitely warranted, but the victim's usual assertion that she was unconscious is obviously not valid in these cases.

Victims who do become unconscious, however, and are sexually assaulted while in this state can be considered incapacitated, and a charge of rape may be sustained if the facts can be proven. Spiked drinks that lead to an unintended increase in alcohol consumption are not uncommon and can be an effective technique to cause unconsciousness. Victims often discover that when they awake they have engaged in unwanted sexual activity and cannot recall what transpired. It is essential that these victims be tested immediately at the nearest medical facility to determine if alcohol or another drug is present before it dissipates from her system. Delays can only impede the collection of crucial evidence that can support the victim's claims. Delays will also preclude the ability to obtain definitive answers as to the cause of unconsciousness.

The frequency with which alcohol plays a role in consensual sexual activity is extremely high in date situations within our society. Alcohol consumption by both the male and the female participant is a generally accepted practice during dates and can often lead to unplanned sexual activity (at least unplanned by the female participant). The sexual predator, however, will attempt to induce the victim to drink to the point of unconsciousness and engage in sexual activity while she is in that state. The questions that arise then are (1) was she unconscious, and (2) did she willingly partake in the sexual activity? Compounding the problem can be the victim's inability to recall how she acted while intoxicated. The intoxication of her male partner may also complicate the issue even further.

Ullman et al. (1999) conducted a study of sexual aggression in college-age men. They noted that increased alcohol consumption by men was not an indicator of increased sexual aggression. They found that those who committed sexually aggressive acts against women were previously predisposed to such behavior and that the frequent use of alcohol as an excuse is fraudulent. Their study also indicated, however, that women who use alcohol are at a greater risk of attack by sexually aggressive men. They found that drinking by both men and women was associated with spontaneous social interactions with unknown individuals and that sexually aggressive men target intoxicated women more frequently in these situations largely because the victim's resistance is significantly reduced. They also found that offenders view intoxicated victims as legitimate targets of their aggression and that the same offenders believe their victims hold some responsibility for the attack. It is also suggested that they target intoxicated women because such women are not likely to disclose the attack, nor will they be believed if they do.

The findings of Ullman et al. (1999) do not suggest that intoxicated women are to blame for attacks by sexually aggressive men. On the contrary, their study showed that alcohol should not be used as an excuse for any abhorrent sexual behavior. Women who drink, however, may find themselves in situations where they become the target of sexually aggressive men more frequently than those who do not. The study concludes that efforts to reduce alcohol abuse alone will not address the problem of sexual aggression in predisposed young men. Institutions, particularly colleges, should focus on the responsibility of males for sexual aggression and reduce the cultural justifications that are used to defend instances of rape.

Rohypnol (Flunitrazepam)

Often referred to as *roofies*, this drug is both legally and illegally manufactured in Europe and Mexico. It is used as a sleeping pill and for short-term treatment of insomnia. It is similar to Valium but is ten times more potent. It was the first of the so-called date-rape drugs to become popular with young adults and was readily available in the club and bar scene. Its normal effects are amplified when mixed with other depressants, and when mixed with alcohol it can be used as a date-rape drug. Indications of flunitrazepam use are a rapid loss of inhibition, loss of consciousness, and possibly coma. Victims typically recall having a drink and then not remembering anything afterward. They awake to find themselves in bed with the offender or they find their clothes disheveled to the point where they suspect that they have been abused.

The frequency and the severity of the problem led to reformulation of the drug so it is readily recognizable when mixed with beverages. Clear drinks will appear blue in color and colored drinks will become hazy. This tactic has greatly reduced the use of legally manufactured flunitrazepam as a date-rape drug. Illicit flunitrazepam, however, is odorless and colorless and is available through illegal producers, primarily in Mexico.

Investigators should be aware of the effects of flunitrazepam while conducting their initial interviews of victims. Particular attention should be given to victims who suspect that they may have been sexually assaulted and report that they cannot recall events after consuming drinks that were handled by someone else. In those cases, it is essential that urine specimens be taken as soon as possible. Although experts report that testing can be done up to 96 hours after ingestion, I have found that urine samples taken more than 24 hours after ingestion typically are of no value but should be taken nonetheless. Ideally, urine samples should be taken within 12 hours of the suspected ingestion. The rapidity with which Rohypnol leaves the system should be taken into account when negative toxicology reports are received. (*Note:* Investigators should not rule out date-rape drugs as a factor in cases when toxicology tests produce negative results from urine samples that were taken more than 12 hours after the suspected ingestion.)

The frequency with which victims do not report acquaintance rapes to the police and delays in reporting are indeed serious problems when it comes to drug-induced rape. Failure to make a report conceals the depth of the problem, and delayed reports, although understandable (see Chapter 5), can affect the ability to collect forensic evidence. Because the failure to undergo testing in a timely fashion impacts the validity of toxicology tests, every effort should be made to ensure that urine specimens are taken immediately and that medical personnel utilize accepted rape collection kits while treating victims.

Case History

A young woman who was interested in modeling went to a Manhattan photographer to have a portfolio made. The photographer, a 30-year-old male, was pleasant and appeared to be very professional. She relates that the photographer noticed that she was nervous and offered her an alcoholic drink to calm her down. She reluctantly accepted the drink. She lost memory of what followed and could not recall anything that happened until she was on her way out of the studio. At that time, she noticed that her clothes were disheveled and she suspected that she might have been sexually assaulted.

She immediately contacted a relative who was a retired police officer and, luckily, he advised her to contact my office without delay. After she called and explained her suspicions, my detectives directed her to report to the hospital, where a rape kit was prepared, but there seemed to be no evidence of rape. When urine samples were taken, however, the results indicated that the victim had ingested Rohypnol. We conducted a background investigation on the subject and found that he had a small photography business. He did not have a criminal record and no allegations of past misconduct had been made against him.

The victim called the subject to inquire about her photographs and he informed her that all of the pictures had been destroyed accidentally. He apologized and said that he would gladly take the pictures over at no charge. A search warrant was obtained for his studio/apartment. Rohypnol was found in the apartment, along with partially nude pictures of the victim in various poses. The victim appeared to be drugged in the pictures. Her eyelids were heavy and she always appeared leaning or laying on something. Additional pictures were found of several other women in similar poses. The investigation uncovered the identities of those victims, and each recounted a similar experience. The suspect was arrested and charged with several counts of assault (administering drugs to unsuspecting victims) and sexual abuse.

Gamma-Hydroxybutyrate (GHB)

The abuse of gamma-hydroxybutyrate (GHB) has grown steadily in recent years. The U.S. Department of Justice reported that, from 1990 through 2000, the Drug Enforcement Administration documented 5600 overdoses related to GHB, with 72 deaths reported since 1995. The Drug Abuse Warning

Network (DAWN) reported only 38 GHB-related cases in 1993, but in 2000 that number skyrocketed to 4969. In February of 2000, President Clinton signed into law the Hillory J. Farais and Samantha Reid Date-Rape Drug Prohibition Act, which made GHB and gamma-butyrolactone (GBL, which is used to manufacture GHB) controlled substances under federal law.

During the 1980s, GHB was widely available over the counter in health-food stores. It was popular as an anabolic steroid to increase body mass and was used extensively by bodybuilders. It was soon discovered that it could also be used as a date-rape drug when Rohypnol became difficult to obtain. The effects are similar to those of Rohypnol, and like Rohypnol, the effects are compounded when mixed with alcohol. It usually comes as an odorless and colorless liquid that has a salty taste. That taste, however, can be masked and undetected by most people when mixed with alcoholic drinks. It can also be obtained as a powder or in a capsule form.

Victims who have ingested GHB often report consuming alcoholic drinks that were handled by others. They are unable to recall events a short time after taking the drink. Others report that the victim may have looked intoxicated but that she appeared to be in good health otherwise. Victims typically come to several hours later and discover that they have had sexual relations but cannot recollect the incident. In date situations, they often find themselves lying in bed naked next to their date of the previous evening. Sometimes they awake to find themselves clothed but disheveled (bra undone, panties missing) and they have no recollection of the previous few hours.

Victims in these situations should *always* be encouraged to seek medical attention immediately and to have blood and urine tests conducted for the presence of GHB. As with Rohypnol, GHB is excreted quickly through the system and any delays in testing will compromise the accuracy of the tests. Although scientists report that testing can show indications of Rohypnol and GHB up to 96 hours after ingestion, investigators and prosecutors should keep in mind that experience has shown these tests to be negative after 24 hours even when they are ingested.

Ketamine

Ketamine was developed in the 1960s as an animal anesthetic and has been widely used by veterinarians for pet surgery. During the 1970s, it became popular as a recreational drug and is commonly known by its street names "Special K" and "Vitamin K". It is available as a liquid, powder, and in tablet form. When injected, its anesthetic effects are immediate, as it affects the central nervous system. It can also be taken orally, and in low doses (10 to 100 mg) it can cause hallucinations, memory loss, slurred speech, and numbness. Larger doses of one gram or more can lead to unconsciousness and even death, particularly when mixed with another drug such as alcohol.

Ketamine is less commonly used as a date-rape drug, but its availability as a recreational drug and the effects it can produce should be considered when drug-induced rape is suspected.

Education and Precautionary Measures

The effort to ensure the prompt reporting of cases when date-rape drugs are used is an ongoing struggle. Education in this area ought to be targeted at potential victim groups to be effective. It could make a significant impact on the amount of reported cases and ensure that victims are aware of the value of reporting cases in a timely manner. Targeting groups such as academic institutions (particularly colleges), community groups, and outreach programs can produce significant results. Each group represents a portion of the affected population. They offer an opportunity to help potential victims understand the depth of the problem, to utilize successful avoidance techniques, to learn about the availability of services for victims, and to become aware of the needs of criminal investigations, particularly the need to corroborate allegations. Unfortunately, these institutions commonly gloss over the investigative portion during their presentations about rape and rape prevention. They address the wide range of issues that are relevant to the topic, but they do not possess the expertise to present the issues that are important to an investigation. I have found that the fault generally lies with investigative agencies for failing to initiate contact with these groups and offer expert investigative spokespersons for incorporation into their programs. Such experts can demonstrate the sensitivity that is expected of sex crime investigators and can articulate the many unique investigative needs that arise while investigating sexual assault.

The problem of drug-induced rape will invariably be an important part of any presentation, especially in college settings. The evidentiary problems that are compounded by victims' actions can be effectively addressed at these meetings by instructing attendees to seek immediate medical attention if a rape occurs or is suspected. Attendees can be made aware of the availability of drugs and the frequency with which they are used to rape women. Beyond the needs of investigations, presentations should also instruct attendees regarding the basic precautions they can take to avoid becoming a victim. As is the key with all crime prevention techniques, awareness is paramount. It is important to discuss with attendees the following guidelines:

- Always be aware of your surroundings.
- Avoid large gatherings where alcohol use is excessive.
- Limit alcoholic drinks to avoid becoming intoxicated.

- Avoid drinking contests.
- Do not drink anything from an open container unless you opened it or someone you trust opened it.
- Do not drink from a communal punch bowl at a bar or club.
- If your drink tastes, looks, or smells strange, do not drink it.
- If you are at a party or bar or are on a date, do not leave your drink unattended; if you do, discard it.
- Go to a party or a bar with friends and agree to look out for each other; tell each other where you are going if you leave the group.
- Get medical attention immediately if you feel strange.
- Call 911 if you suspect that anyone in the group may have been drugged.

Cybersex

The use of the Internet, particularly online chat rooms, has opened up an entirely new area for those seeking companionship. Unfortunately, predators seeking to meet and abuse lonely women and children have also used the Internet to further their perverted needs. The term *cybersex* has been used in relation to pornography, but within the context of this discussion it relates to relationships that have their beginnings on the Internet or are fostered through the use of the Internet.

In recent years, I have seen a noticeable increase in the amount of sexual assaults committed when young women agree to meet men whom they know nothing about and have only chatted with over the Internet. College students seem to be the most likely candidates for this type of assault. Men who are familiar with a college, the particular college environment, and its class schedules can easily carry on a cyber conversation with unsuspecting women regarding contemporary college issues. The clandestine nature of the Internet provides predators with the perfect medium to cunningly convince their potential victims that they are from similar backgrounds and that they share the same emotional and societal concerns. While they gain the trust of their victims, they patiently devise a plan to meet and sexually assault their unsuspecting prey.

As we all know, children are also prime targets of cyber stalkers. Their innocence, their gullibility, and their immaturity make them easy targets. They are readily deceived, and their predators are extremely dangerous. Educating parents to monitor their children's activities and limit the type of activity their children conduct on the Internet, particularly as far as preventing the use of chat rooms, has limited the access of cyber stalkers significantly. Teenage girls, however, are often given greater access by their parents, and they easily become victims. I have seen several lonely young girls attracted to the access that the Internet provides who have gone on to meet their chat partners in person and subsequently become victims of rape. The rape is sometimes by force, but more often than not it is a statutory rape in which the young girl is a gullible and willing participant, a sad episode especially when it is discovered that the victim is as young as 12 or 13 and the predator is in his 20s.

Case History

A college coed met a graduate student in an online chat room. They appeared to have similar interests, and they often spoke about philosophical theories and their individual idealistic philosophies of life. Eventually, they met in a café near the young woman's school to continue their philosophical discussions. The young man acted somewhat effeminate and, although he did not profess to be, their discussions indicated that he was probably gay. She felt safe in his company at the café and did not consider that he would be a threat to her sexually. That night, however, the young man asked her to accompany him to his apartment so he could show her some art that he had collected. She agreed and, once inside his apartment, he tied her up and sexually abused her for over 12 hours.

He went to sleep and she eventually freed herself. She fled the apartment and immediately reported the attack. The investigation could not uncover any additional evidence other then the e-mail conversations, and an arrest of the suspect was made primarily on the credibility of the victim. A search warrant was secured for his apartment and evidence connecting him to the sexual assault was recovered, including data stored on his computer. The investigation also revealed that the subject had been in contact with other women, but that the victim was the first that he had met in person. One of the other women, another college coed, was supposed to meet him on the night of his arrest and did not know why he had not shown up until we arrived. She also believed that the subject was gay and that he was not a threat to her sexually. She was surprised to learn of his arrest, but we were surprised to learn that she had actively spoken with many unidentified men over the Internet. In fact, she showed us some of the chat sites that she had visited, including one called "The Rape Room". Clearly, she was playing with fire, and we hope that his arrest prevented similar attacks and convinced her that her conduct was more than reckless; it was stupid.

Investigating Acquaintance Rape

Some groups find the term *date rape* offensive and even intolerable. They assert that it connotes a pleasant and friendly relationship between two people, and rape is anything but pleasant or friendly. Others maintain that it is merely a term used to describe a situation and that there is no intent to suggest the existence of a bond between the victim and her attacker. Even when those who use the term *date rape* have no intention of degrading the seriousness of the crime and do not use the term in a contemptuous manner, it is not accurate. The term *acquaintance rape*, on the other hand, acknowledges that the victim and the perpetrator are known to each other but does not prejudge the relationship. It is far more accurate and is the term used by knowledgeable investigators, prosecutors, and statisticians as they categorize cases of rapes that include dates, but also include friends, colleagues, co-workers, etc.

Acquaintance Rape: A Difficult Crime to Prove

Clearly, the first step to understanding the difficulty of investigating acquaintance rape cases is to recognize how investigative approaches differ from those in other types of crime. Too often, we look at all criminal investigations similarly and apply the same techniques throughout all of our investigations. Our perspective often does not allow us to consider the many unique issues that can arise, particularly for acquaintance rape. Investigators who are inexperienced at investigating sex crimes conduct their investigations in the same manner as they would when handling any other crime. They are not aware of the crucial differences among the various types of investigations, and they fail to see the special needs that can arise: the need to corroborate; the need for emotional support; the need to understand that the dishonesty of victims can be misinterpreted; and the need to look at the repetitive nature of the attack. Simply put, they fail to acknowledge that it is a different type of crime and that it requires a different type of investigation.

Experienced investigators and prosecutors understand that no other crime will be scrutinized in the same manner as acquaintance rape, nor can any other crime generate the emotions that rape can. Victims of robbery, burglary, and larceny, although upset at their bad fortune, know that they have become victims for the perpetrator's economic gain. They have not suffered the indignity of rape nor have they suffered the near-death experience that accompanies it. They are not fearful of the possibility of pregnancy, nor do they fear contracting a sexually transmitted disease (STD) that may affect their sexuality and their future aspirations as wives and mothers. Although they may be traumatized, they have not suffered the depth of emotional upheaval that is commonplace with rape victims. In short, the crimes of which they are victims are not as serious as those that rape victims have endured. Consequently, rape investigations are far more complex than any other type of investigation, including homicide, where the emotional state of the victim is no longer an issue.

Deception by Victims

It is a known fact that rape victims, particularly acquaintance rape victims, frequently lie. They are embarrassed; their self-esteem and dignity have been attacked, they feel that they are to blame in some way, or they feel that others will blame them for reckless conduct (see Chapter 5). In any event, it is a fact that they will lie. Usually the lie is small and does not have an impact on the seriousness of the situation. Sometimes, however, the lie can change the entire scope of an investigation. For example, it is not uncommon for a victim to lie about the circumstances that led her to be in the company of the male she is accusing of rape. She may suggest that she had entered a bar, had a soda with the suspect, and accepted a ride home. In reality, she may have been intoxicated and was seen by many to be dancing in a suggestive manner with the suspect before getting into his car, where she was forcibly raped. In other situations, victims may report being raped by a stranger because they recognize that they need immediate medical attention but are unwilling to get their male companion in trouble.

In each of these situations, the investigation is likely to uncover that the victim is lying. Unfortunately, the untrained investigator may take this response to mean that, because the victim is lying about one part of the attack, she must be lying about everything. That response is generally acceptable in most criminal investigations, but not in sexual assault, particularly acquaintance rape. Robbery or burglary victims generally have nothing to hide from investigators. If the investigation reveals that the victim is lying about some aspect of the theft, investigators are clearly justified in suspecting that the victim may indeed be involved in some type of fraud.

As we have seen, sexual assault victims do indeed have something to hide and they do indeed lie. Their lies, however, have more to do with preserving their dignity and their self-esteem than they do with intentionally misleading investigators. Those of us investigating these cases must be attuned to these nuances and address them as they occur.

Addressing the Deception

The ability of the investigator to communicate with the victim and to uncover the truth is a principal component in any investigation. It is suggested that the following guidelines be followed when speaking with victims of sexual assault in order to gain their confidence and to ensure that the whole truth is told:

- Advise the victim why you need to know all of the facts. The more she understands about the process, the more likely she will cooperate honestly and openly.

- Advise the victim that you will need to know all of the details, including the clinical details of the attack.
- Advise the victim that hiding embarrassing facts can be damaging and impact seriously upon the prosecution of the case. Explain that you understand that it may be difficult to acknowledge some of the events, but that hiding them can hurt the investigation.
- Advise the victim that your investigation will be thorough and that she should inform you of all details now, no matter how embarrassing, before you learn the truth from someone else.
- Advise the victim that defense attorneys will conduct their own investigation to discredit the victim. The prosecution consequently needs to be prepared to address embarrassing issues that may be uncovered.
- Advise the victim that the path that the investigation takes is based upon the facts that are known to the investigator. False statements or hiding embarrassing facts will cause the investigation to take the wrong course.
- Alleviate the victim's tension by conducting your interview in private, and advise her that part of your job is to protect her.
- Evaluate the circumstances and give the victim an honest account of the investigative needs necessary to arrest and prosecute her case successfully.
- Advise the victim that you will not make her name public. Most police departments have policies in place that prohibit disclosure of sex crime victims.

Victim as Sole Witness

It is an unavoidable fact that the victim and the sole eyewitness in acquaintance rape are one and the same. Both the accused and the accuser acknowledge that they had intercourse. They differ, however, on the issue of consent. He claims that it was consensual, while she asserts that she was forced. Compounding the subject is a perception difference regarding what is consensual and what is force. A victim may stress that she was tricked into consenting and was therefore forced, while the accused may stress that her bruises are the result of rough sex.

Victims' Prior Actions

The prior actions of victims can be of concern when balanced against accusations within a judicial setting. Although victims do not have to convince jurors that they are pure and chaste, they do have to convince them that they are not at fault. Rape shield laws may protect victims from divulging prior sexual activity, but they are not a refuge from discussing the relationship between the two parties in question, nor can they safeguard her from having to disclose the actions that led up to the rape. Victims who are dressed provocatively, who are seen dancing in a sexually suggestive manner with the suspect, who have consumed copious amounts of alcohol, and who then invite the suspect over to her apartment where she is raped will have a more difficult time convincing jurors than a woman in most other circumstances. This is not to suggest that this woman was not raped, only that she will have a more difficult time convincing people that she was. Unfortunately, many victims feel that the burden of proving their case is too strong. They know that they are the sole witness to the crime and they fear that they will not be believed. Their fears are often amplified by what they see and read in the media. Court TV, police shows, and nefarious cases in the news where defense counselors berate victims and perpetrators are set free have created an atmosphere that is not conducive to the reporting of rapes or to prosecuting them.

Lack of Physical Evidence

A lack of physical evidence can emerge from two common situations typical with acquaintance rape. In the first, the victim is threatened by her attacker and succumbs to the sexual assault without resistance. Even though the suspect's semen may be present within her vagina, no physical injuries or vaginal tearing indicate the use of force. In the second situation, the delay in reporting, although normal (see Chapter 5), can sometimes be as long as years and prevents the collection of evidence before it is destroyed. Semen is no longer present, any vaginal tearing that could indicate force has healed, and cuts and bruising have also healed.

Credibility of Victims

As with the general population, some victims simply do not sound as credible as others. Shyness, inability to speak in public, and emotional problems may prevent the victim from sounding credible. On the other hand, some people can sound credible while fabricating attacks that could not have occurred. Compounding the problem is the frequent lack of physical evidence that exists to support the victims' allegations. Establishing (1) that a crime happened, and (2) that the subject committed that crime becomes difficult, if not impossible, under normal investigative avenues. The following strategies are offered as a means to corroborate allegations and to prove cases in court.

Strategies to Address Credibility Problems, Support Victim's Allegations, and Uncover the Truth

The need to establish the victim's credibility can be considered the principal difference between rape investigations and those of any other crime. Investigators need to dissect the victim's allegations thoroughly in order to confirm that she is telling the truth and to ensure that she is divulging all the facts. Experienced investigators and prosecutors know that many of the assertions that will be presented by defense attorneys in sexual assault cases have some merit. Women have lied in the past to even the score with men who have hurt them in some way. They have made false allegations because of jealousy, rage, greed, child custody disputes, or a myriad of other reasons, including financial gain. Investigators need to be on guard for such accusations; if they are not, the defendants' attorneys surely will, and they will have a field day dissecting these cases in court and revealing motivations that were not addressed during the investigation.

The victim's allegations can be corroborated in many ways, each of which may delay the arrest, but if the victim is not in danger or the suspect is not a threat to flee, time is on your side. If, on the other hand, she is in danger or he is a threat to flee, an immediate arrest based solely on her current credibility may be justified and necessary. The factors that have forced the need for an immediate arrest and the evidence supporting the relevance of those factors can be used to help corroborate the victim's account — for example, evidence that the suspect has injured the victim, evidence that he has threatened her, or evidence that he has suddenly planned to move.

Repetitive Nature of Attacks and the History of the Suspect

The repetitive nature of rape and sexual assaults is of great concern to investigators. Experienced investigators know that all rapists are serial rapists or potential serial rapists. If the suspect does not have a criminal history of such conduct, interviews of past female acquaintances may uncover a history of aggressive behavior or of similar attacks that have gone unreported. Armed with this new information and the latest report, investigators and prosecutors can strengthen the foundation of their investigation and proceed with criminal action.

Recorded Conversations

Most states allow conversations to be recorded, provided one of the participants consents to the recording. Meetings between the victim and the suspect can be arranged and recorded when they take place. Investigative personnel should be nearby during these meetings to ensure the safety of the victim.

Public places, such as restaurants, coffee shops, and diners, are the best locations for such meetings. Recording devices come in many shapes and sizes, and the most reliable are often the simplest. It is suggested that a backup device also be affixed to the victim or placed inside her purse. I always found that the most practical way to proceed was to use a transmitting device and a separate recording device. In that way, a team can sit nearby in a car, listen to the conversation, record it, and be alert for any threats made by the suspect. Meanwhile, another simple recording device can be placed on the victim or in her bag to record the conversation. The redundancy is necessary because many things can happen to these devices. Conversations may go beyond the length of the tape, which is not uncommon considering that delays can occur, as when subjects show up late. The victim's unfamiliarity with the equipment may also cause her to accidentally deactivate the device; or noise problems may prevent one of the devices from picking up the entire conversation.

Because the victim will only be in contact with the suspect in a public place, her safety is greatly enhanced and generally not an issue. Moreover, investigators will not be far away should a problem arise. Unlike a typical undercover police operation, the victim will not be subject to a search that could reveal the existence of the recording device. If the suspect decides that she is recording the conversation, he will simply deny any wrongdoing and refuse to discuss the matter further. In that case, it may be possible to enlist the aid of someone who can be trusted to speak with the subject and attempt to record another conversation.

Victim's Role

Before any conversations take place, the victim should be instructed about her role in the planned meetings. She should complain to the suspect that he took advantage of her and that he hurt her seriously. She should ask him why he did what he did and assert that she thought she could trust him. Her role is to get him to admit to the truth. Rarely, if ever, will investigators hear the subject say "I'm sorry I raped you." Instead they will hear comments such as: "I'm sorry I hurt you" or "I'm sorry that I went too far" or "I lost control" or "I don't know what came over me — I've never done anything like that before" or "Can you forgive me for hurting you that way?" At that point, the victim should use the term "rape." She should accuse him of raping her and record his reaction. The tone of the suspect's voice and the context in which these statements are made will either give credence to the allegation or damage her credibility if she is lying. In either event, her role in recording the conversation is to help the investigator uncover the truth. In some cases, where the victim was intoxicated or where the victim may have an ulterior motive, the honest denials of force by the suspect or the assertion that the victim was the instigator may be more plausible than the allegation of rape.

Of course, caution is needed because those denials may also be based upon his knowledge of the law, his actual guilt, and his need for self-preservation. Accordingly, it is imperative that the victim understand what is expected of her during the conversation and that she be persistent about getting the suspect to discuss his motives behind the attack. An evaluation of the recording may produce no new information. More often than not, however, it produces a meaningful look at the relationship and particularly at the sexual encounter in question.

Recorded Telephone Conversations

Quite often, the victim is unable to meet with the suspect to discuss the attack. She may be fearful and unwilling to face him, or the circumstances of their relationship may make it unusual for her to meet him to discuss their last encounter and thus would provoke suspicion. On the other hand, a telephone conversation would not be unusual. I have found that it is easier and more agreeable for victims to record telephone conversations than it is to meet with the suspects in person. The suspect and the victim usually have spent a great deal of time on the telephone together in the past so a call to him would not be out of the ordinary. If the telephone call is taking place at a police facility, investigators must be sure to use a line that cannot be traced by a caller ID system. If the suspect questions where she is calling from, she should inform him that she is staying at a friend's house because she is so upset.

e-Mail and Instant Messages

In the same manner in which in-person conversations and telephone conversations can be recorded, e-mails and instant messages can also be used to uncover the truth. The advantage to the computer is that investigators can control exactly what is being said and can even conduct the dialog without the victim. It is strongly recommended, however, that the victim do the communicating in order to be consistent. Terminologies and language shortcuts that she used in the past should be consistent with any dialog used for this task. The suspect could become nervous and stop corresponding if he feels that he is being investigated.

Eavesdropping Warrant

Some states prohibit the recording of conversations even if one of the parties consents. Maryland is one of them, as Linda Tripp discovered when she recorded conversations she had with Monica Lewinski. In these states, an eavesdropping warrant may be the only means available to gather information needed to convict a suspect. The warrant would be for a short period of time and would only cover as many as two or three conversations. If the victim is credible and the evidence can be collected in no other way, such a warrant may be the only way to obtain it. Judges, however, are reluctant to issue eavesdropping warrants unless investigators can establish two important elements: (1) they have reasonable cause to believe that the subject committed the crime, and (2) they have no other way to collect the necessary evidence.

The Truth

The need to uncover the truth in an acquaintance case cannot be over-emphasized. Investigators will often be burdened with an allegation that is sure to end in a "he said/she said" scenario in which nobody wins and nobody outside of the two people involved knows the truth. In the case of drug-induced rape, the problem may lie in the fact that the victim may not know the truth. She may feel that she had sex but may not know for sure. If she was intoxicated of her own accord, she may not remember what happened. Did she let him have sex with her willingly, or did he force her? The only way to know for sure may be to find out directly from the other person present. Recording conversations can provide victims with the answers they seek, while providing investigators and prosecutors with the evidence they need to effectively arrest and prosecute the suspect. Investigators, however, are not in the business of arresting individuals for crimes that they did not commit; rather, their function is to protect the public from criminals who prey on the weak. If an investigation reveals that the alleged attack was consensual or did not take place, then the investigators involved have done a great service to the victim, the accused, and society through their investigation. On the other hand, if investigators fail to use every means at their disposal then they have done a great disservice that borders on criminal.

Rape on Campus

There has been much discussion given to the problem of rape on campus, and epidemiological studies abound with statistical information regarding the frequency of sexual assault in our nations campuses. Students with new-found freedom and very little experience typically engage in risky behavior that can result in unwanted sexual advances or even sexual assault. No longer under their parents' control, they push the limits of their freedom and become involved with people they barely know. Parties proliferate throughout the campus scene and attendees regularly consume excessive amounts of alcohol. Unwanted sexual encounters flourish in an atmosphere of revelry that few students expected when they left home.

Although epidemiological studies frequently show that the number of rapes on campus is extremely high when compared to the general population, such studies do not take into account the extended definition that many sociologists sometimes give to rape. In some studies, rape has been defined as unwanted advances in which the male attempted to have sex but was rejected by the woman. Under that definition, the frequency of rape is sure to soar. These definitions and studies, however, can be constructive because they heighten the awareness of the problem and bring it to the forefront for examination and discussion.

Colleges are also under a mandate from the U.S. Department of Education to take reasonable steps to prevent and eliminate sexual misconduct under the Title IX nondiscrimination mandate. Consequently, colleges have established sexual misconduct policies to protect their students and to address their legal responsibility.

University Policies

University policies are commonly directed at educating the student population in regard to what constitutes sexual misconduct and at establishing internal mechanisms for addressing incidents when they arise. Policies vary from school to school, but they typically offer aggrieved students counseling and the ability to seek recourse through a university committee consisting of students and faculty members. Once the charges are levied, the offending student is given a hearing where he can refute or admit his guilt. Credence is given to the student making the charges, and the accused can be denied access to confront witnesses. The findings of these committees can then result in punitive action taken against the student if he is found guilty. The penalties range from reprimands to expulsion from the school. Such procedures clearly favor the victim and are designed to placate activists who feel that the school has been too soft on the issue of sexual misconduct. Fortunately, most colleges have rejected such draconian measures because they violate many levels of basic fairness and due process. Many recognize that accused parties must have the right to challenge the credibility of both the victim and witnesses if they are to maintain their intellectual integrity. They have, however, taken up some form of committee structure whereby the accused student is confronted with the allegations and given an opportunity to defend his actions and to refute the charges.

Investigative Impact of Campus Policies

Although such policies may be well intentioned and grounded in the belief that they exist to help victims address the problem, they typically ignore the many criminal and investigative aspects of the attack. Sexual assault cases that are brought before university committees can seriously damage the ability of investigators to corroborate the victims' allegations in many ways. Such policies warn offending students that punitive action is being sought, thus impeding the use of established strategies to corroborate victims' allegations through recorded conversations, recorded telephone calls, e-mails, etc. The offending student is given time to create a defense (e.g., allege that contact was consensual), and a thorough examination of the physical evidence that may or may not have been available is impossible.

Addressing the Issue of Campus Policy

In order to resolve this dilemma, it is necessary for each police department to work closely with colleges and universities within their jurisdictions. In my experience, I have found that most schools cooperate fully with the police, while a few are more concerned with preserving their reputation than they are with justice for the victim. This latter group of schools are governed by policies that may placate the feminist element within the university, but they do a disservice to the victim by preventing the police from corroborating the victim's version and denying the victim her right to justice.

Investigative personnel should be available to address students when they first arrive at the beginning of the school year to ensure them that incidents of sexual assault are taken seriously by the police department and that each case will be investigated thoroughly. Schools can offer students an alternative by allowing them to present cases to internal school committees as long as they inform the student that choosing to work with such committees may jeopardize any investigative strategies that the police may employ. Establishing a protocol with regard to the reporting of cases and providing the victim with all the information she needs to make an informed decision will go a long way toward correcting the problem. Investigators can also train school security personnel on how to safeguard evidence and they can speak with college counselors regarding the availability and needs of the investigators.

I have addressed many school committees over the years and have learned that they have a distorted view of what transpires during the typical sex crime investigation. Unfortunately, they are a product of their environment — an environment that has had little, if any, first-hand knowledge of the police, except for receiving speeding tickets. Committee members picture gruff, unsympathetic detectives who are confrontational and sarcastic with the victim. They envision victims being tormented and ridiculed as they reveal the intimacy of the attack while investigators joke about the incident. Of course, such perceptions are way off base and not held by everyone, but they can influence many within the university and can have a lasting impact upon the schools relationship with the police. I have found that this issue can be dealt with effectively by devoting time to speak with members of the college or university to address their concerns. School personnel are often amazed by the compassion, dedication, and expertise of both sex crime investigators and prosecutors. They are happily surprised to find that investigators can do an excellent job of protecting the victim and prosecuting the perpetrator.

Because colleges and universities still have a public image to deal with, convincing them to have all cases reported directly to the police may be idealistic, but obtaining their assistance by offering students another remedy and for leaving the decision up to the student is not. I have found that schools were more likely to seek police intervention when I supplied administrators with a way to contact me directly. That gave them access to an authority figure, in this case the Commanding Officer of the Manahattan Special Victims Squad. Often, all they want is the feeling that they are being given special treatment and that their case is a top priority for the police.

Rape at High-Security Locations (Hotels, Businesses)

The many sources of useful information that can be found at high-tech, secure locations, particularly hotels, is worth noting. Security systems have become standard in hotels and business establishments and range from video surveillance to card access and timed entry to documented phone calls. They offer an investigative advantage that can be used to corroborate allegations and to identify suspects. Investigators can consult with the director of security for the location in question and utilize the following types of records to enhance their investigation:

- Surveillance camera tapes
- Card access records
- Telephone records
- Computer access records (business locations)
- Personnel records to locate possible witnesses
- Garage entry and exit records

Case History

A technology firm from Seattle sent some of its top-level employees to a convention in New York City. About 30 attendees were present, including the company president, a 40-year-old married man with two children. Due to a hotel shortage, the employees stayed in different hotels within the midtown Manhattan area. One of the employees, a 25-year-old female financial expert, reported to us that she was attacked and raped by the company president inside her hotel room. She claimed that he was flirting with her earlier in the day and that she had rejected his advances. She then claimed that he came to her hotel room at about 11:00 P.M. on the pretense of wanting to speak with her about an important matter (he was staying at a different hotel about six blocks away). She was wearing a robe, and her hair was disheveled because she had been resting in bed watching television. She was stunned that he was there, but because he was the company president she assumed that it must be important. She let him in, but then excused herself and went to the bathroom to comb her hair while he stayed in the main room. When she exited the bathroom she found that he had made himself a drink from the bar and was sitting on the bed watching television. He asked her to sit next to him and when she did she noticed that he was watching a pornographic movie. When she objected to the movie, he grabbed her and forcibly raped her, using a condom. After the rape, he removed the condom and flushed it and the wrapper down the toilet. He then left her room. The victim was hysterical and called a friend in Seattle to tell her what happened. The friend convinced her that she needed medical attention and that she needed to report the incident to the police immediately.

When we arrived, we secured the victim's hotel room for processing by the Crime Scene Unit. We escorted the victim to the hospital, where she gave us a full accounting of the incident. A survey of the hotel and its security procedures revealed that two restaurants, a bar, and several catering halls were located on the first two levels. Access to the individual hotel rooms was limited to guests and was guarded by a security officer at the entrance to the guest elevators. In addition, surveillance cameras documented the activity in many areas of the hotel. The card access system documented when doors were unlocked, the pay television system (e.g., HBO, pay-per-view movies, etc.) documented the exact time that movies were turned on, and telephone records revealed the exact time and length of every call. Many of the same procedures were also in place at the suspect's hotel six blocks away.

We attempted to record a conversation with the subject the next day. We wired the victim and she confronted him, but he refused to discuss the matter. He apologized for any inconvenience, but he did not admit to attacking the victim. We also noticed that he did not *deny* the charges. Clearly, we needed more to support the victim's claims. We had already contacted the hotel security at the victim's hotel and at the suspect's hotel, and they were busy collecting data for us.

We found that surveillance cameras were installed in several areas in the victim's hotel. We viewed the tapes and observed the suspect drinking in the second-floor bar. We also observed him watching the guard at the entrance to the guests' elevators for about 30 minutes. A maintenance worker eventually summoned the guard for some help, and he left his post for about a minute. During that time, we observed the suspect rush to the elevators and enter. The time on the tape indicated that it was 10:52 P.M. when he entered the elevator. Although the card access system at the hotel documents when cards are used to unlock doors, they do not document when the door is opened from the inside. Consequently, we had no documentation regarding the exact time the door was opened. The victim claims that she let him in and then went to the bathroom, during which he turned on a pornographic movie. The hotel documented that the movie was turned on in the victim's room at 10:59 P.M.

The victim claims that the visit and the rape took about 20 minutes altogether and that she called her friend in Seattle a few minutes after the suspect left. The hotel telephone records indicate that she placed a call to Seattle at 11:24 P.M. We subsequently contacted the friend and confirmed that the conversation had taken place. We observed the suspect on the lobby surveillance camera leaving the hotel at 11:22 P.M. At 11:38 P.M., the subject was taped on his hotel security camera entering his hotel six blocks away. We then confirmed that he used his hotel card to enter his room at 11:41 P.M. Because the suspect used a condom and flushed it down the toilet and because the medical exam was not conclusive (vaginal soreness and small abrasions were discovered and some redness was present on the upper arms where the subject allegedly held her down), it was obvious that more evidence was needed. The subject was a very wealthy man, and we were aware that he would hire very competent attorneys who would attack the victim's credibility by arguing that she was merely seeking financial gain.

The security systems and the billing records at the hotels of both the victim and the subject, however, provided excellent impartial corroboration of the victim's allegations. This evidence was also supported by the testimony of the victim's friend from Seattle and the suspect's refusal to deny the allegation when confronted by the victim the next day. His refusal was recorded and presented in court.

Although minimal medical evidence supported the victim's claim and the subject's attorney attacked the woman's credibility by suggesting that she was merely seeking financial gain, the magnitude of the circumstantial evidence was too great for him to overcome and he was convicted of rape in the first degree.

Investigating Domestic Rape

Acknowledging the existence of rape within domestic settings is a relatively new phenomenon within our society. Before the 1970s, the criminal codes in most states did not acknowledge that a husband could rape his wife. Forced intercourse by a husband was considered legal and could not be prosecuted. The marriage license legally gave husbands an exception to the existing rape laws of most states. The advent of the feminist movement brought about revelations that domestic abuse and sexual assault were more common than previously suspected. The affirmation of sexual assault within domestic settings brought about many changes in the rape laws, but most notably it acknowledged that rape was possible within marriage and that it should indeed be prosecuted.

Changes in the law, however, do not bring about social and psychological changes, particularly within domestic settings. Cultural influences still can dictate dominant roles for men and submissive roles for women. These roles can have serious assault and sexual assault implications if the male is aggressive and the female views herself as subservient. Male partners and ex-partners often feel that they can get away with rape because they have repeatedly gone unpunished in the past and because cultural bias is on their side, even if the law is not. Husbands who have subjected their victims to forced sexual contact and physical abuse over time foster an oppressive relationship that instills a constant fear in the victim and renders her incapable of confronting her attacker. Eventually, she may acquiesce repeatedly to demands for sex in order to avoid the unpleasantness of physical force and/or abuse. Acquiescence in and of itself, however, does not constitute rape. Rape occurs only when force is used or threatened. Consequently, the category of domestic rape is the least likely to be reported to authorities. Mahoney (1999) conducted a study regarding sexual assault within domestic relationships. Her study revealed that the relationship between the victim and the rapist is the most important factor when victims decide whether or not to report incidents to the police. The closer the relationship between the victim and the rapist, the less likely it is that victims will report the attacks. Accordingly, domestic rapes, with their intimate relationship status, are less likely to be reported than stranger or acquaintance rapes. Mahoney also found that domestic sexual victims are more likely to experience multiple sexual assaults than any other category of sexual assault.

Because the vast majority of domestic cases also involve a history of psychological and physical abuse, of which rape is only a part, the emotional factors are clearly much deeper and more permanent and commonly involve multiple incidents. Once the victim decides to seek help and report attacks to the police, she may still be fearful. Her assailant, whether he resides in the same household or not, will often continue to be a threat to her physical and emotional well-being. He obviously knows where she lives, he has access to her residence, and he knows where she works and where and from whom she would seek help. These factors combine to put the victim in jeopardy when she commits to prosecuting her partner for assaulting her.

Consequently, it is rare that domestic cases are reported while both parties are still living together, despite the frequency of attacks. Usually, cases are not reported until one of the parties moves out. Even when they are no longer living together, there is usually some contact between them that can place the victim in danger. Fear for her safety and resistance to police intervention are not uncommon in such situations.

Divorce or separation proceedings frequently involve custody battles, visitation rights, and alimony. Compounding an already complicated issue is the fact that both parties know that accusations of abuse can go a long way toward deciding divorce proceedings and can provide a distinct advantage to the accusing party, even if the accusations are false. A man who rapes his wife is aware that he can convince others that his wife's accusations are fabricated by asserting that the woman is merely seeking an advantage in court. As detectives conduct their investigations, it is imperative that they obtain the details of such proceedings in order to address the issues likely to arise and to help verify the validity of the accusations.

Custody battles can easily give rise to false allegations of abuse and sexual assault against a spouse or even against the children. Such matters need to be investigated thoroughly and without prejudice. If an allegation of abuse is proven to be false, justice demands that the accuser be arrested. If, on the other hand, the accusations are valid, investigators have a duty to pursue every prosecutorial avenue available to ensure that the perpetrator is prosecuted and convicted.

Agency Rules That Require Arrests in Domestic Situations

For good reason, most agencies require its members to effect an arrest once an allegation of assault or sexual assault involving a domestic relationship has been made. History is replete with incidents of police failure in domestic situations. In the past, policies did not demand an arrest, and both the police and prosecutors routinely overlooked the seriousness of the victim's situation. Publicity regarding such failures was generated when victims' rights advocates demonstrated that many women and children continued to be maimed or even killed because the police and prosecutors failed to act when the first incident was reported. They proved over and over again that if action had been taken against the violators then the victims would have been spared. Survivors united and brought lawsuits against the police, charging them with failing to protect some of the most fragile members of society, and the courts granted substantial awards, not only to compensate the victims but also to punish the police for their failure to act. The awards subsequently changed the way police departments conducted business. No longer would domestic cases be subject to individual interpretation. Departments instituted policies that mandated their officers to make arrests when accusations of domestic crimes were made. Such policies have served them well and prevented accusations of unfair treatment by domestic survivors and their families.

Although immediate arrests are often necessary to protect victims from future harm, frequently there is ample time beforehand to conduct investigations without endangering their safety any further. The mandate to make an arrest and the need to conduct an investigation need not be mutually exclusive. If the safety of the victim can be secured while investigators corroborate the victim's allegations and gather evidence, the mandate to arrest can be delayed, but by no means disregarded. The delay can provide investigators with the time needed to secure the evidence required for a conviction and provide for the long-term safety of the victim. If no further evidence can be obtained, then the mandate to arrest based upon reasonable cause and the victim's allegation must be preserved.

The delay can also give investigators the time they need to uncover false allegations made by alleged victims that otherwise would have resulted in the arrests of innocent individuals. I have seen many domestic investigations, particularly those that involve child custody, concluded when evidence of a false allegation was found. In those cases, the accuser (usually the mother) was arrested for falsely reporting an incident. If, however, that proof was not found, then the department mandate to arrest the husband was maintained, even in the absence of any evidence beyond the allegation to support the victim's claim.

Recorded Conversations

Recording conversations, as with acquaintance rapes, may be the best way to corroborate the victim's allegations. Whether the recordings are done in person or by telephone, I have found that recordings are more successful in domestic cases than in any other type of sexual assault. The victim's intimate knowledge of what can make the suspect talk can be very useful as the conversation progresses towards the subject of rape. Her knowledge of his likes and dislikes can help steer the conversation more effectively than acquaintances with limited knowledge of the attacker. This intimacy can also facilitate a more open and honest discussion. Apologies by the perpetrator for the attack or his insisting that it was his right to force sex upon his wife can make compelling corroborative evidence to support the woman's allegations of rape within a court setting. Recordings, however, cannot always be made. The safety of the victim or her children and the likelihood that the suspect will flee are persuasive arguments for effecting arrests based upon an accusation alone. This does not preclude securing corroboration after an arrest is made. The interrogation of the suspect can often produce some form of corroboration or even a confession. Meanwhile, a search can reveal evidence of the rape, and interviews of witnesses can substantiate the victim's claim.

Uncovering the truth can be an illusive pursuit. Investigators will sometimes discover that accusations may have to stand alone without any corroborative support. Evidence may not be available, and the credibility of the victim may be the only reason to proceed with a prosecution. Although most police departments are mandated to arrest those alleged of domestic violence, prosecutors are not bound by the same guidelines. They can refuse to take legal action in cases that have no prosecutorial merit. The victim's ability to articulate the crimes committed against her in a clear and methodical manner may be the only credible evidence available for presentation to a jury. In weighing this evidence, prosecutors will ultimately be forced to make the decision based upon their subjective analysis of the victim's credibility and her capacity to communicate well. Conversely, victims who cannot articulate well and are not convincing may have a very difficult time, particularly when no supportive evidence is found.

The legal system may not be perfect, but it does make certain legitimate demands of the prosecution. Questioning the victim's motivation is a justifiable concern in domestic cases, particularly when divorce, child custody, and alimony are at stake. Sex crimes, particularly domestic sex crimes, are fraught with complications that attack the credibility of the star witness, the victim. The dilemma for investigators is to uncover all possible evidence in order to expose the truth and to corroborate the victim's allegations despite the many complications that can attack her credibility.

Case History

A young New York mother, 24 years old, was involved in a custody battle with her ex-husband over their two children, ages two and three. He had a new job in Seattle and was due to move within a couple of days. He still had a key to her apartment, and one day he used the key to enter the apartment unannounced, allegedly to discuss their relationship. He overpowered her, forced her into the bedroom, and raped her while the children slept in the next room. He used a condom during the rape, and he flushed it down the toilet when he was done. The victim had no visible facial or extremity bruising. Hospital personnel, however, documented recent bruising to the lower abdomen and the interior of the upper legs. They also documented tearing in the vaginal wall, which was consistent with rough sex.

This case had both elements that made an immediate arrest necessary. Because the ex-husband had a key to her apartment, she was clearly in danger of being attacked again, and, because he was moving to Seattle, he was an obvious flight risk. Although it would have been preferable to obtain incriminating evidence against the suspect before making an arrest, in this case there was little time to do so, and department procedures mandated an arrest in domestic cases such as this. We attempted to record a telephone conversation between the two while the victim was safely in our custody, but we only obtained his answering machine. He was due to leave for Seattle within two days, and a decision to arrest without additional evidence was made. She appeared credible, and the case relied heavily on her testimony and the modicum of supporting medical evidence that existed.

Bibliography

Acierno, R. and Resnick, H., Health impact of interpersonal violence. 1. Prevalence rates, case identification, and risk factors for sexual assault, physical assault, and domestic violence in men and women, *Behav. Med.*, 23(2), 53, 1997.

Bureau of Justice Statistics, *Criminal Victimization 2000: National Crime Victims Survey*, Office of Justice Programs, U.S. Department of Justice, Washington, D.C., 2001, p. 8

Mahoney, P., High rape chronicity and low rates of help-seeking among wife rape survivors in a non-clinical sample: implications for research and practice, *Violence against Women*, 5(9), 993–1017, 1999.

McGregor, M. J., Weibe, E., Marion, S. A., and Livingstone, C., Why don't more women report sexual assault to the police?, *Can. Med. Assoc. J.*, 162(5), 659–660, 2000.

Ullman, S., Karabatsos, G., and Koss, M., Alcohol and sexual aggression in a national sample of college men, *Psychol. Women Q.*, 23(4), 673–689, 1999.

Investigative Strategies for Stranger Rape

7

Sexual assault by strangers, sometimes referred to by sociologists as predator rape, is one of the most insidious crimes committed by men. Although members of either sex may and do perpetrate sex crimes in domestic and acquaintance cases, the commission of stranger rape and stranger sexual assault is almost exclusively the domain of men. During my tenure as the Commanding Officer of the Manhattan Special Victims Squad, I directed the investigation of over 7000 cases, and I can recall only one incident of a stranger attack that involved a female perpetrator. In that case, the victim was raped and mutilated by a gang of four individuals, one of whom was female. Although she did not actually rape the victim, as an accomplice she was just as guilty as her male companions. In domestic and sometimes in acquaintance situations, sexual assault by female perpetrators is more common, albeit still rare. These cases usually involve children under the perpetrators' care and occur in the privacy of their homes. It is not uncommon for male companions to also be involved in the assaults.

The repetitive nature of the rapist and the impact he can have on communities are significant. Stranger rape produces an atmosphere of fear that is much more disturbing than any other crime. Although rape is certainly not as serious as homicide, its impact can influence entire communities in a way that no other crime can. Like homicide, it is a fundamental attack upon our way of life. Unlike homicide, it affects a wider range of people as communities recognize that rapists are unrelenting and that they pose a threat that can seize control of an entire community. Not only are the victims and their immediate circle of family and friends affected, but the entire community is forced to make lifestyle changes to address the need to protect potential victims. Women modify their habits and avoid being alone, especially in secluded locations. Men become more protective and alter their plans in an attempt to secure the safety of female friends. Similarly, businesses, schools, and institutions are forced to enhance their security measures to counteract the threat to their female population.

The atmosphere throughout the entire community changes drastically. A stranger is looked upon with suspicion for fear that he may be the rapist. The psychological devastation to victims of rape is unparalleled, altering their outlook toward men and their capacity to socialize with others henceforth. Likewise, the social implications for the community can transform the character of a neighborhood overnight from one that is friendly and open to one that is inhospitable and even hostile. Consequently, police departments are forced to utilize every resource at their disposal to attack the problem. If they do not, they will have failed their constituents and their duty to protect the public. That failure will inevitably generate substantial community pressure that will ultimately force the investigative agency to make a substantial commitment of resources to facilitate the investigation and to rid their community of the threat posed by the rapist.

Victim Profile

Rapists frequently describe their victims as easy prey. I have found that sex predators are inclined to pick victims who appear shy and unable to put up a fight. It may be the demeanor of the victim as she passes by, or it may be her observed interactions with others. In either event, the rapist selects his victim because he feels that he can accomplish his assault with the least amount of resistance from the victim. If she resists, he feels that he can easily overpower her. The age and the physical beauty of victims are not as relevant for rapists as is their vulnerability. Although young attractive women are frequently the targets for rapists, they are not the sole targets. Rapists are opportunists and they strike when they feel the conditions are suitable for achieving their goal. The lifestyles of young women, as opposed to older women, tend to put them into the rapists' category of suitable victims. School, work, and social engagements often compel them to travel alone. Whereas older women or young children do not typically walk home alone or drive to secluded parking lots late at night, young and middle-aged women do. Whereas most elderly women and young girls are usually in the company of someone else, young and middle-aged women are frequently alone. Stevens (1999) conducted a study in which he interviewed a number of rapists and found that they attacked regardless of physical beauty, age, or physical condition.

When rapists do discriminate it is based on their personal perceptions of a victim's vulnerability prior to the attack. Women who are considered weak and defenseless in the eyes of the rapist are potential targets, while those whom the rapist perceives as strong or challenging are not. Stevens (1999) concluded that a rapist's decision to attack is based upon his perception of the victim's vulnerability. If an offender perceived that a potential victim was easy prey, he was more likely to strike; 69% of the offenders in Stevens' study felt that their assessment of the victim as easy prey was a primary factor in their decision to attack.

After interviewing many stranger rapists myself, I have found Steven's conclusions about how rapists select their victims to be accurate and insightful. They target their victims based upon situational circumstances more than any other factor. I have also found that rapists, as with other criminal elements of society, are very attentive to the actions and mannerisms of potential victims. They have developed a keen sense of awareness in order to make quick decisions regarding potential victims and situations. If they are wrong, then they leave themselves vulnerable to injury and/or capture. Usually, however, their need to survive and their criminal nature have honed their skills of observation to the point that they can make superior calculations regarding their ability to succeed. Unfortunately, most victims have not sharpened their skills in this area. Their experiences have not taught them to fear for their safety nor have they been conditioned to be aware of the danger posed by sexual predators.

Case History

On two occasions, a serial rapist attacked women after they exited taxicabs in front of their apartment houses at about 3:00 A.M. In each case, the victims did not see the suspect and were unaware of his presence as they entered their apartment buildings. In the first case, when the victim exited her taxicab, she passed several people who were walking by on the street in front of her building. She unlocked the door to the building and began to walk up the stairs. The rapist had obviously been searching for a victim and had hidden himself among the people walking down the street; when he saw the victim he made an instant decision to attack. He followed the woman into her building before the front door could close completely. No one on the street had noticed anything unusual at that time. Once inside the relative safety and isolation of the building, he produced a gun, forced her up the stairwell, and raped her.

In the second incident, the victim had also exited a taxicab in front of her building. She did not notice anyone on the street and entered her building. The front doors to the building are made of glass so the first floor is visible from the street. The outer door was unlocked, but she had to stop to unlock the inner door. Again, the rapist was obviously searching for a victim and this time had hidden himself in the darkness when he saw his potential victim exit her taxicab. When she stopped to unlock the inner door, he attacked. Fortunately, she had yet to open the door and he was never able to get her into the relative isolation and safety of the building. She threw down the keys and began to fight him off, screaming as loud as she could. The rapist fled before any help could arrive.

Both investigations revealed that in each case the rapist did not follow the victim for any length of time; instead, he was searching for victims when he discovered women whom he considered to be vulnerable and under circumstances that were ideal. He had been planning an attack and searching for victims, but his decision to strike these particular women was based upon his perception of their vulnerability under the circumstances at hand. His decision in the second case, of course, was obviously flawed and could easily have ended with his apprehension.

Targeting Potential Victims

The rapist will use the following factors to target potential victims and to strike when conditions are right:

- *Locations and circumstances that allow rapists to be in control* — Locations are preferred that isolate the victim from any help, thus ensuring that the confrontation will not be interrupted, and that provide the rapist with a means of escape (e.g., quiet streets, quiet park areas, vehicles, inside victim's apartment).
- *Women whose demeanor makes them appear unable to resist* — They may or may not be shy, reserved, or introverted, but the rapist's perception is what matters, not the victim's actual manner. Women who carry themselves in a confident and assertive manner will appear prepared to strike back and are less likely to be targets.
- *Women who do not appear to be attentive to their surroundings* — These women do not glance behind them when they walk down the street. They do not have their keys in their hand as they approach their building or their car; instead, they are unaware of their surroundings and often fumble through their bag to find their keys while the rapist approaches unnoticed. Other factors that can have an impact on the attentiveness of potential victims are alcohol consumption, drug use (both prescribed and illegal), and temporary health problems such as headaches, the flu, or a cold.
- *Women that appeal to the rapist's needs* — Although most rapists do not target specific types of women, some target victims because of their physical characteristics, their age (generally younger women), or because of an emotional need to punish a certain type of woman.

The Blame Game

Although stranger rapists have been known to attack women under many different circumstances, they typically attack those falling into one or more of the above categories. The tendency, however, to blame victims for placing themselves in these positions is a problem that must be addressed continually by investigators if we are to gain the confidence of victims. Blaming victims erodes any chances of their cooperating to the fullest, and such blame is the most common reason why victims do not report assaults immediately after they occur. It is also the most common reason why evidence is lost and sexual predators are allowed to escape prosecution, roaming free to strike again. As discussed in Chapter 5, investigators must be sensitive to the needs of the victim and her emotional state. They should do everything possible to ensure that she is not subject to criticism for being in the wrong place at the wrong time. Criticism will only inhibit the investigation by embarrassing the victim and influencing her ability to be honest and forthright about the attack. Investigators should remind those close to the victim that, despite all of the factors that caused the victim to be targeted by the rapist, she is not to blame. She did not initiate the attack, and she is not responsible for the criminal actions of her attacker.

Victim Selection

As a sex crime investigator, I have observed that sexual assault victims come in every shape, size, and age. I have seen elderly women attacked, as well as young women and children. As far as the stranger rapist is concerned, the only prerequisite seems to be that the victim must be female. Beyond that, stranger rapists discriminate little in regard to their victims, but they do discriminate quite a bit in regard to the situations in which they find their victims. The victim selection process has more to do with the victim's vulnerability than any other factor. Predators seek out victims they perceive as vulnerable. They hunt for and eventually find women in isolated settings and strike more because of the location, the time of day, and the demeanor of the potential victim than any other factor. Rapists, like any other criminal, do not want to pay the price for their crimes. They act in a cowardly manner and only strike those who have no hope of preventing the attack. They will not attack victims who they feel will resist or cause them harm or under situations where the potential for apprehension is amplified. They only attack women who they think will offer the least resistance and under circumstances that expose their victim's vulnerability. If the conditions are not right, the rapist will simply wait for another opportunity to strike. Remember, 51% of the population is female.

Rape during Burglary, Robbery, and Other Felonies

Although most rapists initiate their crimes with the intention of raping their victims, others begin their forced sexual behavior while committing crimes like robbery and burglary. During the commission of their theft, they discover that they have total control over their female victims. They seize the opportunity to act upon their sexual urges and add rape and/or sexual assault to their criminal repertoire. Typically, I have observed that, once robbers and burglars have seized the opportunity to sexually assault their victims, their criminal careers enter into a new phase that determines their future criminal conduct. Each time these criminals graduate from forcible theft to forced sexual assault, they are no longer satisfied with just stealing property. The sexual assault becomes their primary objective and the burglary or robbery is secondary. They continue to sexually assault female victims each and every time they break into homes or rob victims from that point forward.

Frequently, an underlying sexual aspect of this rapist's criminal activity escalates from crime to crime. When the suspect is apprehended, a review of his past criminal history and interviews of his prior victims often confirm a deviant sexual progression. Earlier victims may report instances where some form of forced sexual gratification was perpetrated against them during his attacks, and that gratification generally intensifies with each successive attack. The process may begin with the suspect using sexual references that demean the victim. He may infer that the victim would enjoy sexual contact with him or he may simply leer at her during the attack. With each succeeding attack, however, the sexual aspect of the assault becomes progressively more pronounced. Soon victims are fondled as the suspect searches for property, first over their clothes and then more intimately. With time, the sexual aspect of the crime increases in intensity and takes the form of forced sexual abuse, forcible sodomy, and forcible rape. The transition for some is short. They relish their newfound power over women in vulnerable situations, and they immediately begin to act upon their own sexual desires without regard to the victim. Others fight to control their urges and their progression is more gradual.

In both cases, however, the progression can be seen when the criminal history of apprehended suspects is examined closely. Interviews of past robbery victims can reveal a sexual nature to the attack that may not have been reported initially. Embarrassment, combined with the minor role the sexual advance played during the attack, however, frequently prevents them from divulging that information to investigators. Victims can report robberies and leave out information about the sexual nature of the attack, particularly if they thought is was insignificant. The more aggressive the sexual assault, however, the more likely victims are to report it.

As investigators search for leads in serial rape cases, linking one case with another can produce vital information that can lead to the identity of the rapist. The more cases that can be connected to the same perpetrator, the closer investigators will be to discovering his identity. Consequently, sex crime investigators are frequently called upon to search through different types of crimes when looking for correlations between a current pattern of rapes and past criminal activity. Caution, however, must be exercised to ensure that unrelated crimes that can lead investigators down the wrong path are not included. To remedy this problem, investigators who are trained to deal with sex crime victims should conduct extensive interviews of past crime victims. Thorough interviews by trained investigators can reveal correlations that others may not find. Those same interviews can eliminate suspected cases from further review and save time and resources.

Risky Behavior

Typical victims of stranger rapes do not engage in what one might consider risky behavior. They do not get intoxicated in public, they do not go to single bars alone and flirt with men they do not know, and they do not arrange to meet men without knowing something about them. Instead, they live ordinary lives and take typical precautions regarding their safety. When they are attacked, they are merely going about their everyday lives and are doing the things that ordinary people do. They may be on the way home from work or school, they may be on their way to meet some friends, they may be shopping, they may be out for a walk, or they may be out exercising when the rapist decides to strike. A stranger rapist targets those in situations that provide the best opportunity for him to accomplish his assault and provide for his escape. They do not necessarily target those involved in a particular type of risky behavior.

Of course, an intoxicated woman walking home alone in a deserted neighborhood easily provides a predator rapist with the situational requirements he needs to accomplish his assault and avoid apprehension. Investigators should be careful, however, in these situations not to place any blame on the victim. Investigators should also ensure that those coming into contact with the victim (medical personnel, friends, family, etc.) do not blame the victim. They may feel that the victim engaged in risky behavior, but they should be made to understand that the victim was not targeted because she was out alone and intoxicated; she was targeted because the perpetrator felt that the situation coincided with his goal. Blaming the victim will only discourage her further and generate animosity toward those involved in questioning her about the details of the incident. Clearly, the victim's behavior did not cause the attack. It may have made her more vulnerable, but it did not make the rapist do what he did. Making her responsible is not only wrong but it is also counterproductive and will limit the ability of investigators to obtain the details they need to pursue their investigation. She was merely in the wrong place when a perverted mind decided that she should be raped. The fault unmistakably lies with her assailant, not the victim.

Initial Response by Uniform Personnel and Mobilization of Personnel

Initial Response

Uniform members on patrol will typically be the first to respond to the scene of crimes and their initial actions are crucial to the future of most cases. Their first responsibility is, of course, to ensure the safety of the victim. If she is suffering from injuries, they are obliged to render aid and call for additional medical assistance immediately. Usually, that can be done without compromising the crime scene or hindering the search for the suspect. All uniform members should be trained thoroughly in this area. It is imperative that the crime scene be preserved intact, if possible (see Chapter 4), and that victims be advised not to destroy evidence, particularly semen that may be present on or in several specific locations, including:

- On the victim's body where he ejaculated
- In the victim's vagina
- In the victim's anus
- In the victim's mouth
- On the victim's clothing
- On the bedding
- On the floor where the attack occurred

Because stranger rapists often strike at random, picking victims who appear vulnerable and who provoke their rage, the evidence found at the scene or on the victim is likely to be the only link between the suspect and the victim. With it, identifications and connections between cases can be made; without it, predators will frequently escape punishment.

Mobilization of Personnel

As we have seen, a delay in the sexual assault reporting process is common. Victims often ponder what to do and whether or not to report attacks to the police. While they ponder their predicament, precious time passes and immediate responses to secure evidence and begin searches are prevented. In those cases that are reported immediately, however, the search for suspects can commence without delay by utilizing all available personnel and every resource at the department's disposal. In many large departments, prearranged mobilization plans have been instituted to respond to the various levels of emergencies for which they are responsible. Those mobilization plans are typically used to address large disturbances such as riots and impromptu demonstrations. Since September 11, 2001, police departments nationwide have updated those plans and augmented them to address the new threats posed by international terrorism. Smaller departments have also seen the wisdom of establishing mobilization procedures and have joined forces with neighboring jurisdictions to address the needs of their area.

These plans can benefit the investigator by utilizing their instant-response capabilities to facilitate the needs of a stranger rape investigation. They provide a prearranged structure to redeploy personnel instantly and in significant numbers to address the threat posed by civil unrest, natural disasters, and terrorism. Such plans can be modified with little effort to mobilize the personnel needed to initiate the search for a suspect and to assist in the recovery of evidence. The New York Police Department began utilizing mobilization plans for this purpose, and they found that not only did it address the needs of individual crimes it provided a system by which managers could evaluate individual mobilization responses and make adjustments as needed. This win–win situation has made mobilization the preferred approach when searching for perpetrators of major crimes such as stranger rape. If the suspect is still in the area, the chances of apprehending him are increased significantly with the mobilization of additional personnel.

Departments that establish mobilization plans and review them regularly provide a valuable tool to administrators by providing input from the diverse segments involved. Logistic problems, communication issues, and various levels of mobilization can be discussed and resolved before the need actually arises. Mock deployment drills frequently expose impediments to the successful deployment of personnel that were unrecognized before and provide input from areas that are normally overlooked (investigative units, support units, and outside agencies). Solutions can be incorporated into the plan and adjustments can be made to ensure that every resource is utilized to its maximum.

Once a pattern of serial rape has been identified, mobilization plans can be incorporated into the tactical plan (discussed later in this chapter) to address the immediate need to maximize the capabilities of the department. Those agencies that deal with serial rape patterns on an *ad hoc* basis and attempt to coordinate the needs of the investigation with a search for the suspect without a preplanned mobilization strategy in place will find that their responses are flawed and inadequate in most cases. Unplanned responses do not give managers a strategy to coordinate personnel in an efficient manner nor do they address the needs of the investigation properly. Opportunities to apprehend the suspect can be overlooked, and the search for evidence can be inadequate.

Established plans, on the other hand, can integrate responses from all units and agencies within the jurisdiction in an immediate and tactically superior manner. Agencies in charge of bus terminals, train stations, colleges, and other institutions can also be of enormous help in finding and apprehending suspects. I have frequently found that these agencies can be a valuable source of information and can supply another set of eyes and ears in the search for a suspect, provided they are informed and given direction. Even if they cannot provide any assistance, nothing is lost. Their involvement in the mobilization plan can be used to help assure the public everything is being done to address the crisis at hand, and can provide a positive public image for the department.

First Officer

The actions of the first officer on the scene are crucial to the outcome of stranger rape investigations. The ability of this officer to secure evidence while dealing with the needs of the victim will determine whether or not crime scene technicians are able to isolate and collect evidence. Unlike acquaintance and domestic rapes, this evidence may be the only connection that exists between the suspect and the victim. Chapter 4 delineates the duties of the first officer which should be carried out carefully, as the first officer's actions can make a substantial contribution to the investigative effort and their importance cannot be understated. Training should be reinforced continually, and detectives can provide realistic examples of how to secure evidence properly.

Case History

A rapist had attacked two women as they entered their apartments during the evening hours in separate areas of Manhattan. His description, his *modus operandi*, and his mannerisms reinforced our belief that we were dealing with the same individual in both cases. The existence of a pattern was announced, patrol personnel were given details regarding the rapist, and instructions on how to preserve crime scenes were reinforced by investigators at roll calls. Although we had DNA evidence from both crimes, no individual on file matched that genetic profile. When the suspect attacked a third time, alert patrol personnel cordoned off the entire block where the victim lived. She had been followed into her building and forced into her apartment, where she was raped and sodomized. After interviewing the victim, we found that she had seen the suspect near two cars parked on the street, and a witness identified the suspect walking past another parked car on the next block after the attack.

I asked the crime scene unit to search for latent prints on those cars and on several others parked in front of the building. I found that the lobby door had been compromised by several uniform police officers, and ambulance attendants had understandably touched it with their bare hands before they understood its significant forensic value; nevertheless, I had the crime scene unit process that door for prints. A fingerprint that did not belong to any of the responding officers, the ambulance personnel, the building residents, or the victim was found on the door. The perpetrator had a prior criminal record and was identified through that print. He was arrested before he could attack again. In subsequent lineups, two of the three victims positively identified the suspect. A court-ordered DNA sample was then obtained from the suspect, and the sample positively linked him to all three sexual assaults. He is now spending 25 years to life courtesy of the New York State Corrections Department and is unable to hurt any more innocent women.

The officers acted superbly by safeguarding the area. Their need to respond quickly to ensure the safety of the victim obviously justified disturbing the crime scene; at that point, they were unaware of the victim's status as a victim of a stranger rape, and their primary duty was to secure her safety. Once it was discovered that the suspect followed the victim into the building, however, they sealed off the entire area until detectives arrived. The crime scene unit was able to retrieve the relevant latent print from the lobby door, and the actions of the first officers, the ability of the investigators to elicit pertinent information from the victim, and the capabilities of the crime scene unit combined to solve a major sexual assault investigation.

Uniform Supervisor

Once a sexual assault has been confirmed:

- Mobilize personnel and begin a coordinated search for the suspect.
- Ensure that the crime scene is safeguarded and assign personnel to search areas for additional evidence (weapon, blood, condom, etc.).
- Ensure that the name, address, and telephone numbers of all potential witnesses are obtained for delivery to the investigating officer.
- If an investigator is not present, ensure that an officer accompanies the victim to the hospital. Instruct this officer to be sensitive to the victim's needs while ensuring that evidence she possesses is secured properly (semen or blood on clothing, on skin, in mouth, in vagina, or in anus).

Initial Investigative Response

A professional investigative response utilizes the talents and resources of the various units at its disposal to gain insight from their different perspectives. Uniform personnel, paramedics, hospital staff, and crime scene technicians play a crucial role in identifying and securing evidence. Uniform police are usually the first to arrive, and they can provide important information regarding their actions, their observations, and the victim's statements. They are the first to render first aid to the victim, and their actions are critical to the preservation of evidence and the crime scene. They are in an advantageous position to identify witnesses, and their observations are invaluable. The paramedics provide the victim with her initial medical care. Their observations regarding the victim's medical condition are important, while their verbal exchange with her can provide a valuable insight into the victim's emotional state. The hospital staff not only provides treatment for the victim but also serves to collect evidence for the investigator and for presentation in court. They document the injuries sustained by the victim for presentation in court. They also collect samples for laboratory analysis and they provide expert opinions regarding the vaginal and rectal examinations.

Team Approach

During the initial response to a stranger rape, a number of investigative duties must be coordinated simultaneously. To facilitate a more efficient approach to the coordination of investigative resources, an investigative team approach is required. The team approach distributes the workload among the investigative resources to prevent an enormous burden being placed on the lead investigator. Experience has shown that the ability to solve a crime often diminishes with the passage of time. Allocating investigative resources effectively and coordinating those resources to deal with the multitude of issues that arise before too much time passes is essential in the early stages of an investigation. Consequently, sufficient personnel and resources are needed to perform the many tasks required at this early stage. Allocating too few resources and taking just one step at a time can have a deleterious effect on the investigation. Potential witnesses can disappear before they are interviewed. They may leave before anyone has even sought their assistance, they may be identified but refuse to wait for investigators to get around to them, or they may decide that the process is too protracted and creates too much of a burden for them. Furthermore, insufficient resources can result in lost leads and missed opportunities that will not be available as time passes.

An investigative team approach coordinates the investigative resources quickly and assigns duties to maximize the effectiveness of these resources. The investigative commander assembles as many investigators as needed and directs them to perform the various tasks at hand. Witnesses can be inter-viewed swiftly, and investigators can consolidate and evaluate the information obtained before any leads go cold. Prompt interviews also prevent witnesses from becoming disgruntled, thus preventing the loss of vital information while giving witnesses the individual attention they need and deserve. Like-wise, a team approach allows commanders to institute a quick response to canvass for additional witnesses before they depart (for example, nearby workers such as doormen, garage attendants, or delivery people who may be finishing their shifts soon), and it frees the lead investigator and his partner to deal with the victim and the hospital staff and to confer with the crime scene unit. Probably the most important aspect of the team approach is that it frees the investigative commander to assign personnel to pursue important leads before they go cold.

The fundamental investigative duties of the lead investigator cannot be delegated, but the investigative commander is free to assign other personnel and resources to the many duties that arise during this early stage of the investigation. It is important to note that, although certain fundamental investigative duties must be performed in every thorough investigation, each investigation is unique and requires a unique approach. Geberth (1996), one of the most respected and experienced police homicide commanders in NYPD, noted the importance of not falling into a set routine. He found that experience may be invaluable, but new twists require flexibility and adapt-ability. Each case is unique, and different perspectives are needed to address the various issues that arise. The following duties are important and should not be overlooked; however, they are only a guide and should be modified to address the needs of individual cases.

Lead Investigators

The responsibilities of lead investigators begin with notification of the assault from a patrol officer on the scene. Any duties that do not directly involve the victim can be delegated to members of the investigative team; however, interactions with the victim should be limited to the lead investigator, the investigator's partner, and the investigative supervisor to protect her from repeated questioning and added stress. Lead investigators must make every attempt to:

- Document each step in the investigative process, including the initial notification; document how it was received (telephone, in person, radio, etc.), the date and time of the notification, and the reported criminal allegation.
- Confer with uniform supervisor and first officer and confirm that the crime scene is secure; expand or contract the crime scene as needed.

- Obtain an account of the first officer's response, but do not allow the victim or any of the witnesses to be present at the time.
- Interview the victim (see Chapter 5) in private.
- Evaluate the validity of the victim's statements (see Chapter 10).
- Separate the witnesses to prevent them from discussing their observations before an investigator interviews them. In this way, witnesses will not be able to influence each other, and an honest exchange of observations can be elicited from each. Those who have something to hide will be deterred from lying because they will not have the chance to conspire with others to cover up the lies. The dishonesty of those who do lie is often exposed when their statements contradict those of the other witnesses.
- Accompany victim to hospital and obtain a detailed statement of the attack.
- Confer with medical personnel to ensure that all evidence is collected (see Chapter 4); obtain a detailed description of the victim's injuries and the results of the vaginal and rectal examinations.
- Ensure that medical evidence is secured properly and submitted for analysis.
- Confer with the crime scene unit to ensure they have all the information they need to process the scene properly; obtain a detailed listing of the evidence collected at the crime scene and discuss the crime scene with the technicians to confirm that all evidence has been collected.
- Discuss the evidence to be tested with the lab technicians and/or forensic biologist.

The crime scene response and the interviewing techniques are outlined in Chapters 4 and 5, respectively.

Investigative Supervisors

Investigative supervisors must:

- Take charge of the crime scene and the investigation.
- Verify that the crime scene is properly established and expand or contract it as necessary.
- Ensure that personnel are posted to keep the crime scene secure, with instructions regarding who is allowed access.
- Confer with the uniform supervisor to render any assistance in the search for the suspect, ensuring that all possible avenues of escape are being searched; utilize the resources of all units at their disposal in a

multifaceted approach to address the immediate need to search for the perpetrator.

- Confer with the lead investigator to discuss the location of possible evidence, witnesses, and the perpetrator.
- Have the investigative team interview the witnesses.
- Assign investigative personnel to canvass for additional witnesses (e.g., neighbors or passersby; see Canvass section below).
- Obtain record of police calls at the location of occurrence and have investigators interview callers for information about their observations.
- Obtain a record of police calls in the surrounding area.

It is not uncommon to discover police calls made prior to the incident that could involve the perpetrator. Calls reporting, for example, "a suspicious person" or a "possible street robbery" may reveal the perpetrator's prior actions when he pursued his prey. It is also not uncommon to find police calls regarding the same suspect as he flees. Investigative supervisors, then, should also:

- Have the callers interviewed, establish if the same suspect is involved, and seek their assistance in identifying the suspect.
- Assign investigative personnel to immediately follow up on any leads that arise.

The coordination of personnel is a fundamental responsibility of investigative commanders. Their skills in this area will ensure the most efficient use of personnel and the success of the investigation. Leads are frequently lost when initial investigations are not coordinated properly; these lost leads could have resulted in identifying and apprehending the suspect.

Canvass

During a canvass, investigators query people in the vicinity of the attack to obtain information and identify possible witnesses. Assigned investigators are directed to interview residents, workers, delivery people, etc. and to document their interviews for review by the investigative commander and the lead investigator. Witnesses with important information are prioritized and that information is immediately given to the investigative commander. The perpetrator's approach and escape routes should also be canvassed for information.

When canvassing residential areas late at night, common sense should prevail. Residents who are clearly awake (lights on, looking out open windows) can be interviewed immediately. It is hoped that investigators will find that they were awake during the incident and can provide additional information. The rest of the area can wait until a reasonable hour. Such consideration will yield more cooperation and will provide investigators with a more accurate and complete canvass.

When conducting residential or workplace canvasses, all the occupants or workers should be interviewed. Document the names of those not present at the time of the canvass and interview them at a later date during a re-canvass. In each interview, obtain basic information such as name, address, and date of birth; employment information; and additional contact information (e.g., cell phone number, pager number, names of relatives). Also, seek answers to the questions:

- Are you aware of the sexual assault?
- How did you hear about the incident?
- Do you have any information about the sexual assault?
- Have you seen anyone suspicious in the neighborhood recently?
- Do you know the victim? Can you tell me about the victim? (Do not reveal the victim's identity if it is clear that the person being interviewed does not know her.)

Prepare a report documenting each interview. A common mistake is to list those interviewed and to indicate their lack of knowledge by marking "N/R" (negative results) after their names; however, those reviewing the canvass will not be able to tell whether:

- No one was home.
- The occupant was uncooperative and refused to answer the questions. (Further examination of such people is obviously needed to determine their reason for not cooperating; they may simply dislike the police or they may have something to hide.)
- Only some of the occupants were home and they reported that they did not see or hear anything; it is not known if the other occupants might have heard or seen anything. (In this case, a re-canvass is obviously needed.)
- All of the occupants were interviewed but none of them heard or saw anything.
- The occupants heard a noise but did not investigate and had nothing to contribute. (This witness can at least corroborate the victim's allegation that something transpired.)

Commuter Canvasses

In highly populated areas, it can be helpful to conduct canvasses of commuters during their trips to and from work. In order not to inconvenience everyone on their commute, flyers can be prepared and distributed seeking the public's help in identifying the perpetrator. Investigators should be present at each distribution point to interview those who may have some information. Flyers can be distributed at train stations, bus stops, toll booths, and busy intersections near the attack. Each flyer should describe the attack and provide a description of the perpetrator, if possible. If a sketch is available, it should be displayed clearly on the flyer. A 24-hour hotline telephone number should be displayed for the public to call with information.

Documentation

Geberth (1996) notes that no matter how experienced investigators are, during the early stages of an investigation they can never be certain what information or what witnesses will eventually prove to be important; therefore, complete notes and documentation of every detail are essential. Likewise reports must be thorough and complete in order to ensure that every aspect of the case is reviewed properly and to prevent investigators from being humiliated in court. Defense attorneys have the luxury of scrutinizing paperwork in depth as they prepare their cases. When their clients are guilty of attacks, they have no choice but to dissect every aspect of the investigations and attempt to exploit weaknesses when they find them. The massive amount of paperwork makes it easy for them to find errors and question and criticize the investigation.

The investigative strategies outlined in this book are intended as a guide. Although these investigative standards have proven to be successful, the unique characteristics of each case require that strategies be adjusted to address the distinctive issues that can arise. As one of my more experienced colleagues frequently liked to proclaim, "Investigation is an art, and we are artists." He understood that, although no standard investigative model can address every case, investigators can base their investigations on certain features common to every investigation and adapt their strategies as needed to move their investigation in the appropriate direction. Investigators should demonstrate an attention to detail, an ability to adapt strategies to changing circumstances, a methodical nature for pursuing all leads, and superior interviewing and interrogation skills. Often overlooked, however, is their competence in keeping proper records, their ability to organize those records in a chronological and cogent fashion, and their persistence in documenting every aspect of an investigation. Every experienced prosecutor will assert that those who maintain excellent records and document every aspect of the investigation leave little for defense attorneys to criticize. Those that do not soon find that their memory is not capable of absorbing and maintaining all of the minute details of an investigation. The vague and often contradictory testimony that results can be an easy target for defense attorneys who are all too happy to manipulate any doubts that will favor their client's standing with the jury. Consequently, the massive amount of paperwork generated in major criminal investigations coupled with an often unpredictable investigative model offers defense attorneys a prime target for exploitation. Investigators who take excellent notes and convert them into logical and cohesive records validate their own actions and leave few prospects for attorneys to criticize. Accordingly, care should be taken when preparing reports from notes. Geberth (1996) notes that this involves three steps: (1) collecting the information, (2) collating the information and organizing the notes, and (3) writing the report. His assessment is as valid for sexual assaults as it is for homicides.

When taking notes:

- Start with a new notepad for each investigation.
- Begin with the initial notification. Describe who made the notification, how it was received, your location at the time of the notification, and the time and date of the notification.
- Take note of your time of arrival, the weather conditions, lighting, and persons present at the scene (e.g., victim, witnesses, police officers, ambulance).
- Document all injuries to the victim, her appearance, her dress (indicate torn clothing), her ability to communicate, etc.
- Document the presence of evidence. Although crime scene technicians will take pictures, it is recommended that investigators take Polaroid pictures of the crime scene upon their arrival. This serves a twofold purpose in that the photographs provide an instant reference for discussing the case with the investigative team and such photographs also provide a reference that can be used while interviewing the victim.
- Document all times accurately.
- Document the interview with the victim.
- Document the interview of the first officers and the supervisor. (Remember, do not interview them in front of the victim or witnesses.)
- Document the interviews of possible witnesses. As with a canvass, obtain the complete "pedigree" information of the witnesses, including residence, contact numbers, occupation, telephone number at work, cell phone number, beeper number, etc. (Remember, keep

witnesses separated and interview them individually in order to get independent and candid responses free from the influence of others; do not let other witnesses overhear the interviews.)

The Ongoing Investigation

In many ways, the investigative techniques used in stranger cases are similar to those used in nonsex crime investigations, with two notable exceptions. First, the interaction with the victim requires trained and skilled investigators to discover all the facts. As we have learned (see Chapter 4), the investigator's abilities in this area will have a profound impact upon the crime scene and upon the forensic technicians' attempts to determine the location and substance of potential evidence. Second, the repetitive nature of the sexual offender makes it likely that he will attack again. Sex Crime Units are therefore mandated to treat every unsolved sexual offense, particularly stranger offenses, as part of a larger pattern of abuse committed by the same offender, thus making the investigative process markedly more complex. The following discussion addresses the steps to be taken at the scene of stranger sexual assault attacks to ensure that every investigative avenue is pursued.

Prior Criminal Activity of Sexual Offenders

If the immediate investigative efforts do not yield positive results, cases cannot be dismissed as unsolved after all the leads have been exhausted. Instead, the investigator and the investigative commander need to consider the repetitive nature of the assailant and search for correlations that may exist with crimes reported to the police in the past. Units that do not routinely search through reported crime intelligence are missing opportunities that can help solve the current case under investigation. After determining that the case under investigation lacks sufficient evidence to identify the perpetrator, a search should be made through past crime data in an effort to identify similar crimes committed by the same individual. If links can be established between past criminal activity and the current investigation, the accumulation of evidence can help identify the suspect or at least help identify his movements and his transitions from one crime to another. Consequently, reviews should be made of all solved and unsolved cases in an effort to search for additional victims and to hold offenders accountable for all their criminal activity.

Similar sexual assaults committed within the same geographic area are easy to identify as part of a pattern, and every investigative agency/unit is responsible for conducting continual reviews to ensure that they identify them immediately (after the second incident). I have often found, however, that predators sometimes graduate to rape after committing lesser nonsexual offenses. Identifying a relationship among these earlier cases and the latest case can be difficult due to the obscure nature of the similarities and the lack of information from past victims. When the connections can be established, however, they have a significant impact on the investigation. They provide additional evidence, additional background information (including geographic information), and additional witnesses who can help identify the suspect.

Once a sexual assailant is apprehended, a quick look at his past criminal activity, however, may not reveal a connection that is recognizable at first glance. This is particularly true when the current arrest is the first one of a sexual nature. Extensive interviews of his prior victims will be necessary to dig deeper and to uncover the similarities that certainly exist. Mannerisms are often the same, and his method of attacking his victims are frequently similar, but even more important is the underlying sexual tone that will become apparent in all of his past criminal activity. Prior victims will typically avoid divulging such information to investigators unless it is relevant to their assault or specific questions are asked. They do not wish to be embarrassed further, and they frequently feel that the slight sexual tone to the attack was both immaterial and unimportant.

Nevertheless, when sex crime investigators interview a suspect's past victims, they will undoubtedly discern a distinct degeneration in the suspect's actions. It will become apparent to the investigator that, as the predator has become more proficient and accomplished in his criminal activity, the underlying sexual tone has become more readily apparent. Similar phrases will often surface in the interviews, such as phrases that the suspect finds useful for threatening his victims and forcing them into submission. Likewise, the amount of and type of force he has used is generally the same (physical force, knife, gun, etc.). Investigators should keep in mind, however, that the type of force used by the rapist could change drastically from one attack to another. His emotional state at the time of his attacks, his previous experiences in forcing victims to submit to his will, and the amount of resistance from his victims are factors that can change the amount of violence he exhibits. That violence can easily escalate if one of those factors is altered during an attack.

Criminals, like everyone else in society, develop their own way of dealing with the obstacles they encounter in life. Once they find a method that is successful, they will tend to duplicate it and even refine it as similar obstacles are encountered. In this way, criminals develop their *modus operandi*, which can be described as behavior that is learned. It changes over time as offenders gain experience by committing crimes or associating with the criminal element of society. Each develops his own *modus operandi* because he finds that certain things work well for him and fit within his abilities. As criminals gain more experience, they refine their skills and become more proficient.

Investigators will find that the circumstances leading up to the assailant's previous criminal activity and the methods he used to accomplish his attacks may not be identical, but they are frequently similar. Potential victims may have been entering their cars in a parking lot, they may have been entering their buildings late at night, or they may have been walking alone in the park when they were attacked. The choice of which woman to attack is based upon personal preferences that have been developed over time. Consequently, the records of robberies, burglaries, assaults, etc. should be examined closely for any similarities to the current attacks. The same mannerisms are frequently evident, as is the amount of force used to accomplish the crime. The sexual undertone and the correlation among these cases can seem obvious once identified but may be difficult to detect at first for several reasons. The lack of details in the original case may not be sufficient to make correlations. The victims may not have been candid with investigators in the prior incidents, or the predator may not have developed a distinctive method of attacking his victims at that time.

Past attacks may have also occurred within different jurisdictions. Well-run Sex Crime Units routinely reach out to these surrounding jurisdictions to obtain their cooperation in the search for criminal connections. They establish a rapport with these jurisdictions and communicate frequently to ensure that nothing is missed. Developing a good rapport works well for all jurisdictions involved and facilitates an atmosphere where reciprocal requests are given priority. Searching through thousands of crime files is certainly difficult, time consuming, and often unproductive but absolutely necessary to ensure that all leads are exhausted thoroughly.

It is, of course, possible to make associations between cases where they do not exist. An unidentified perpetrator who robs a female as she walks down a deserted street may or may not be a good suspect for inclusion in the current sexual assault case. His description, his demeanor, the words he uses, and the manner in which he treats the victim are items that can help investigators narrow the search efficiently. The more details investigators have regarding the current attack under investigation and an older attack, the more likely it is that they will be able to identify or eliminate correlations between cases. Skilled investigators who are proficient at interviewing sexual assault victims (see Chapter 5) will speed up the process by obtaining as much information as possible, including sensitive information, from the victim and from witnesses. This investigator is then in a better position to connect cases that require further examination and to eliminate suspects that may on the surface look similar. An investigator's ability to gather minute details from sexual assault victims in a methodical and comprehensive manner is vital to this effort and its importance cannot be understated.

Computer Analysis

Computer systems have greatly enhanced the efficiency of the investigative process and have generated many correlations among cases that would have been missed in the past. In New York City, computer systems are available to search through crime data, narcotics investigative data, warrant investigative data, criminal justice data, and in some cases federal investigative data. Unfortunately, like the rest of the country, New York does not have databases that communicate with other local jurisdictions. Perhaps one day these databases will be available, but for now investigators are left to their own devices. Although Teletype messages or e-mails can be sent nationwide to request searches from local jurisdictions, the searches are limited by the inconsistent attention that each agency gives these requests. Typically, investigators find that the most effective way to ensure that a thorough search is conducted is by developing a comprehensive network of reliable investigators who hold similar positions throughout the nation. Fraternal organizations and professional associations are helpful in finding colleagues that can be of assistance if needed. Although requests to these investigators are typically cordial and dependable, they are still limited by the data existing in local jurisdictions and by the manner in which the data are collected. Unfortunately, a great deal of investigative manpower is necessary to communicate individually with each local agency. It is currently, however, the only way to ensure that requests are given the attention they deserves while ensuring that each criterion is searched thoroughly. Currently, spending long hours on the telephone in a search for an investigative lead is a necessary element of every stranger rape investigation. Investigators should keep the following in mind when trying to find similarities from case to case:

- Similarities in perpetrator description can include race, height, weight, clothing, neatness, mannerisms, hygiene, genital description, scars, and tattoos, among others.
- Similarities in *modus operandi* can include, but are not limited to, the words used by the suspect during the attack or after completion; the manner in which the victim is accosted (entering car, entering building, etc.); actions during the sex act and the order and manner of forced sexual activity (e.g., oral sex followed by vaginal or anal sex); ability or inability to maintain an erection; methods used to obtain an erection (masturbation, demand for physical stimulation by victim); physical injuries inflicted on the victim (strangulation, punched in face, use of weapon, etc.); or robbery of the victim (noting the type of items stolen). It is important to understand that rapists do not always attack in exactly the same manner each time. Sometimes it is very difficult to determine the similarity in actions until suspects are

arrested, debriefed, and their criminal history is examined in detail (unless, of course, DNA or other forensic evidence can connect them). Past criminal activities (even petty offenses) often show similarities in language or actions when they are examined closely.

- Similarities among victims can include race, age, hair color, etc. Do not confine the search, however, solely to these similarities. The only requirement for many rapists is that their victims must be female. Victims are usually targeted because of where they are at the time of the attack, not because of individual victim characteristics (see Victim Profile section). Investigators who restrict themselves to a specific type of victim confine their investigations and are certain to miss opportunities.
- Similarities in victims' actions prior to the attack can include walking home at night alone, exiting a bar, entering an apartment building, or getting into a vehicle. By far, the most common attack occurs as victims enter their residences or their vehicles, when they are most vulnerable. These environments frequently provide the rapist with all the situational elements necessary to complete his attack.
- Similarities in geographic locations can include assaults taking place in a residential area, business area, or commercial area.
- Similarities in timing could include time of day, day of the week, or time of the year.
- Similarities in escape methods could include escaping on foot, by bicycle, in an automobile, etc.
- Forensic comparisons of fingerprints, hair, blood, semen, etc. should be made; also, compare crime scenes for partial prints and palm prints that are not in the computer databases.

Do not confine the search to cases that incorporate *all* of these similarities. Instead, start with cases that contain as many similarities as possible. If no cases fit all of the criteria (and probably none will), expand the search by eliminating similarities one by one.

Conclusion

Investigators will find that stranger sexual assault cases are more complex and puzzling than those involving domestic or acquaintance cases. Advances in forensic biology, however, have provided investigators with a powerful tool that can support the victim's assertions. Whereas acquaintances and domestic partners can easily claim that the sexual act was consensual, a similar claim by a stranger is more difficult to sustain. In stranger cases, the following circumstantial evidence comes into play and makes it difficult for suspects to show that the sexual act they are accused of was not rape:

- Lack of a relationship between the victim and the suspect
- Existence of injuries to the victim, particularly injuries that are consistent with forcible sex
- Location and time at which the rape occurred
- Circumstances surrounding the attack that confirm the suspect's motivation

Identification of the suspect is the key element in stranger cases. In the past, we would rely upon the victim to identify the suspect in a lineup. Today, we have forensic science to back up that identification. This, of course, makes the preservation of evidence at the crime scene by uniform and investigative personnel critical to the investigation of stranger cases. Such evidence is usually the only link between the victim and her assailant and therefore is the only way to positively identify the suspect.

Uniform personnel are typically the first to arrive at the scene of sexual assaults, and the importance of training these first responders cannot be overstated. Proper training produces officers who know the value of evidence and who know how to preserve it properly. Their actions at the scene can often mean the difference between a solved and an unsolved crime.

Understanding how rapists select their victims will help investigators understand that the victim should never be blamed for her conduct. Friends, acquaintances, and relatives of the victim often make the mistake of assigning some of the blame to the victim. Investigators will need to educate those around the victim to ensure that they understand the victim is not to blame. Perpetrators select their victims because situational circumstances are suitable for the completion of their attack, not because of anything the victim did.

Investigators will find an enormous demand on their time at crime scenes. Only a team approach directed by the investigative supervisor will provide adequate investigative resources to address the many tasks required in stranger sexual assault case. Without a team approach, witnesses will be lost, and victims will become frustrated as they wait for investigators to complete tasks that can be performed by others.

The likelihood that sexual assailants limit their criminal activity to sex-related cases or that the case under investigation is the only one ever committed by the perpetrator is extremely small; consequently, every stranger sexual assault case investigation should include a search through the available crime data to look for correlations that can help solve the current case. In doing so, investigators are likely to find victims who originally hid the sexual aspect of their attack from the police because they were embarrassed or ashamed or felt that it was to trivial to mention.

The threat posed by a stranger sexual assault can have a profound impact upon the lifestyle of residents within the targeted community who will express their displeasure with police departments that do not use the full resources of their agency to address the issue at hand. A collaborative effort headed by a specialized unit consisting of highly trained and sensitive investigators will go a long way toward alleviating those fears. The ability to deal with the victim effectively and to apply its expertise is clearly the best response an investigative agency can have.

Bibliography

Geberth, V. J., *Practical Homicide Investigation*, 3rd ed., CRC Press, Boca Raton, FL, 1996, pp. 76, 808.

Stevens, D. J., Victim selection techniques, in *Inside the Mind of a Serial Rapist*, Austin and Winfield Publishers, San Francisco, CA, 1999, pp. 55–67.

Investigative and Tactical Plans for Serial Sexual Assault

8

Experience has shown that those who sexually assault strangers become addicted to the feelings of power and the sexual gratification they achieve when perpetrating their assaults. Their obsession takes control of their lives, and they continue to assault unsuspecting women until they are removed from society. Men who commit these crimes are empowered not only by the successful completion of each assault but also by their ability to avoid apprehension. With each successive attack, they become progressively brazen and arrogant. They also become more and more skilled at intimidating and subduing their victims while refining their ability to elude detection. The reader should be reminded that serial sexual assaults occur in all categories of rape: domestic, acquaintance, and stranger. This chapter, however, addresses only the issue of serial cases committed by strangers. The strategies concerning domestic and acquaintance cases have been delineated at length in Chapter 6. Those strategies are excellent for dealing with suspects who are known to their victims, and should be employed even when multiple attacks occur. They are, however, significantly different from what is needed to address the issue of a serial stranger case. Therefore, for the purposes of this discussion, the term *serial rape* is used only in reference to stranger cases and includes all types of sexual assault (sodomy, sexual abuse, etc.) for simplicity's sake. It will be used to address the issue of multiple sexual assaults committed by men who are not known to their victims and who appear to strike at random.

The seriousness of serial rape and the havoc that such attacks can cause demand that every available resource be utilized to address the issue. The most appropriate response that police agencies can have is to establish a collaborative climate in which the investigators, patrol personnel, and the support units work in tandem to attack the threat posed by the rapist. As the reader will see, an investigative plan along with a tactical plan can effectively formalize the process. Such an approach provides a system to document the responsibilities for every unit involved, and it verifies the commitment of resources by the various commanders involved. This arrangement has proven to be the most effective way police departments can address the threat of serial sexual assault, as it provides a comprehensive approach to achieve the ultimate goal of apprehending the perpetrator.

Investigative and Tactical Plans Defined

An *investigative plan* is a detailed plan to coordinate the *investigative resources* that have been assembled to address a particular sexual assault pattern and to obtain the assistance of *investigative units* from within the department and from outside agencies. The extent and intensity of each segment of the plan will depend on the needs of the particular investigation, the perceived threat to the public, and the commitment of the investigative agency. The *tactical plan*, however, is a detailed strategy to use every resource at the department's disposal to address the threat from an overall perspective. It incorporates a nontraditional investigative response to formulate an intense strategy to apprehend the predator who remains at large and to address the needs of the investigation. Personnel are drawn from patrol, transportation, and narcotics divisions, among others, and are placed under the control of the division/precinct commander in a strategic effort to search for and apprehend the predator at large.

Sexual Assault Patterns

Sexual assault patterns can be described as multiple sexual assaults (rape, sodomy, sexual abuse) forcibly committed by the same person upon unsuspecting victims. Within every Sex Crime Unit, analytical personnel are needed to review stranger assaults and search for similarities that may indicate that the same person is responsible. A pattern team consisting of two detectives is typically needed to interview victims and interrogate potential suspects in a relentless search for connections to avoid overlooking patterns when they occur. Relationships should be established with adjoining jurisdictions to expand the search area and to find patterns as soon as possible. A pattern can involve as few as two cases and should be established as soon as possible to prevent more women from being attacked.

The Investigative Plan

The first step in any investigative plan is to recognize that the enormity of the investigation at hand requires a formalized process that coordinates intelligence and provides sufficient investigative personnel to examine every lead quickly and thoroughly. Once the plan is established, the investigative commander can then coordinate with the division/precinct commander regarding the tactical plan. The investigative team should consist of a supervisor, the lead investigator, and as many investigators as are necessary to complete the tasks listed on the following pages under the command of the Sex Crime Unit's commanding officer. I have commanded several investigative teams that have ranged in size from 4 to 25 full-time investigators and from 1 to 3 supervisors. The size of the investigative team depends on the scope of the investigation and the urgency of the case in question.

Case Familiarity

All investigative team members should study the case file and discuss the merits of the investigative strategies as soon as they are assigned. A detailed background is required before the team can interview persons or review data. Each investigator and supervisor should also review on a daily basis every lead, every tip, and all data that have been generated. Doing so will ensure that the entire team is up to date, that each member is aware of every facet of the investigation, and that the potential to match incoming information to the perpetrator is maximized. Often the amount of information coming in to investigators is staggering. Excess data can accumulate if supervisors do not ensure that every investigator reads and is aware of the latest updates. The need to prioritize information will soon become apparent. Geographic and psychological profilers (see Chapter 9) can be of enormous help to investigators in their efforts to manage the overabundance of information. Profilers will not solve the crime, but they can help investigators prioritize their search for the perpetrator and manage information more efficiently.

Public Announcement

Once a sexual assault pattern is uncovered, strategic plans can be developed to ensure that all resources are dedicated appropriately. The public should immediately be made aware of the existence of a pattern. The public statement will serve to:

- Warn the public of the danger.
- Alert the public to the specific method in which perpetrator operates.
- Educate the public in regard to how to avoid dangerous situations.
- Provide a 24-hour phone line (hotline) for use by the public to call in tips.
- Publicize a reward, if one exists.
- Solicit the public's assistance in identifying possible suspects.
- Seek the public's assistance in reporting any unusual activity.

Intelligence Reporting Structure

Because many large departments are compartmentalized into a number of individual geographic areas and specializations, the intelligence reporting structure for those departments is much more complex and subject to error. Investigators must reach out to these many levels within the organization to coordinate their efforts with the investigative and tactical plans and to ensure that the intelligence gathering capabilities of the investigative unit are maximized. Investigative counterparts throughout the department, in adjoining geographic jurisdictions, and on the state and federal level can frequently be of enormous help in identifying similarities for cases under their jurisdictions. Likewise, uniform members on patrol can become the eyes and ears of investigators within the targeted areas by talking to neighborhood sources and reporting possible leads to investigators. Plainclothes officers can seek information from street sources and stake out areas where the suspect is likely to strike. Traffic officers can be alerted to the perpetrator's *modus operandi* and description, and they can assist in closing off escape routes if the suspect attacks again. Canine units can help search for the suspect if and when he attacks again. Outside government agencies (e.g., transportation agencies or schools) and private entities (e.g., hospitals or colleges) can be recruited to generate intelligence that can be channeled for investigative use. Meanwhile, aviation, harbor, and transit units can be utilized to search for suspicious persons and to assist in the search if the suspect strikes again.

The bottom line for the investigator is that all of the above are valuable sources of information and every good investigator knows that information is power. Sorting through the information generated, however, can be cumbersome and sometimes tedious but necessary if no stone is to be left unturned. Providing a structure for reporting leads to investigators is the responsibility of the investigative commander, who must also ensure that every one of those leads is investigated thoroughly.

Many variations on the best ways to manage such massive amounts of investigative leads will surface within each serial case. Some investigative agencies utilize computer programs to coordinate the amount of information coming in, while others still utilize logbooks and paper documentation. In each case, however, a central repository for information must be maintained. Each lead must be given a number, and documentation of every investigative step associated with that lead must be maintained to ensure that all incoming information is investigated fully. Although each lead must be investigated, geographic and psychological profiles (as mentioned earlier; see Chapter 9) can help investigators evaluate and prioritize information to maximize the use of resources in the most efficient manner possible.

Logbooks and Paper Documentation Model

Many departments do not have the resources available to dedicate specific personnel to updating their information technology systems. Computer technology and interface systems are expensive and beyond the means of many local jurisdictions, for which old-fashioned methods will have to suffice for coordinating investigative leads. Leads can be described as any information about the pattern of attacks and may or may not be specific to one case within the pattern. Generally, such leads provide information that may help identify the unknown sexual predator. It may be necessary to establish a Tips Book (Figures 8.1 and 8.2) to coordinate the large amount of information that

Page 76

Tip #	Time/Date Received	Details
364	3/11/02 –1410	From: Hotline - Detective Smith. Anonymous female called hotline - 1345hrs, 3/11/02, and reports that a male fitting the description of the rapist lives in apartment 22 of 956 E. 75th Street. His first name is Troy. No further info. Det. Mayor

Figure 8.1

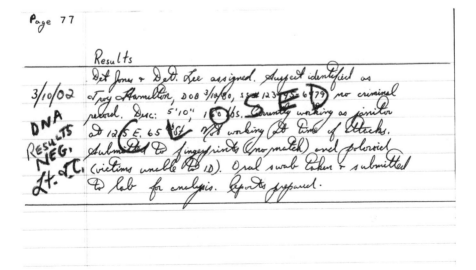

Figure 8.2

investigators will receive. Information will come from several sources: from other investigative units, from uniform and plainclothes members of the department, from civilians who call the 24-hour hotline, or from any other source who has some (no matter how small) investigative value. The Tips Book provides a structure to document every lead coming into the investigative unit along with the results of the investigation into that lead. Those tips that are deemed to be of no value can be eliminated. Each tip, however, will require that investigators prepare a separate written report to document any interviews with the person calling in the tip and of the investigative steps taken. The assigned tip number can be used to file that documentation for future review. Supervisors and investigators will be required to read through each tip, but the authority to close tips should be limited to supervisory personnel.

Computer-Generated Model

In this model, all information is entered into a computer or a series of computers designed to interface with each other. Tips generated from the 24-hour hotline are entered and can be retrieved by the investigative unit. Communication from the various investigative units is documented and sent to the lead investigative unit. All reports are input into the computer database, which allows investigators to search for names, addresses, descriptions, or even for phrases that have been used (in a manner similar to that of many Internet search engines). The obvious advantage of this model is its dependability and its ability to make correlations without relying on the memories of individual investigators. The disadvantages are the costs of the system, the cost and time required for training, and the amount of time needed to input data.

Dissemination of Intelligence to Noninvestigative Units: Overcoming Cultural Bias

Regrettably, some investigators develop a cultural bias against sharing information. Their approach can frequently create resentment in the very people whose help they need when serial cases occur. Their reluctance, of course, has some historic foundation. Every seasoned investigator has seen apprehensions thwarted, evidence lost, and suspects set free because some well-meaning but uninformed officers took action even though he/she lacked the information needed to make that decision logically. In sex crime cases, they also lack the necessary expertise to contend with the personality issues that are unique to sex crime investigations. Consequently, actions have been taken that have alerted suspects to pending apprehensions, provided suspects with the time necessary to discard evidence, or have aggravated already strained relationships with victims and witnesses. Within that context, investigators' reluctance to share information is understandable and often justified.

All information, however, does not have to remain confidential. Investigative commanders can decide what can and should be disseminated to those involved in the tactical plan in order to fulfill strategic needs. Each commander's ability to lead by example can engender an atmosphere of cooperation and understanding between investigators and those whose help they seek. Certainly, a description of the perpetrator, the manner in which he operates, and the type of victims who have been attacked are details that should be disseminated to assisting units. The commander and the investigative team should make themselves available to patrol personnel to answer questions and to provide a synopsis of the perpetrator's *modus operandi*. Patrol personnel should also be encouraged to call investigators whenever questions arise. Calls should always be taken cordially and patrol officers should be made to feel that they are part of a team effort to capture the assailant. The investigative team, however, should maintain control of the information at all times and keep certain details confidential, particularly investigative leads and identifying indicators (such as peculiarities of the suspect's genitalia or his blood type) or information that could jeopardize the victim. Establishing a rapport with those on patrol and encouraging their input creates a cooperative climate that can be a valuable tool to the investigator.

When New Attack Patterns Occur

In an effort to develop investigative leads, the following investigative steps should be considered and expanded when appropriate. This checklist can be utilized in pattern cases and is most effective when an investigative team can respond swiftly to take charge of the investigation. These steps incorporate many of the those I have found useful when responding to serial rape cases and are designed to help investigators coordinate their resources effectively. Investigators should note that these steps augment those already discussed in Chapter 4 as they relate to the crime scene and in Chapter 5 as they relate to the victim interview. The steps provided here particularly pertain to the response taken when an attack occurs which requires a resourceful use of personnel in an often confusing and unstable situation. These steps can be used in singular stranger sexual assault cases as well. When new cases occur:

- Have the investigative team respond immediately and assign team members to tasks in such a way as to maximize the use of personnel.
- Interview first officers on the scene and any paramedics who responded to determine, for example, the state of the victim, statements she may have made (including a description of the perpetrator and what

he said during the attack), any other observations made, and locations
of possible witnesses and/or perpetrator.

- Contact all 911 callers and interview them.
- Canvass the crime scene location for possible witnesses.
- Canvass the neighborhood to locate people working in the area who may have seen the suspect (doorman, custodians, storeowners, etc.)
- Document vehicles parked in vicinity and contact the owners.
- Check parking summonses issued in the neighborhood and interview the owners.
- Check moving summonses issued in vicinity and interview those drivers.
- Check parking garages for videotapes and payment receipts and interview the drivers.
- Check toll plazas and electronic pass use (EZ Pass, Fast Lane, etc.) before and after the attack.
- Canvass the routes taken by victims; search for surveillance cameras and pull tapes and interview possible witnesses along the route.
- Search garbage and sewers along the route of escape by the perpetrator.
- Search rooftops and alleys where the suspect may have hidden prior to the attack; establish a secondary crime scene if necessary.
- Check the database of calls to the police and search for similar crimes or reports of a suspicious man who fits perpetrator's description.
- Check the database for a criminal record of the victim.
- Interview friends and relatives of the victim for information, particularly any who currently live with the victim; check the database for their criminal records.
- Establish a response protocol for investigators in the event of another attack.
- Establish a response protocol for nightwatch investigators and provide direct access (cell phone numbers, home telephone numbers, beeper numbers) between them, case detectives, supervisors, and the commanding officer of the investigative team.
- Request that investigators from all units with informants debrief them regarding the description and *modus operandi* of perpetrator.
- Debrief prisoners arrested for any crime regarding their possible knowledge of the suspect or the crime.
- Confer with adjoining investigative agencies and personally debrief any of their prisoners or witnesses who appear to have some knowledge of the attacks or the attacker.
- Plan narcotics and vice sweeps in targeted areas and provide investigators for debriefing.
- Canvass the neighborhood 24 hours after the attack for witnesses (particularly important when witnesses may have been in transit

during the attack, such as during rush hour, after a movie, or when a theatre performance concluded). Some events, such as church meetings, may be held on a weekly basis; check with those groups for information.

- Re-canvass the neighborhood with the victim in search of the suspect, if she is capable of doing so. Repeat if victim is available to do so.
- Search jewelry shops and pawnshops for stolen property.
- Expand the search for stolen jewelry to adjoining geographic areas, if necessary, or to areas where the suspect may be located.
- Search databanks for past criminal activity in the vicinity of the attacks. Interview those victims to see if the same suspect may have been responsible.
- Search databases for persons arrested for sexual assault.
- Search databases for persons arrested fitting the description of suspect.
- Search corresponding correctional database to identify suspects released prior to attacks; conduct a similar search when suspects are identified to ensure that they were not incarcerated during the attacks.
- Contact surrounding jurisdictions and ask that similar database searches be conducted.
- If drugs are involved, attempt to identify the type and contact narcotics informants.
- Check phone records of the victim.
- Address roll calls of uniform personnel to advise them of the threat and how to contact investigators directly; also, address other units operating in the target area (narcotics, vice, etc.).
- Have a sketch of the suspect prepared and disseminated throughout the department and to the public.
- Distribute a sketch (photograph, if available) of the stolen property.
- Publicize the sketch or photograph and disseminate information to the media.
- Announce a reward if one has been posted.
- Establish a 24-hour telephone number for the public to call in tips.
- Utilize a database or log to coordinate tips, but do not remove the human element from reviewing all tips.
- Investigate every tip thoroughly. Set up a procedure whereby tips are investigated and closed; those that cannot be closed positively should remain open as possible leads.
- Search parole and probation databanks for the suspect (state and federal).
- Plan sweeps of persons wanted on warrants (even minor offenses) and provide investigative personnel to debrief prisoners.

- Have the victim view photographs of persons fitting the perpetrator's description (gathered from the databases).
- Collect DNA samples from possible suspects and submit them for comparison with the rape kits.
- Compare the samples with DNA databases in other jurisdictions (using, for example, CODIS, the Combined DNA Index System administered by the FBI).

Old Cases

Sexual predators do not always confine their criminal activity to sexual assault. Their predisposition to ignore the needs of others is generally not confined to women, or to sex. Prior criminal activity that is not sex related is common among sexual predators. Although these crimes are not part of the sexual assault pattern, they can be useful to the investigator once they are identified. They can expose facts that, when combined with current information, can help identify the perpetrator or expose his vulnerability to apprehension.

The following steps should be taken after making an arrest in sexual assault pattern cases. It is not uncommon to find that past victims omitted sexual assaults that were committed against them while they were being robbed to avoid embarrassment or because they felt that the sexual abuse was minor and inconsequential. A thorough interview of these victims often reveals the development of the suspect's sexual nature and his advancement from crime to crime. It can also result in additional sexual assault charges that can have a considerable impact upon the suspect's sentencing.

Search for similar types of crimes in his past. Do not limit the search to sex crimes. As mentioned earlier, crimes such as an attempted robbery of a female on the street may actually have been attempted rapes that were thwarted by the victim's screams. The sudden appearance of a witness or events that interrupted the suspect may also be reasons for the suspect not completing a sexual attack. Re-interview the victims and witnesses of past attacks and review the evidence. Use the new cases checklist, as applicable, and have the laboratory examine and compare evidence suspected to be from the same perpetrator (DNA, fingerprints, hair, fibers, etc.)

The Tactical Plan

Establish a Lead Unit within a Multifaceted Approach

The only responsible investigative approach to an unsolved stranger pattern case is a multifaceted one in which several police resources are utilized and coordinated by the investigative team. This approach will require the assistance and approval of the uniform division/precinct commander in order to facilitate the patrol forces response in an organized and effective manner. The precinct/division commander, after conferring with the investigative commander, can develop a tactical plan that utilizes the various resources available to assist the investigation and to set up a strategic response if the rapist attacks again.

Although the command of the personnel assigned within the tactical plan will remain under the precinct/division commander, the familiarity that the investigators have with the intimate details surrounding the case and the manner in which the perpetrator strikes makes them the obvious choice to coordinate the use of manpower and resources, while ensuring that the integrity of the investigation is maintained. Of course, this also gives them a tremendous responsibility. Not only are they accountable for the investigation, but they are also crucial to the effectiveness of the tactical plan and the coordination of department assets.

Executives will understandably and appropriately demand oversight and the right to approve or disapprove any plans that arise. The investigative commander will be responsible for developing an investigative plan in order to manage the investigative process and, along with the uniform division/precinct commander, will also be responsible for developing a tactical plan. That plan will address the ongoing coordination of uniform and investigative resources to search for the suspect and to pre-plan tactics in the event of another attack. The tactical plan will incorporate every facet of the department that operates within a particular geographic area, as well as nonpolice agencies and private entities.

The information disseminated within the department and to outside agencies, of course, will differ. Law enforcement personnel should be given every possible detail and instructed not to reveal certain facts that investigators do not wish to be made public. Outside agencies, on the other hand, should generally be given only the information that investigators feel the public should know.

The following steps are only suggestions. I have found them useful in the numerous pattern investigations I commanded within New York City. Although the plan will certainly need modification to address particular requirements of various geographic areas and to cope with the limited resources available, it is a positive response to the problem at hand. Plan modifications will be necessary with each successive attack to incorporate new information and to improve tactics. The latest information and the modifications needed to address those issues will maximize the utilization of all personnel and ensure that every available resource is utilized in an efficient and effective manner. Plans of this magnitude, of course, require approval at the highest level within individual departments. Such approval will also ensure that every subordinate unit cooperates fully and that the plan carries the full authority and commitment of those in charge.

Coordination Conference

Before the tactical plan can be developed, it is necessary to organize a meeting of all commanders that operate within the affected area and within adjoining areas. This group can include, but is not limited to, investigative units, patrol units, plainclothes units, narcotics units, vice units, federal law enforcement, traffic enforcement units, transportation units, harbor units, aviation units, police laboratory units, communications units, crime scene units, crime analysis units, public information personnel, paramedic units, corrections personnel (e.g., sheriff's office), parole and probation units, and any other support unit that can be of assistance. The high-ranking official chairing the meeting must have authority over those present in order to ensure compliance, and the commanders present must have the authority to commit their personnel and resources. The meeting has many purposes:

- Inform everyone attending of the investigative needs.
- Discuss the resources available from all the commands present and how each can improve the effectiveness of the tactical plan.
- Obtain a commitment from the various units present.
- Give commanders the details they need to operate effectively. Disseminate information (e.g., sketch and/or description of the suspect, his *modus operandi* and psychological profile, and geographic profile).
- Instruct various units to gather information on possible suspects from their respective databases and establish a protocol to disseminate information to the lead investigative unit.
- Ensure compliance and commitment of units.
- Formally document the plan and elicit every unit's commitment to it. The executive approving the plan should have authority over all units involved to ensure compliance.
- Schedule frequent follow-up meetings with the same personnel to review the plan and to make modifications when necessary. If another attack occurs and the perpetrator remains at large, a meeting should be scheduled as soon as possible. Modifications can be made to address the effectiveness of the response to the new attack and to make adjustments to address any new issues that have arisen.
- Meetings that do not have the authority of a high-ranking official will not be successful. The cooperation of all of the units present must be demanded, not asked for. The authority to order cooperation is necessary for tactical plans to be successful.

Assist Patrol with Investigative Personnel

If resources allow, assigning investigative personnel to work with officers involved in the tactical plan (see following section) will go a long way toward creating a cooperative atmosphere while encouraging the officers to be diligent and resourceful. Assign investigative personnel to tours that coincide with the period during which the perpetrator is likely to attack. Also, have the victim (if possible) patrol with investigators during this same time frame to search for the suspect in the neighborhood. Have investigators respond when persons suspected of the attacks are stopped by patrol personnel. Positively identify all persons stopped, and if they are considered possible suspects ensure that they are fully identified. Carry photographic equipment and obtain a voluntary picture of persons stopped. Investigators can then place these photographs in albums that can be viewed by victims (see the following case history). If deemed necessary, obtain a DNA sample (buccal swab, see Chapter 4) of each person stopped for comparison with evidence.

Case History

During the investigation of the East Side Rapist in Manhattan, we established a plan that included approximately 120 officers from various units on patrol during the days and hours that the perpetrator attacked. Soon hundreds of men fitting the description of the suspect were stopped and questioned. Investigators on patrol responded and verified the identity of all who were stopped. They also corroborated the explanations each person gave for being in the neighborhood by questioning friends, acquaintances, or co-workers to verify their recent movements.

Because no reason was found to hold these people and because the victims were usually not available at the time, lineups could not be held. I then made the decision to take photographs of these men whenever possible. Investigators were instructed to explain the seriousness of the investigation to each person stopped and to request their assistance. They were asked to allow their picture to be taken while they were stopped on the street. Because they were not inconvenienced for a long period of time, they generally agreed to have their picture taken. These pictures were subsequently viewed by the victims and kept as part of the case file.

It was anticipated, of course, that some people would eventually think that this was a violation of their constitutional rights (either the Fourth or Fifth amendment). Eventually, an attorney complained to the media that the police were using photographs taken of his brother to conduct photographic lineups in a variety of cases. That, of course, was not the case, as these photographs were used only for this particular case and were kept locked and secured in a confidential file. They were not part of any other photographic database and were not used in connection with any other crime.

The authorization for instituting this procedure became an issue, and my decision was being criticized in many circles. I knew that I stood on solid legal ground, but the press was having a field day accusing the department of infringing on the rights of innocent individuals. The department, of course, was not happy with the criticism. Eventually, the mayor, a former U.S. Attorney, was pressed for a response by the media. My decision was vindicated when he said that taking the photographs was a good investigative tool and commended the innovativeness of the investigators. Those who questioned the decision then agreed with the mayor, and I was given accolades for instituting an innovative solution to a cumbersome problem. Such are the ups and downs of life in large departments such as the NYPD.

During this time, the attorney who complained was contacted. We offered to remove his brother's photograph from our files and deliver it to his brother, but he refused to answer our calls. Needless to say, he was not interested in his brother's constitutional rights; he merely wanted the publicity and his name in the paper, an objective he certainly achieved.

This case history is an example of an innovative technique that can be applied during the course of an investigation. In my experience, including team personnel in brainstorming sessions can be very productive and can generate creative solutions to existing problems. The picture-taking strategy came out of one such session. I have personally observed the innovative talents of investigators countless times as they construct sound and legal strategies to address the problems at hand. They need only be given the latitude to be creative; their desire to find a solution is already there. Commanders who neglect to utilize the talents of their investigators to address problems are destined to failure. Commanders are often preoccupied with a number of issues that stem from the responsibilities of their commands; investigators, on the other hand, are not. They have conducted the interviews and are keenly aware of the intimate details of the case. They are often in the best position to judge the effectiveness of a particular strategy and can help refine strategies to maximize effectiveness. Final decisions, of course, lay with their commanders, as does the responsibility.

Personnel Commitment

Obtain the commitment of personnel from each unit involved in the tactical plan. The assigned personnel should be performing only those duties that are consistent with the tactical plan. Each officer or investigator should be assigned on a full-time basis, except those assigned to units that are only supplying statistical information. Statistical information, however, should be prioritized and collected without delay. It is the responsibility of the precinct or division commander to verify that the assigned personnel are confined to the location and that their duties are limited to those agreed upon at the meeting. The tendency to utilize personnel for discretionary enforcement must be avoided. An example of documentation of personnel assignments is provided below. This is an illustration of the large personnel commitment that was mustered to address a series of rapes that occurred on the upper east side of Manhattan. Most tactical plans, of course, are not this large, but it offers an example of what can be done if the need exists.

Detectives

- Assignment of personnel will be under the direction of the Commanding Officer of the Special Victims Squad.
- Assign 2 sergeants and 20 detectives: 2 sergeants and 6 detectives from the Special Victims Squad and 14 detectives temporarily transferred from other commands. Personnel will be used for both investigative duties and tactical response to assist supporting commands.
- One supervisor and 4 detectives will be assigned to every first platoon (deployed during the time that the rapist is known to strike) to assist patrol units in identifying suspects stopped, eliminating those who do not fit the profile, and responding to any new attacks to take charge of the investigation immediately. During the weekend (Friday and Saturday evenings), when the suspect is more likely to strike, 4 additional detectives from outside commands will be assigned (from the 22 precinct detective squads throughout Manhattan).

Uniform Patrol

- Assignment of personnel will be under the command of the precinct commander.
- In addition to the normal precinct patrol strength within the precinct (1 sergeant, 5 patrol units, and 2 anticrime units), the following extra personnel are assigned during the first platoon, 7 days a week:
  - Eight zones have been established that correspond to the areas in which the perpetrator is most likely to strike again. Two sergeants and 18 police officers are assigned; two officers in one vehicle will patrol each zone. The four zones (1 through 4) in the southern half of the precinct are to be monitored by one sergeant, while the northern zones (5 through 8) are to be monitored by the other. Each Sergeant will have a police officer assigned to patrol with him or her.
  - On the first platoon (12 × 8) Saturday and Sunday (Friday and Saturday nights), an additional sergeant (with a vehicle and a

driver) and 18 police officers (2 from each command with a vehicle) will respond from different commands throughout the borough.
- The borough task force is to supply 1 sergeant and 10 police officers.
- From the Precinct Anticrime Unit, 6 additional plainclothes personnel will be assigned on the first platoon Saturday and Sunday (Friday and Saturday nights).
- The Transit Unit will assign an officer to each of the 8 stations within the precinct during the first platoon (i.e., 1 sergeant for 8 officers).
- The Highway Unit will assign two units to patrol the East River Drive (i.e., 4 officers).
- From the Plainclothes Unit, the Street Crime Unit will supply 1 sergeant and 6 officers to patrol on the first platoon during the week. On the first platoon Saturday and Sunday (Friday night and Saturday night), 2 sergeants and 16 officers will be assigned to the same zones as the patrol units.
- The Canine Division will supply one unit for patrol within the precinct on the first platoon, 7 days a week (i.e., 1 officer with dog and vehicle).
- The Mounted Unit will supply 2 officers for patrol within the precinct on the first platoon.
- The Emergency Service will patrol the precinct when not on assignment (i.e., 2 units, or 4 officers).
- The Narcotics Division will assign 1 sergeant and 8 investigators to conduct enforcement activities and debrief prisoners.
- Total personnel on the weekend: approximately 100 to 120.

All personnel (except the narcotics unit) were equipped with radios tuned to the division frequency and patrolled within their assigned areas. At the beginning of every tour, a roll call was conducted of all personnel and assignments were coordinated to maximize coverage. As the commanding officer of the investigating squad, it was my responsibility to ensure that the assigned personnel were instructed properly. At each roll call, we shared what we knew about the rapist. We gave them a summary of the suspect's psychological profile and his *modus operandi*. We also instructed them to summon one of my detective units if they found a suspicious person who fit the criteria. The detectives would then, if necessary, verify that person's identity, question him further, bring him in for a lineup, take his photograph, and/or collect a DNA sample. Every person stopped was thoroughly investigated by the detectives to see whether or not he could be considered a suspect. Officers were continually updated with the latest information and instructed on every platoon to keep them informed and to make certain that they were targeting the appropriate individuals.

Continuing Efforts

In addition to the preceding commitment of personnel, the following efforts should be maintained to manage the resources supplied through the tactical plan and to expand the search beyond the local community:

- Alert all commands within the department regarding the pattern and description of the suspect, as well as his manner of operation. Deliver sketches to all commands and ensure that all personnel have a copy.
- Alert surrounding jurisdictions and supply them with the same information.
- Have all detectives in the targeted area and surrounding areas debrief every prisoner arrested in regard to serial rapes. Have sex crimes investigators respond immediately when positive information is received.
- Set up a protocol to debrief all persons arrested to solicit information about the rapist.
- Set up a protocol to have investigators respond and debrief suspects who have been stopped and questioned by the patrol force.
- Set up a protocol to take voluntary DNA samples from suspects (see Chapter 4).
- Ensure that persons stopped are properly identified and that backgrounds of each are verified.
- Instruct local patrol officers to seek help from individuals in the neighborhood (storeowners, homeowners, apartment building residents, workers, etc.).
- Alert the public to the existence of the pattern and advise them how to avoid becoming a victim. Seek their help in identifying the perpetrator and provide a 24-hour telephone number to call with information about possible suspects.
- Attend community meetings to warn those in attendance about the presence of the assailant, to provide prevention information, and to request their assistance in identifying suspect.
- Obtain reward monies if available and publicize.
- Instruct the radio dispatcher assigned to the targeted area to transmit information regarding all calls reporting suspicious persons, calls for help, or calls regarding residential burglaries, assaults, etc., even when no personnel seem available to respond. Commanders will ensure that personnel assigned within the tactical plan are always available

(investigators, plainclothes officers, traffic officers, etc.) to respond immediately.

- If overhead command maintains a task force (such personnel are to be used at the command's discretion), assign sufficient personnel to address any needs that may arise.
- Assign narcotics and vice personnel to engage in enforcement activity within and around the targeted area. Have narcotics and vice investigators debrief prisoners and notify sex crime investigators when prisoners disclose pertinent information.
- Assign units to surveillance of targeted areas and equip them appropriately (surveillance vans, night-vision devices, etc.).
- Have personnel periodically check alleys, rooftops, abandoned buildings, etc. in the targeted area.
- Reassign specialized units (emergency service, mounted, etc.) to patrol the targeted area when not responding to calls.
- Have highway, harbor, and aviation units prepare a response plan in the event of a new attack.
- Update all personnel with any new developments to ensure that everyone involved is kept informed properly.

In the Event of a New Attack

- Establish a response plan with radio dispatcher to ensure that the call is given the highest priority and that units are dispatched properly. The plan should provide dispatchers with the ability to notify all affected units simultaneously to ensure a prompt and proficient response.
- Have units respond to the scene in a coordinated manner.
- Have two units respond to the scene with the supervisor and investigators.
- Assign units to escape routes; a plan should be in place assigning personnel to specific locations (east, west, north, and south of scene).
- Have officers stop traffic and search vehicles, taxis, buses, and trains for the suspect.
- Notify transportation units to search train stations, bus stations, etc.
- Notify highway units to stop and search the highway.
- Notify the aviation unit to search area (with infrared, if equipped).
- Notify the harbor unit to search escape routes along the shore.

Upon verifying that an attack has occurred:

- Have the radio dispatcher notify all units involved in the tactical plan about the attack and alert surrounding areas to be on the watch and to search for the suspect (utilize a preplanned notification system for the radio dispatcher).

- Institute preplanned mobilization of additional personnel to the scene.
- Utilize available personnel to assist in the search for suspect.
- Have investigators verify the identity of all persons stopped.
- Have show-ups conducted if the victim is available.
- Take voluntary DNA samples (buccal swabs) and photographs of persons stopped.
- Interrogate those deemed to be suspects.

If the suspect is not apprehended, conduct a meeting of all units involved in the tactical plan to review the response plan and to make corrections as needed. This meeting is not designed as a punitive measure to attack those who failed to follow the plan but is intended to be a corrective measure to make the plan more effective. Any attempts to make it punitive will only create an antagonistic relationship amongst the participants and limit the collaborative tone that is necessary for a successful operation.

Police Surveillance Cameras

Security cameras are common at many business locations where personnel are frequently assigned to keep stores, parking lots, and malls under surveillance. Security personnel frequently monitor these locations, in addition to keeping tapes, and act as dispatchers to their security force. Many locations, however, are not manned. Most banks, ATMs, and small stores do not have security personnel on the premises to watch customers; instead, they maintain tape recordings to be used in the event of a theft and to serve as a deterrent to those who might have larcenous intent. In the past few years, public entities have begun using cameras to augment patrol capabilities, to act as a deterrent, and to aid investigations when crimes do occur. These cameras have been used successfully in a number of locations. In New York City, programs were instituted to make subway stations and housing developments more secure. Surveillance cameras installed in strategic locations have had astonishing success in deterring crime and in facilitating the identification of perpetrators when crimes do occur.

As is the case with any rape pattern, investigators are constantly searching for innovative ways to help the investigation. After one brainstorming session that involved a pattern of rapes in Manhattan, I decided to use surveillance cameras in a way that they had not been used before. The infrequency with which the rapist struck posed a problem for manning the cameras, as did the locations themselves. Attacks were often separated by 3 to 6 months, and the location of each attack was different; the attacks covered a large area of 175 square blocks in one of the busiest areas of the city. After studying the crime pattern and conferring with the geographic profiler (see Chapter 9), I decided to put several unmanned surveillance cameras at key locations. Instead of focusing on an entire block, as was usually the case, I decided to focus on specific street corners that provided good lighting for the cameras and where the rapist was likely to pass.

Prior experience with extracting images from surveillance cameras has shown that when they cover large areas they do serve as excellent tools for those monitoring them to direct their personnel effectively; they provide a wide range of observation and can be used to direct officers to locations where trouble is suspected. Their ability to help identify suspects, however, is limited. Cameras that span large areas often show suspects as small dark figures on the screen that cannot be enhanced enough to supply recognizable features for identification.

Armed with this knowledge, we placed our cameras at specific well-lit street corners and made sure that the areas they covered were small enough to make passersby recognizable. We confirmed that, as individuals passed, we were able to extract images that clearly showed the features of their faces. We knew that if the rapist attacked again we would not see him in the act (highly unlikely, as all the attacks occurred indoors), but we suspected that he would pass by one of the monitored locations. The victim could view the tape to search for the suspect, and, if he was identified, his face could be disseminated to the press, who would be sure to show it on every television station and publish it in every paper along with the reward announcement and the 24-hour hotline number. It was hoped that someone would be able to identify him and call us. Clearly, this use of surveillance cameras was different and may be controversial to those who consider it a form of "Big Brother" (particularly the ACLU). It is, however, an innovative, legal, and appropriate use of technology given the threat to the public and the large area involved.

DNA Indictments

The latest weapon in the investigator's arsenal is DNA. It positively links individuals to their crimes, and it has proven to be a marvelous tool for investigators and prosecutors alike. With little training, investigators can readily collect DNA samples from crime scenes and from suspects, allowing forensic biologists to positively link suspects to their crimes, even in cases where victims cannot make identifications. The abundance of DNA material that is frequently left by sexual assailants has made the verdict of these cases more certain. Juries are more likely to convict based upon scientific evidence, even in those cases where the victim's identification is in question. Those who have been falsely accused have also reaped the benefits of DNA technology. A particular male's semen extracted from the victim's vaginal exam is incontrovertible evidence that cannot be denied. The presence of semen that is not the suspect's also cannot be denied. Of course, in domestic and acquaintance cases, the suspect will assert that the sexual act was consensual, thereby justifying its presence (see Chapter 6 for domestic and acquaintance strategies). In stranger cases, however, such assertions are irrelevant. Advances in DNA technology have opened up a new world for the criminal justice system. Where the testimony of victims and the identification by witnesses could sometimes be contradictory and problematic, the evidentiary links made with DNA are incontrovertible.

Unless a suspect's DNA is on file, however, it cannot be used to identify him, just as fingerprints do not identify suspects unless prior corresponding prints exist on file. As all investigators know, when fingerprint matches are made, the location where they are found may be problematic and may not be sufficient to link a suspect to the crime. For example, the existence of a fingerprint on a banister within the subject's apartment building may be meaningless. That identical print on a murder weapon, however, can positively link the perpetrator to the crime. In the same manner, the presence of a stranger's semen within a victim's vagina, on her body, on her clothing, or near the crime scene is virtually impossible to explain away plausibly. Consequently, because the reliability of DNA technology is nearly unquestionable and because the presence of body fluids such as semen and blood conclusively implicate only one individual, the use of DNA has become the standard when linking individuals who commit sexual assault to their crimes.

Occasionally, through no fault of their own, investigators will work on cases that go unsolved. Many of these cases cry out for justice to be done but can go unpunished if the statute of limitations expires. The threat to society continues as long as the perpetrator goes unpunished. The threat will not end when the statute of limitations no longer allows police and prosecutors to pursue criminal sanctions against the sexual predator. The innovative use of DNA technology, however, can help prevent these limitations from impeding justice and can provide prosecutors with a new tool that was not available a few short years ago.

Prosecutors have long recognized that initiating a criminal proceeding against individuals before the statute of limitations lapses satisfies the mandatory legal requirements. This is not a new idea. It has been used frequently when identified suspects have fled to avoid prosecution. Indictments for such individuals are regularly obtained within the statute of limitations period, thereby satisfying the need to commence proceedings within the specified time. When indictments are obtained, they typically identify the indicted person by name and may list identification numbers used by the individual (e.g., date of birth or social security number). Sometimes, however, the identity of a suspect is not completely known. In those cases, indictments may read "known to the informant as [...]." Similarly, prosecutors in narcotic cases have regularly obtained indictments of unidentified individuals based upon a description given by undercover officers. Indictments may read "JD Red Shirt," "JD Scar Face," "JD Big Nose," etc., where JD stands for John Doe and the descriptive name given the indicted person is the one used by the undercover officer. These individuals can then be prosecuted when they are apprehended; no matter how long that takes, as long as the undercover officer can positively identify the suspect and connect him to the case.

Prosecutors quickly discovered that the existence of reliable DNA technology offered an option that did not exist before in that they could list the perpetrator's DNA profile as the identifying factor when seeking indictments. Prosecutors argued that an indictment listing an individual's genetic code is much more accurate than any name, description, or identification number. They have sought and obtained "John Doe" indictments that, instead of providing a description such as "Red Shirt" or "Scar Face," list the genetic code for the individual who perpetrated the crime. Forensic biologists can testify that this distinct genetic code came from the evidence submitted by investigators. The source of that evidence could be semen found in the rape kit, on clothing, on bedding, or on the floor of crime scenes. Clearly, such genetic codes are unique to individuals and are far more accurate than any identification used in the past.

Such DNA indictments allow investigators to continue the search for rapists who elude them for long periods of time, and they provide law enforcement with a conclusive way to identify suspects. Most states currently mandate that convicted felons provide DNA samples for inclusion in state DNA databases and the federal database, known as CODIS. These systems have just begun to reap rewards for investigators. Perpetrators in a number of unsolved stranger rape cases have already been brought to justice when they were convicted on unrelated crimes and their DNA samples were matched to evidence from crime scenes. As advances in DNA technology begin to lower the costs of processing, the frequency of testing will surely rise, and as the databases grow their ability to make connections will increase exponentially.

Case History

The East Side Rapist had attacked 17 women in 16 different incidents that spanned a period from 1994 through 1998. In each case, he followed a young woman (the youngest was 20 and the oldest was 37) as she entered her apartment building late at night. He would typically push his victim into the stairwell, where he sexually assaulted them. This pattern was identified two weeks after I took command of the Special Victims Squad. A massive manhunt was begun and lasted through my 5-year tenure as commander. The rapist was never identified, but he left behind his semen in four of the cases. No semen was available for the other cases for a number of reasons. Some attacks were reported too late to extract DNA during a pelvic exam, some attacks were attempts that were never completed, and some victims mistakenly destroyed evidence before the police arrived. In the four cases where DNA was extracted, it was confirmed that the same individual was responsible for those rapes. The oldest DNA case dated back to March 1995. In March of 2000, the 5-year statute of limitations that exists in New York was about to prohibit any prosecution of that case.

Earlier that same year, Milwaukee prosecutors had been successful in indicting a John Doe with a particular DNA profile for an unsolved rape. We met with the District Attorney's Office and discussed the possibility of a John Doe indictment based upon a DNA profile. They researched the case and found that it was an appropriate legal remedy. The witnesses, including the victims, the investigators, and the forensic biologists, were assembled and the four cases were presented to a grand jury. An indictment was then handed down days before the statute of limitations would have restricted prosecution of the March 1995 case. The only downside to the indictments was that under New York law the right to counsel attaches once criminal proceedings are commenced. That would prevent us from interrogating the suspect, but because we had enough evidence to convict without a confession it was a small price to pay.

DNA Indictment Protocol and Statute of Limitations

Before retiring from the NYPD, I discussed the possibility of setting up a protocol with the District Attorney's Office to indict stranger cases that had gone unsolved. Every unsolved stranger rape, of course, is not suitable for indictment, and a review process is needed to ensure that only those cases that are deemed appropriate are indicted in this manner. The suitability of cases can be determined by several factors:

- *DNA* — Obviously the perpetrator's DNA must have been extracted from evidence in the case and his DNA profile must be complete.

- *DNA Search* — A search through all available DNA databases should be conducted to ensure that the perpetrator is not incarcerated for another crime or that a connection cannot be made to another case that may provide additional leads for the investigator.
- *Exhaust All Possible Leads* — DNA indictments should not be considered unless all possible leads have been exhausted.
- *Witness Availability* – The victim must be willing to proceed with a prosecution, and she must be available to testify. I have found that rape victims, especially those who have no permanent ties to any area, frequently relocate after the attack to avoid being reminded on a daily basis of what happened to them.
- *Witness Credibility* — As mentioned in the previous chapter, false reports are more common in stranger cases than in domestic and acquaintance cases. If investigators and prosecutors do not believe that the victim is credible, they will have a difficult time convincing a jury and should not proceed with an indictment. To do so would only erode their integrity and the integrity of future cases.
- *Time Frame* — It is not necessary to wait until the statute of limitations is about to expire. When it was determined that cases could be indicted based upon a perpetrator's genetic code, I established a year for each case as an appropriate time to review the case for possible DNA indictments. Although we had not encountered any problems with the victims of the East Side Rapist, I was concerned that complications could easily arise in other cases. The victims of the East Side Rapist had been given every consideration, and detectives contacted them on a regular basis to keep them involved. That is generally not feasible in every unsolved stranger case. I was concerned that if we waited until the end of the 5-year period in every case, the likelihood of encountering problems would increase significantly. Victims might move within that period and not advise investigators of their whereabouts. When found, they may be out of state and unable to return in time to stop the statute of limitations from making their testimony irrelevant. A long delay could also change their outlook. Some victims may no longer wish to get involved or pursue the prosecution of their assailant. Delays frequently produce a desire in victims to get on with their lives. Many have gotten over the rape to some degree and have no desire to testify and relive the traumatic and life-altering crime they experienced. Others suffer from serious emotional conditions that were caused or aggravated by the sexual assault. Those conditions may not have been resolved and investigators may find that the victims are no longer able or are unwilling to help prosecute the case. Still others may have become convinced by

friends and relatives that it is time to move on and that the police should simply leave them alone. Just too many variables could emerge over the 5-year statute of limitations period that could influence the victim in a negative way.

Consequently, it is clear that establishing a shorter time frame to commence proceedings could avert many of the problems associated with long delays. The advent of DNA technology in criminal cases has meant that a victim's assertions can easily be sustained in court and cases in which victims cannot identify their assailants are no longer automatically lost. The suspect's genetic code can establish his identity, and the only requirement of the victim is that she credibly communicate to a grand jury that she was not a willing participant in the sexual encounter. In stranger rape cases, unlike domestic and acquaintance situations, that is usually not a difficult burden to overcome. The surrounding circumstances and the evidence supporting those circumstances (bruises, torn clothes, vaginal injuries, etc.) will clearly show that she was indeed a victim and that she did not know the subject.

Conclusion

The impact of serial rape upon communities can be staggering. Fear of the predator extends to everyone, not just potential victims. Friends, relatives, acquaintances, and co-workers (both male and female) are forced to adjust their daily routines to ensure the safety of potential victims. They find themselves monitoring the activities of potential victims, much as they would for a young child. They ensure that the victim is not alone and placed in potentially dangerous situations, and they find themselves making adjustments within their lives to accommodate the need to protect them. The impact of serial stranger rape has such a debilitating effect upon communities that only a multifaceted approach by the police that utilizes every possible resource should be considered acceptable.

Many large police departments utilize mobilization plans to deploy personnel quickly in riot situations, major conflagrations, or when natural cataclysmic events occur. Modifications to these plans can address the need for personnel when major crimes occur. These modifications can be accomplished with minimal effort while serving to acclimate personnel to the procedures and address obstacles as they occur. Mobilization plans can be used to maximize the use of personnel to search for the suspect, to collect evidence, and to find witnesses.

The development of an investigative plan is designed to address the need for a strategic response to the investigation. That response incorporates a team approach to address the following concerns of serial sexual assault investigations: response plans, the search for and collection of evidence, the interview of witnesses, the management of information, the search for correlations between attacks, and the search for the suspect.

The tactical plan, on the other hand, is an ongoing multifaceted response that incorporates the many resources of the department (uniform, investigative, and support personnel) and of the community. It assembles them in a coordinated manner to alert the public of the threat, to search for the suspect, and to prevent future attacks.

Advances in DNA technology have opened up new opportunities for investigators to solve crimes. Genetic codes are regularly placed in databases in which searches can be made to match suspects to their crimes and correlations made between cases. Prosecutors have also discovered that DNA can be used to forestall the statute of limitations. DNA can positively identify perpetrators by their genetic code, as well as to identify those who are otherwise unknown and not apprehended. Indictments can be sought utilizing that genetic code to identify the perpetrator, thereby satisfying the legal requirement to commence criminal proceedings within the time frame set by the statute of limitations. Once the requirement to commence proceedings within the statutory time limit has been satisfied, it cannot be used as a refuge by sexual predators to avoid prosecution.

Recent legislation in many states has mandated that DNA samples be collected from all prisoners upon their convictions for certain crimes. As the database of genetic codes increases, so does the likelihood of matching criminals to their crimes. Because the evidence in sexual assault cases frequently includes bodily fluids, the likelihood of identifying sexual predators through their DNA increases significantly. In the past, prosecutors frequently relied upon the victim's identification of a suspect in a lineup to prosecute stranger rape cases. The emotional state of victims during the attacks, however, has often prevented them from positively identifying their attackers, even when other evidence points toward particular individuals. Consequently, many sexual predators have been set free to attack again. DNA technology has changed that outcome by providing conclusive evidence that points to only one individual. Those who have been falsely accused have also reaped the benefit of this latest advancement in forensic biology, as they can now prove their innocence even when false identifications are made.

The Profile of the Rapist: Understanding and Interrogating Rapists

9

As with any criminal investigation, and particularly in serial rape investigations, understanding the offender's psychological preferences can be an invaluable tool to the investigator, particularly when making investigative choices. In serial rape cases, the investigative choices that confront us are multiplied exponentially with each attack. The insight that profilers provide is an extra dimension that can help investigators navigate through the many choices by steering the investigation in a logically sound and efficient manner. Profilers provide an insightful view of the criminal activity under investigation that helps investigators understand the motivational aspects of the assailant's crimes. Once investigators are able to step into the rapist's shoes, they can gain valuable information regarding his preferences and can be more receptive to new leads that might emerge. This added information could be used to mount a more comprehensive campaign to find the attacker before he strikes again and to deploy personnel more efficiently.

Psychological and geographic profiles also serve as a case management tool, as they provide a means to sort through the massive amount of information that these cases generate. Investigators should be cautious, however, not to disregard any information that might not agree with the psychological or geographic profile. The profiles are merely tools that can help investigators prioritize information, not discard it. Profiles are based upon psychological and geographic data that conform to what is known about past criminal activity. These profiles are theoretic, and individual cases under investigation may or may not fit totally within that theory.

Effective investigators utilize the information provided by profilers to assist them in the investigation, but they do not disregard any information that does not conform to the profile; they merely use the profile to prioritize that information. Experienced investigators know that they need to utilize all possible information when making choices regarding the relevancy of information. Their decisions are made based upon sound investigative methodology, which includes the input of psychological and geographic profilers. Profilers are able to give investigators a general psychological and geographic perspective, but their input cannot replace the information that can be developed through the myriad sources utilized in the normal investigative process. Those sources include, but are not limited to, the following:

- Forensic evidence developed at the crime scene and during the medical exam
- Leads developed from the interviews of witnesses, suspects, and the victim
- Leads initiated through criminal database searches (local, state, and federal sources)
- Information developed from noncriminal database searches (e.g., Customs, Welfare, Division of Motor Vehicles, Immigration and Naturalization Services)
- The collective knowledge and wisdom of the investigative team
- Tips called into investigators that do not conform to the profiles

Psychological and geographic profiles have also proven to be invaluable when limited resources force difficult choices on the investigation. These choices can be in regard to prioritizing potential leads for investigation or deploying personnel. Clearly, having some idea of the preferences of the attacker and the locations where he is most likely to strike again is important when faced with these choices. Although profilers may not be in a position to capture offenders, their insights have improved the efficiency of the investigative process when a large amount of information must be prioritized. Their support can frequently improve the efficiency of the investigation by helping investigators narrow the search for the assailant and by providing insights into the evaluation of evidence.

Abnormal Psychology of the Rapist

Those of us who have dealt with sexual assault and interviewed offenders can attest to the fact that certain abnormal traits appear to prevail among most sexual offenders, particularly those who commit stranger attacks. They may appear normal at first, but they lack certain qualities that are ingrained in and typical of the rest of us. Their inability to empathize with others who are suffering and their complete disregard for the feelings of others make them abhorrently different. Even though some rapists may appear to be more

compassionate than others because they try not to harm their victims physically during their attacks, they are still missing an essential psychological
component that exists in most of us. They live in a selfish world where only
their needs are important. The needs of their victims are not considered, and
they appear to be unable to feel compassion for those who are suffering.
Simply put, they are not normal. They may appear normal at first, but
experience has shown that when investigators spend any time at all interrogating sexual offenders they consistently uncover the true persona of the
assailant. All too frequently, we find that sexual offenders lack certain inhibitions and are not disturbed by the moral compass that regulates the actions
of the vast majority of the population. Consequently, investigators who try
to understand these predators from their own perspectives are often at a loss.
They need to step into the minds of sexual predators to understand their
motivations. This will help them predict the predators' next moves and
facilitate their cooperation when they are apprehended.

Rice and Chaplin (1994) conducted a study of imprisoned rapists and
compared their responses to sexual stimuli against those of nonrapists. In
their study, they exposed their subjects to 32 different audiotaped stories
describing various encounters between men and women. A variety of situations were described in detail, including consensual sexual relations and
forced sexual relations. The subjects were fitted with a device to measure
penile responses as they listened to each story. They found that the sexual
arousal of nonrapists was inhibited during stories of rape because they empa-
thized with the victim and experienced some of her suffering. Those who
were incarcerated for rape, however, experienced little or no empathy for the
victim, and their responses were quite different. Rice and Chaplin found that
rapists preferred to hear stories of forcible sex to those of consenting sexual
relations. They also found that violence and the distress of victims added to
the sexual arousal of the convicted rapists.

Consequently, criminal investigators who rely upon their own experiences with the opposite sex to deal with rapists will be at a severe disadvan-
tage. As the Rice and Chaplin study shows, a distinct difference can be
observed between men who rape and those who do not. The enjoyment that
rapists obtain from demeaning their victims and the pleasure they sometimes
receive from inflicting pain are antithetical to what most of us would consider
normal when dealing with the opposite sex. Their abnormal behavior, however, needs to be understood from a psychological perspective in order for
investigators to direct the investigation properly.

The distinct psychological differences between rapists and nonrapists,
however, should not be considered as an excuse for their crimes and are only
important from an investigative standpoint when they can provide investigators with an idea of the motivation behind an offender's conduct and his

choices. Naturally, like the rest of society, some offenders do suffer from some form of severe mental disorder; these individuals may be motivated by their mental illness, and their legal culpability may come into question. Their numbers are few, however, and their fate is up to the criminal justice system to decide, not law enforcement.

Why Psychological and Geographic Profiles Are Useful

Efficiency

Profilers do not apprehend criminals; rather, they provide information to be used by those in charge of the investigation. They assist the case by helping investigators become more proficient and resourceful, as their input provides a logical basis for narrowing the search and gives investigators some insight into the mind of the rapist. Without profilers, the massive amount of information generated during a serial rape investigation can overwhelm the investigative effort and cause extensive backlogs that can result in inefficiency and additional opportunities for the assailant to strike again.

Narrowing the Geographic Area of the Search

The psychological profile will frequently indicate the type of environment in which the assailant is comfortable, and the geographic profile can help narrow the geographic area of the search. Geographic profilers analyze data and visit crimes scenes to produce a scientific analysis of where the attacker most likely resides, thereby helping investigators prioritize suspects within that area.

Provide Public with Protective Information

Both the geographic and psychological profiles can be used to provide the public with a detailed description of how and where the assailant operates. Sharing this information with the public has several objectives. The first is to help potential victims avoid situations that will make them susceptible to attack; providing a description of the assailant (including a sketch if possible) and details regarding how he selects his victims can be very useful. The second reason is to solicit information from the public about potential suspects and to provide a means to contact investigators with that information. There are witnesses who do not consider information they possess as important. Seemingly insignificant information, however, can provide the vital link investigators need to identify the assailant. Involving the public serves a twofold purpose: it helps investigators gather previously unknown information, and it gives the public the opportunity to observe the depth of the investigative effort. These insights into police work can have a positive public relations impact by reassuring the public that the police have dedicated sufficient resources and are doing everything humanly possible to capture the assailant. Of course, if adequate resources have *not* been devoted to the problem, then the media will be the first to criticize the actions of the police, and the public will make demands that can divert the attention and resources of investigators. Generally, however, it makes sense to involve the public, let them know what the dangers are, and assure them that the resources dedicated to addressing the problem are sufficient and being used intelligently.

Case History

One particularly heinous case during my command involved a rapist who sexually assaulted his victims as they walked home alone late at night. In each attack, he raped his victims and forcibly removed their valuables. He operated in a rather large area that encompassed two boroughs within New York City (Manhattan and the Bronx), and his attacks were spread out over a 2-year period. No discernable connection seemed to exist among the various locations, times of the attacks, or victims. These two boroughs alone have a population of over 2.8 million people, which does not count those who travel into the city for work or entertainment each day. The task of finding the perpetrator within this population would prove to be a gargantuan task.

Investigative plans and tactical plans (see Chapter 8) were established, and every investigative avenue was pursued. The prior actions of the victims, their social contacts, and the locations of the attacks, however, were all dissimilar. The victims seemed to have little in common other than the fact that they were young women and that they were all walking down isolated streets late at night when they were attacked. The public was warned to be alert for strangers, and women were instructed to avoid situations that would place them in jeopardy. A request for assistance from the public to help identify the assailant went out. A detailed description (including a sketch) along with his method of operation were distributed in the metropolitan area with the help of the media.

Soon, a massive amount of information began to come in from many sources. The law enforcement databases produced thousands of possible suspects that required further investigation. The officers assigned to the tactical plan identified thousands of additional individuals who lived, worked, or were seen in the areas of the attacks. The public provided information on possible suspects, and the number of tips rapidly grew into the thousands. Every tip and every suspect required a thorough investigation. Clearly, the amount of perpetrator possibilities was staggering. Something had to be done to narrow the search for the suspect in an intelligent manner and to utilize personnel in a creative and productive way. Without a plan, investigators would easily get bogged down and important leads could be overlooked. The logical approach, then, was to seek the assistance of psychological profilers. We also sought out the help of a geographic profiler to assist us in narrowing our search from a geographic perspective.

The psychological profilers gave us an idea of what type of individual we were seeking. They put together a psychological profile of the suspect based upon the details of his actions, his statements to the victims, his mannerisms during the attacks, and the preferences he revealed. Their profile helped us concentrate our efforts by prioritizing the investigation of those who fit the profile. Those who did not fit that profile, however, were not ignored and were also investigated thoroughly; they were simply not prioritized.

In the same manner, the geographic profiler helped us to concentrate our efforts in specific geographic areas. Although the techniques of psychological profilers are well established and have been applied successfully in many cases, geographic profiling is a relatively new area that has only begun to be used within law enforcement circles. We were hopeful that it would help, but we were also skeptical because it had never been tested in a city such as New York. After conducting his analysis, the profiler urged us to concentrate our efforts within a particular area of the Bronx. His examination of the past attacks had revealed strong ties between this particular area and the suspect. Our profiler theorized that the assailant probably lived there in the recent past or currently lived there. When the case was concluded successfully, we found that, to our surprise, the geographic profile was exceptionally accurate.

A break came in the case when stolen jewelry from one of the victims surfaced in a Bronx pawnshop (there are hundreds of pawnshops in Manhattan and the Bronx). The law requires that all pawnshops document the names and addresses of every person who pawns property. The sellers are also required to show some form of identification, which is documented by the pawnshop. In this case, a woman sold property that was stolen in a recent rape/robbery. Unfortunately, however, the identification she used was counterfeit. She used a forged college identification card, and the social security number on the card belonged to a man who was deceased. Further investigation revealed that the same woman sold jewelry in a number of Bronx pawnshops over a 2-year period, each time using the same fake identification. Detectives staked out several of the shops, and 2 months passed before the same woman returned to sell more jewelry. She was apprehended inside the pawnshop, and her boyfriend, who was waiting in a parked car, was apprehended. Her boyfriend was subsequently identified in several lineups and his DNA proved that he was the person responsible for these rapes and terrorizing a large area of the city for over 2 years. Interestingly enough, his girlfriend knew that the property was stolen, but she was unaware that they were stolen during sexual assaults. She accepted his explanations that he had taken the jewelry during burglaries of unoccupied apartments, and she was genuinely shocked to learn that he had sexually assaulted over 30 women. She became very cooperative and helped us confirm much of what the profilers had told us about the suspect's personality, his traits, and his preferences. She also helped us confirm his actions and his whereabouts during his reign of terror.

The accuracy of the geographic profiler was amazing. The profiler had given us a map and circled areas that indicated the most likely residence of the suspect. On this map, the profiler circled a large area of the Bronx and indicated the likelihood of the perpetrator living within that area. Smaller areas within that larger area were highlighted to indicate an increased probability that the suspect resided there. As it turned out, the suspect and his girlfriend were residents of an apartment building located within the most probable area, and the police sketch of the suspect had been taped to the lobby wall of their building. Unfortunately, even though the suspect looked very much like the sketch, no tips had been called in. Our efforts to obtain information from the public had been disregarded. A recent police shooting had created a tense situation between the community and the police in that neighborhood, and the ensuing volatile climate created a precarious situation between the police and the community that hindered efforts to gain cooperation in all police matters. Efforts to gain community confidence were further frustrated by activists who fueled the unstable conditions to gain recognition and turned potential witnesses against the police. Although we will never know, I am confident that the attacker's apprehension would have come about much sooner had our relationship with the community been better.

Even though the attacker's apprehension came about without the assistance of the psychological or the geographic profiler, their accuracy in this case cannot be denied. They were both on target, and their insights provided a means to analyze and prioritize information effectively. Had the rapport with the community been more conducive to cooperation, investigators would surely have been able to gain the information they needed to bring about a quicker end to these attacks.

Preparing a Case for Profilers

In order for a profiler to analyze offender actions, investigators should be prepared to provide a detailed account of the attack. The profiler will need to know every exhaustive detail in order to make the analysis as accurate as possible. The more details the profilers have, the more accurate their analyses can be. It will be necessary for investigators to:

- Chart the times of attacks, including month and day of week.
- Map locations of the attacks.

- Describe locations of the attacks (e.g., residential private home, residential apartment, commercial building), in addition to describing the location within the building and the surrounding area.
- Describe the victim in detail, including emotional and physical condition at the time of the attack. Was she alert? Was she preoccupied? Was she intoxicated? Was she on drugs?
- Describe each victim's actions prior to the attack in detail.
- Describe how the offender approached each victim.
- Describe each attack in detail, including clinical details of the sexual act and the order in which sexual activity occurred. Did the offender have trouble maintaining an erection? What did he say? What type of force was used? Did he try to demean the victim during the attack or did he try to compliment her?
- Describe each victim's reactions. Did she physically resist or was she intimidated by the offender's threats and succumbed to his demands?
- Describe the offender's reaction to the victim's resistance or lack of resistance. Did the victim plead with him? If so, what was his reaction?
- Was property stolen? If so, what was stolen?
- Describe how the offender fled.
- Describe the police response, crime scene, and evidence that was recovered.
- Describe the results of forensic analyses.
- Describe what investigative steps have been taken and the current status of the investigation.

Investigators should be prepared to make a presentation to the profilers on each case and describe all of the above information assembled in a cohesive manner. Remember, the profilers are not the investigators. They have not interviewed the victims nor were they present while the crime scenes were processed. They will only be able to work with what you give them. The more you give them, the better they will be able to assist your investigation.

Psychological Profiles

Classifying rapes into specific categories is helpful to investigators who seek a greater knowledge of unidentified stranger offenders. It allows a structured, academic evaluation of the offender that is useful in understanding the motivations that cause him to act. Profilers try to view the criminal activity from the offender's perspective. In doing so, they are able to assess the offender's preferences and provide some insight into his motivation. Hazelwood and Burgess (2001, p. 134) noted that "… the objective of a profile is to describe an individual in the same way as those who know him would." Armed with this type of knowledge, investigators can make superior investigative decisions. With an improved understanding of what drives each offender, investigators are in a better position to evaluate both the evidence and potential suspects as they are developed. For example, if the profile shows that the suspect stalks his victim, the investigator knows that evidence might be found in areas other than the immediate crime scene. If the profile shows that the suspect has certain emotional traits, the investigator can concentrate on suspects who possess those traits. Remember that knowledge is power — the more that can be learned about an offender, the more accurate and efficient the investigation will be.

As we have seen, the need to understand the motivational characteristics of rapists is important in sexual assault investigations. Many traditionalists, however, are skeptical of the impact that profilers can have on an investigation. They view profilers as academics who hide behind vague psychological descriptions that are not useful or productive. They point to the many investigative successes in which profilers were *not* used, and they see no reason to change. They see the desire to understand the rapist as a liberal attempt to justify the offender's actions and excuse his crime. They view their job as simply to apprehend the offender and put him in jail for as long as the law allows.

Understanding the offender in complex cases, however, is a necessity. Those engaged in the criminal investigation of sexual assaults, particularly those that involve multiple assault investigations, are obliged to pursue every possible lead. Understanding what makes offenders tick can be a very useful investigative tool that helps investigators pursue those leads efficiently, and it can help narrow the search for the suspect in many important ways.

Interrogating Tip

Profiles can also be useful when interrogating the rapist after his apprehension. Remember that these individuals are not like the rest of us. Their feelings toward others are what most of us would consider callous and heartless. The 1994 study conducted by Rice and Chaplin, discussed earlier in this chapter, illustrated that rapists are quite different from the rest of us and that they possess a distorted view of the role of men and women within a sexual context. In their study, they found that convicted rapists experience sexual arousal in situations that most of us would find shameful and unacceptable. Their value structures and their relationships with women do not allow them to empathize with their victims. Because they are self-absorbed and care only for their own situation, the suffering of others is not relevant to them nor does it have an impact upon their decisions. During interrogations, investigators need to understand that certain sexual predators care only about their own need to express control and power over physically weaker individuals while satisfying sexual desires; others may seek affection and validation of their masculinity from their victims. Certainly, these are important factors to be considered during interrogations.

Two General Rapist Categories

Before discussing the specific categories of sexual assailants, it is important to understand that each category can be assigned to one of two general psychological groups. Hazelwood and Burgess (2001) described these groups as selfish rapists and pseudo-unselfish rapists. Although the term *unselfish rapist* may seem inappropriate and insensitive, it does accurately describe the psychological makeup of a particular type of rapist.

Selfish Rapist

Hazelwood and Burgess describe the selfish rapist as an offender who has no regard for the well-being of his victims. When this offender attacks, he displays a deep-seated anger and will cause varying degrees of injury to his victims. He has no concern for the welfare of the victim. His only interest lies in his personal physical and psychological needs. With a disturbing attitude such as this, he will readily torment and mistreat victims to gain their cooperation. If a victim resists, he will escalate the amount of force needed until she succumbs to his will. He will also engage in activity that demeans his victims. He will make his victims perform degrading acts, and he will humiliate them as much as he can. He is the type of rapist who will call his victims names such as "whore" and "cunt" during his attacks and take the victim's clothes when he is finished. By doing so, he forces his victims to walk naked through the streets and thereby demeans them even further. He has a very low opinion of his victims, and his conduct constantly displays that opinion.

Case History

A young teenage Hispanic girl was walking alone in a secluded area of an upper Manhattan park. A Hispanic male approached her and produced a knife from inside his coat. He placed the knife to her throat and threatened to kill her. She pled with him not to hurt her and she began to cry. Although she did not physically resist and cooperated with his demands, he punched her and knocked her to the ground. He then hit her over the head with a rock, causing her to lose consciousness. When she gained consciousness, she found that her clothes had been torn off and that her attacker was having vaginal sex with her. She pled with him to stop and he cursed at her, called her a whore, and then forced her to orally sodomize him. When he had ejaculated, he pushed the victim down a hill, causing her further injury. He then fled the scene, not knowing whether the victim was alive or dead.

The assailant in this case can clearly be described as a selfish rapist. Not only did he have no regard for the victim, but he also clearly had a deep-seated anger that took several forms. First, there was no need to hit the victim with a rock; he had already knocked her to the ground, and she was not resisting physically nor was she screaming to attract attention. She only pled with him not to hurt her and he answered with more violence. Second, the order of the sex act indicates an attempt to humiliate the victim. He forced her to orally sodomize him after vaginal sex. As Hazelwood and Burgess indicate, a selfish rapist, in order to humiliate his victim, may also force the victim to orally sodomize him after anal sex. Third, he called the victim a whore during the forcible sodomy. And, finally, he had no reason to push the victim down the hill and injure her again. The actions of the offender indicate that he had no regard for the well-being of the victim, and he appeared to have a deep-seated hatred of her. From his perspective, he was only interested in asserting his power over the victim, demeaning her as much as possible, and satisfying his sexual desires.

Interrogation Tip

Any attempt to appeal to the attacker's sense of right and wrong will fall on deaf ears. An interrogation of a selfish rapist should concentrate on the needs of the offender. He will only be responsive to issues that will impact his quality of life and his personal needs. Interrogators should consider explaining how serious the charges are, the time the suspect will spend in jail, the conditions in jail, and the certainty of a conviction. Only then will a selfish rapist consider talking, provided he feels that his statements will help him in court. His confession, however, will not be complete. He will lie about the brutality of the attack, and he will frequently assert that he and the victim engaged in a consensual act or that the victim's injuries were self-inflicted. Frequently, all that is needed is for the suspect to place himself at the scene of the attack. His statements, however, when coupled with the physical evidence will usually be enough to convict him in court.

Pseudo-Unselfish Rapist

The unselfish rapist, on the other hand, desires to win the victim over. In his own perverted way, he views the rape as an encounter. He will seldom inflict injury to his victims and uses only the minimum amount of force necessary to obtain his objective. If the victim is aggressive and fights back, he will usually abandon the assault. During the attack, the unselfish rapist will attempt to win the victim over. He may compliment her physical appearance while putting himself down. He will frequently refer to himself in unattractive terms and will typically assert that the victim is too good for him and that she would never consider dating a guy like him. Afterwards, he may even warn her to be careful when she walks in deserted areas and offer tips on how to protect herself. The unselfish rapist has no desire to degrade the victim. Instead, his desire is to persuade her that he is not a bad guy and to win her over.

Case History

A 34-year-old woman was attacked as she entered her apartment at 11:00 P.M. on a Thursday evening in October. Her assailant threatened her with a knife and forced her into her apartment. As he threatened her with the knife, he told her that if she did what she was told she would live. He then ordered her to undress and attempted to compliment her by telling her that she had a nice body. He softly caressed her and then placed her on the bed and forced her to have vaginal sex. When he was done, he lamented that someone like her would never go out with a guy like him. He told her that she was beautiful, and that her boyfriend was very lucky man. He also told her to be careful when she walks home late at night and offered advise on what to do if she sees someone suspicious on the street. He cut the telephone cord and then fled the apartment. The victim did not sustain any injuries other than the rape itself.

Clearly, this rapist could be classified as a pseudo-unselfish rapist. He was obsessed with involving the victim in the sexual act and he continually complimented her while putting himself down. If the victim had resisted and screamed, the suspect probably would have fled without hurting her further. Unfortunately, however, the victim had no way of knowing that she was dealing with this type of rapist. It was only after analyzing the offender's actions following the attack that we were able to make this determination. When he was apprehended, he expressed deep feelings of remorse and quickly confessed to two rapes, one of which had not been reported yet.

Interrogation Tip

The unselfish rapist frequently has feelings of remorse about his attack. He feels sorry for the victim and he is ashamed of his actions. Those feelings may not prevent him from attacking again, but investigators can use that information to solicit a confession from offenders when they are in custody. Unselfish rapists are clearly more willing to confess their crimes in order to unburden their conscience than selfish rapists are. By exploiting the assailant's feelings of remorse, interrogators can set the tone for a complete and detailed confession that can withstand the scrutiny of judicial review.

Specific Rapist Categories

Identifying a rapist within the general category of selfish or unselfish adequately serves the purposes of investigators in the vast majority of rapes. Those stranger cases that have gone unsolved, however, frequently require some added insight in order to identify the motivational aspects of the offender's personality. Rapists are not all alike. The impulses that drive them have different psychological triggers. Psychologists have frequently attempted to delve into the complex reasons that cause men to rape, but they have differed in their classifications of rapists. Several typologies have been developed, the most commonly used one being that developed by Groth et al. (1977), who identified four types of rapists: two power-type rapists (*power assertive* and *power reassurance*) and two anger-type rapists (*anger retaliation* and *anger excitation*). I have found that these categories are deficient in that they leave out one very important category. Hazelwood and Burgess (2001) list a fifth category with which I agree and have found to be particularly troublesome in my career — the *opportunistic rapist*. I have added that category to the typology of Groth et al. (1977) because opportunistic rapists are not uncommon in stranger cases, and investigators will find that they encounter them more frequently than the other types of rapists. Consequently, I have found the following classifications to be the most accurate and most useful from a practical standpoint for those of us involved in investigating sexual assault.

The Power Assertive Rapist

The power assertive rapist maintains that it is his right to demand and force sexual relations. He feels that as a man he must dominate women and that he is entitled to demand sex whenever he wants. He has no concern for the well-being of his victims. He is a completely selfish individual, and during the attack he is only concerned with his dominance over the woman and his own sexual gratification. Although he may come to the attention of the police because he engaged in a forcible rape with a stranger, further investigation frequently reveals that his relationships with his spouse or female acquaintances also included forced sexual attacks. Unfortunately, most of those will have gone unreported. That, however, does not mean they cannot be prosecuted.

Investigative Tip

Once an arrest is made, investigators are advised to interview those who know the suspect well, particularly the women in his life. Conduct the interviews in private and be alert for signs of abuse. If investigators are patient and persistent, it is very likely that they will uncover additional unreported sexual assaults. In these cases, however, a prosecution against the suspect may not be possible. The victim may not want to prosecute, enough evidence may not be available to proceed with a prosecution against the suspect, or the statute of limitations may have expired, thus precluding any further action. The prosecutor, however, may be able to use the testimony of additional victims to refute any testimony on behalf of the suspect's character, including his own testimony. The accounts of additional victims are powerful corroboration of the events for which the assailant is charged.

The Power Reassurance Rapist

The power reassurance rapist suffers from feelings of inadequacy. He is uncertain about his own masculinity, and his sexual assaults are attempts to reassure himself in regard to his virility and his ability to be dominant over women. He lies in wait to catch his victims in vulnerable situations, looking for situations in which he can control the victim's actions and play a dominant role. By doing so, he reinforces his self-esteem and, in his peculiar and despicable way, his abilities as a man. He will generally use the minimum amount of force needed to control his victims because he wants his victims to desire him. He does not want them to find him repugnant. Instead, he fantasizes that his victims will enjoy the encounter and want to be with him voluntarily. The power reassurance rapist will frequently target several victims prior to an attack. He will strike the one who he finds is the most vulnerable at the moment.

Investigative Tip

If investigators know that they are dealing with a power reassurance rapist, their search for witnesses should not end at the scene of the attack or along the path taken by the victim prior to the attack. The assailant may very well have pursued similar potential victims in nearby areas and abandoned the attack only because he could not complete the assault due to some unforeseen event. Consequently, after investigators have searched the scene of an attack nearby areas should also be examined. A canvass for witnesses in these areas could uncover someone who saw the assailant lingering in the neighborhood and produce useful leads that could help the investigation. Witnesses may reveal locations where forensic evidence might be found (discarded cigarette, saliva, fingerprints, etc.) and may be able to provide a vehicle description, aide in identifying the assailant, or offer important information on the assailant's whereabouts prior to the attack. Posting a sketch of the suspect along with a detailed description and requesting the assistance of the public in these secondary areas have frequently proven to be useful when additional information is sought.

The Anger Retaliatory Rapist

The anger retaliatory rapist is motivated by revenge. He hates women and he perceives that they have wronged him in some way. His mistreatment may be real or imagined, and if it is real it is usually distorted and exaggerated. He strikes out at those who have characteristics in common with those he despises. Attacks of older women can be very revealing psychologically. Clearly, a rapist who attacks an elderly woman has deep-seated hate toward an older female in his life. This type of rapist will use excessive force and display extreme rage during his attacks. He is sadistic and will assault all parts of the victim's body. He will use profanity and be verbally abusive to his victims. Groth et al. (1977) noted that this type of rapist uses the attack to expresses his hostility and rage while degrading and humiliating his victims.

Interrogation Tip

An interrogation of this type of suspect would go well if the interrogator understands that the suspect holds this hatred for the dominant women in his life and should steer the interrogation to take advantage of that hatred.

The Anger Excitation Rapist

The anger excitation rapist is a sadistic coward who enjoys the excitement he gets from the suffering of women he can physically control. His objective is to see his victims in pain. Their suffering arouses him, and the more they suffer the greater satisfaction he derives from the attack. His victims will suffer serious injuries as a result of the severe physical and sexual assault. In order to intermingle the victim's suffering with his own sexual gratification, he will cause injuries that are sexual in nature. He will typically insert objects into the anus or vagina of his victim which results in serious injuries and inflicts substantial pain in a sexual manner. The severity of his attacks, however, can be so brutal that they result in the victim's death. The victims are not chosen because they meet any known criteria for the rapist. His attack is not based upon any connection with the victim. Instead, his victims merely meet circumstantial demographic criteria. They are simply at the wrong place at the wrong time.

Interrogation Tip

Be aware that the suspect enjoys inflicting pain and feels that his victims deserved what they got. Guide the interrogation toward attributes of the victims that produced this hate in order to make him relive and enjoy his memory of the attack.

The Opportunistic Rapist

The emergence of an opportunistic rapist can be a particularly troublesome phenomenon for law enforcement. This type of rape occurs during the commission of otherwise nonsexual crimes. Typically, the rape occurs during the commission of a robbery or a burglary when the assailant suddenly discovers that he has total control of a female victim he finds sexually attractive. At that point, he decides to rape. He has no preconceived plan to rape and only does so because he finds himself in an advantageous situation. Investigators will find that his verbal commands to the victim indicate that he was not prepared to commit a sexual assault and that he was only taking advantage of the situation after finding his victim sexually vulnerable. I have found that the problem with the opportunistic rapist is that once he begins to sexually assault his victims, he becomes obsessed with the sexual aspect of the attack and continues to rape every chance he gets. I have seen several serial attacks that began with robbery, escalated to rape, and became rape patterns in which the victims were also robbed. Investigators will find that these rapists may or may not possess some of the traits characteristic of the previous typologies in which power and anger are found to be the controlling factors. Unfortunately, what is certain is that once these predators begin to engage in sexual assault they consistently rape their victims every time.

Investigative Tip

Do not limit the investigation to past sexual assaults or sexual offenders. Look at past robberies and burglaries for similarities and additional evidence. Search databases of robbery and burglary perpetrators in addition to sexual offenders.

Investigative Preparation for Profiling

In order to accurately classify rapists into the subgroups discussed in this chapter, information gleaned from several attacks is usually necessary. A singular incident can be revealing, but the circumstances surrounding one unsolved case may give rise to too many unanswered variables that can affect the outcome of the profile and make it unreliable. The aspects of the attacks that profilers will need to examine include, but are not limited to:

- Choice of victim
- Amount of resistance by the victim, including her assertiveness or her passivity
- Assailant's reaction to the victim's assertiveness or passivity
- Verbal exchange between the victim and the suspect (can be very revealing when analyzed)
- Geographic circumstances surrounding the attacks, including the proximity to help
- Situational circumstances
- Theft of property from the victim (particularly the type of property taken)
- Sexual acts (including the type of sexual contact and the order in which the sexual acts were performed)

Although profilers can work with one case, multiple cases give profilers a clearer picture of the offender and allow them to make a more thorough evaluation. Consequently, investigators will need to gather every minute detail of every case to help the profilers accurately classify and describe the assailant. Profilers will prepare a detailed presentation, describing each attack thoroughly, including the geographic elements and the forensic ties. Investigators will find that accurate profiles will equip them with the tools necessary to guide their investigation in the right direction.

Geographic Profiling

Geographic profiling can be an extremely useful tool that, when incorporated with a psychological profile of the offender, allows law enforcement to manage information more effectively and prioritize leads as they develop. Rossmo (2000), an accomplished geographic profiler, stresses that "… geographic profiling does not solve crimes, but rather provides a method for managing the large volume of information typically generated in major crime investigations." He further states, "Geographic crime patterns are clues that, when properly decoded, can be used to point in the direction of the offender."

Although the concept of geographic profiling is relatively new, the use of maps to analyze crime patterns is well established. Law enforcement officials have long used pin mapping to uncover spatial commonalities of crime and their relation to other chartable factors. Since the early 1990s, police departments have made tremendous strides by using a computerized pin-mapping technique known as the Graphic Information System (GIS) to deploy personnel and to address emerging crime patterns quickly and accurately. GIS has become an integral tool used by progressive strategists to address criminal activity. The NYPD's innovative techniques for addressing crime and the success experienced since adoption of the COMSTAT (Computerized Statistics) process during the 1990s are well known and well documented. The cornerstone of the COMSTAT process is the crime strategy meeting. In these meetings, uniform commanders and detective commanders are called upon to validate their response to criminal activity within their respective commands and to defend their strategic decisions. GIS crime maps are displayed to illustrate the spatial connections of criminal activity. By displaying this activity in combination with the enforcement actions taken, upper level managers can readily evaluate the effectiveness the strategies currently employed by precinct, detective, and narcotics commanders. For example, shooting incidents can be mapped together with narcotics activity. This map can then be combined with the various types of enforcement activity of the different units. Frequently, narcotics activity and incidents of shootings will show a spatial commonality. If the GIS illustrates that enforcement activity is lacking, the logical response emerges: Reduce the incidents of shootings by increasing enforcement in areas of narcotics activity. The success of NYPD's COMSTAT strategy can be attributed to the timely (weekly) updates in crime statistics and enforcement activity coupled with a structure that continually reevaluates strategies and adjusts them to address changes as they emerge.

Likewise, geographic profiling attempts to find the commonalities in serial cases by identifying *anchor points* used by the offender. Anchor points are locations that the offender visits frequently. The strongest anchor point is usually the offender's residence. Strong anchor points can also include the location where the offender works or a place where he spends a significant amount of time. Such secondary locations may include a bar, a park, or a relative's residence.

By examining the spatial patterns produced by the location of an offender's attacks, the geographic profiler can establish the area where the offender is most comfortable hunting his prey. In doing so, the profiler can then identify anchor points within the area of the hunt. Geographic profiling, however, is much more than preparing a pin map of locations and searching within the area created by that map. Like the COMSTAT process, it incorporates a number of strategic factors to develop a comprehensive profile.

Anchor points are not simply locations within an area of attacks. Several details must be considered by the profiler to determine the positioning of anchor points. The profiler must take into account the psychology and the behavior of choice that come into play when people (particularly the offender) move from one place to another. We all make choices as we move through life that are based upon our preferences, but what makes us choose one path over another? What makes us choose to walk on one side of the street as opposed to another? What makes us take a certain route as we travel? Rossmo utilized Stea's (1969) assertion that an individual's perception of distance is influenced by several factors, including:

- Relative attractiveness of origins and destinations
- Number and types of barriers separating points
- Familiarity with routes
- Actual physical distances
- Attractiveness of routes

Furthermore, Rossmo noted that even though an individual's perceptions are affected by several social, educational, and environmental factors that also influence movement, similar mental maps are common because most people perceive things in a similar manner. He cited Lynch (1960), who found that the image compositions, or mental maps, of most people are based upon the following elements:

- *Paths* — Routes of travel that tend to dominate most people's images of cities (e.g., highways, railways)
- *Edges* — Boundaries of lines that help to organize cognitive maps (e.g., rivers, railroads)
- *Districts* — Subareas with recognizable unifying characteristics and possessing well-established cores but fuzzy borders (e.g., financial districts, skid rows)
- *Nodes* — Intense foci of activity (e.g., major intersections, railroad stations, corner stores)
- *Landmarks* — Symbols used for orientation but which typically are not physically entered (e.g., signs, tall buildings, trees)

Just as law enforcement would use the crime map to determine future criminal activity, the geographic profiler uses spatial mapping to identify an offender's anchor points. As stated earlier, however, anchor points do not merely lie within the center of the criminal activity. They are influenced by those factors that mold the mental map of individuals, coupled with the previously identified perceptional factors that influence an individual's perception of movement. The geographic profiler takes these forces into account and combines them with the known investigative data to pinpoint anchor points. Those anchor points can then be used as a management tool to reevaluate the concentration of resources and to prioritize leads that materialize in or near anchor points.

Conclusion

Investigative techniques have been forced to change over the past half century, partly due to the limitations placed on an investigation by an increasingly litigious society that protects offenders' rights and partly due to the benefit of technical advances. Just as it would be reckless not to learn to live within the legal constraints set by society, it would be irresponsible not to take advantage of the technological advances that have been developed. The achievements made in DNA testing are well known. They have made the task of proving a suspect's guilt far simpler and more accurate than was previously possible, particularly in sexual assault cases. Just as no competent investigator would ignore the presence of DNA to help identify a suspect, neither should investigators ignore the ability of profilers to aide in their pursuit of sexual predators. Psychological and geographic profiles are tools that can be used to the advantage of an investigator who is aware of their usefulness and their limitations.

Profiles can help investigators in several important ways. They offer new clues to help the investigator understand the impulses that cause the offender to act; they provide an instrument to help prioritize the massive amount of leads generated by serial sexual assault cases; and they provide a means to prioritize personnel deployment to prevent future attacks. Investigators, however, cannot expect profilers to solve their cases for them. The function of the profiler is to augment the investigation by providing knowledge about the assailant that is consistent with known psychological and geographic profiling methodology, not to take over the investigation. Profilers provide an expertise that lies within the nebulous world of psychological and geographic theory. Their ability to apply that theory to concrete situations is what makes them useful. Their expertise adds another dimension that can help investigators sort through information they already have and concentrate resources more effectively.

Reliable profilers are the first to tell investigators that they are not responsible for the investigation; the investigative agency maintains that responsibility even when profilers are used. Investigative agencies have the expertise and manpower to integrate the several resources at their disposal. They are the ones who evaluate evidence, conduct interviews, interrogate suspects, and gather the corroboration needed to support their charges within the current legal constraints imposed by law. Psychological and geographic profiles, although important, are merely two of the resources available to investigators. They will never replace the instincts of an investigative team nor will they challenge an investigator's ability to interview, interrogate, and analyze evidence effectively. It is the investigator's ability to integrate all of these resources into the investigation that cannot be replaced.

Bibliography

Groth, A. N., Burgess, A. W., and Holmstrom, L. L., Rape: power, anger, and sexuality, *Am. J. Psychiatry*, 134(11), 1239–1243, 1977.

Hazelwood, R. R. and Burgess, A. W., *Practical Aspects of Rape Investigation: A Multidisciplinary Approach*, 3rd ed., CRC Press, Boca Raton, FL, 2000, pp. 134, 141, 147.

Lynch, K., *The Image of the City*, MIT Press, Cambridge, MA, 1960.

Rice, M. E. and Chaplin, T. C., Empathy for victims and sexual arousal amongst rapists and nonrapist, *J. Interpersonal Violence*, 9(4), 435, 1994.

Rossmo, D. K., *Geographic Profiling*, CRC Press, Boca Raton, FL, 2000, pp. 2, 87–91.

Stea, D., The measurement of mental maps: an experimental model for studying conceptual spaces, in *Behavioral Problems in Geography*, Cox, K.R. and Gollege, R.G., Eds., Northwestern University Press, Evanston, IL, 1969, pp. 228–253.

False Allegations of Rape

10

False allegations of rape create dilemmas not only for the police but for communities, activists, and government officials as well. Identifying these types of allegations and minimizing their potential impact are crucial to maintaining the integrity of the investigative process and removing the infectious fear that false reports of sex crimes can have on communities. Unfortunately, experience has shown that the frequency of false reports in rape investigations is much larger than for any other criminal endeavor. Activists and sociologists argue that the available statistical data are incomplete anyway because they do not include those victims who do not report sexual assault. Many victims fear reprisal, others are ashamed, and many others simply feel that they will not be believed by the police or the criminal justice system. Such victims feel that reporting sexual assaults will expose them to yet another cruel ordeal that will result only in their further humiliation and distress. In any event, activists point out that the statistics are not representative of the true problem. The reasons for this disparity are many, and we will discuss those, but first let us look at the impact of false rape investigations.

Impact

Although false rape investigations inflate the number of reported crimes in a particular area, their numbers are relatively small when compared to the overall crime rate. The resources required to conduct sex crime investigations and their impact upon communities, however, are much greater than the statistical data would show.

Police

We have discussed the need for specialization in sex crime investigations. Enormous resources are put into the investigations of sex crimes, particularly those that involve stranger attacks (see Chapter 7). Those resources may be committed over a prolonged period if the attacks continue and the fear within the community persists. Consequently, other types of investigations can suffer due to such false reports, and personnel will be unavailable or resources will be stretched thin when *bona fide* cases are reported.

Communities

I have seen the character of entire communities change in response to reports of rape, particularly stranger rape. Reports of rape that are domestic or involve acquaintances generally do not create the climate of fear that stranger cases do, unless they involve people of prominence (see Chapter 1). This fear can change the way communities view themselves and view others. Areas that are normally friendly and open can become inhospitable and wary of outsiders. Women will change their habits to avoid placing themselves in dangerous situations. Many will become wary of strangers and curtail their activities so as not to place themselves in jeopardy. For many, this may require a complete lifestyle change. Single women who once felt free to congregate in certain areas frequently avoid those situations until the perceived danger is gone. Both the community and the police may look upon strangers differently as long as the danger exists. In short, the attitude of an entire community can be affected by false reports of rape.

Activists

Like it or not, activists play an important role in our society by bringing attention to issues that need to be discussed. It was women activists who changed the way we deal with sex crimes. Prior to their intervention, it was almost impossible to obtain a conviction for sex crimes. These activists have brought about countless changes that now give several rights to victims that did not exist before. They have also brought pressure to bear on legislatures to change the legal statutes in order to allow convictions while providing due process to the accused. All of their progress, however, has been tarnished by false reports. Activists have argued that the victims of sex crimes must be treated differently than those of other crimes and that the emotional and social repercussions of reporting sex crimes are far different than for any other crime. The arguments put forward by their opponents are reinforced whenever a false allegation unfairly damages the reputation of someone or when convictions are overturned. False sex crime allegations, then, can validate the viewpoints of the activists' opponents and can negatively impact the ability of activists to promote their platforms. These repercussions can even result in legislative changes that negate any gains made over the years.

Government Officials

Elected officials frequently get involved in high-profile cases. They may call for community meetings to address the issue of safety, they may hold press conferences to support or increase the efforts of the police, or they may request information about the investigation. Because they are frequently in a position to bring about legislative change, they can use high-profile cases to reinforce their arguments to effect that change. If the case they are citing is a false report, however, they may be doing more harm than good to their cause.

Historical Viewpoint

During the 1970s, a number of social issues gave rise to increases in the number of reported rape crimes. Certainly, these social changes, including the sexual revolution and an inundation of sexual references in the media, gave rise to increased expectations on the part of men in regard to sex. The chief cause of the increased reporting, however, came in the form of legislative changes that made it easier for women to report rape. Prior to that time, most states required that, in order for an arrest to be made for rape, independent corroboration of the attack was needed from an uninvolved third party. This situation favored men and at the same time made it virtually impossible to prosecute the vast majority of rapes successfully.

Gradually, legislative changes were implemented that treated rape the same as any other crime. Allegations of rape, just like an allegation of a robbery, gave police officers the reasonable cause they needed to make an arrest. Police forces soon learned, however, that the number of false reports in rape cases far exceeded that for any other type of crime. Why was that the case? For the most part, the answer to that question can be found in the many emotional connections that surround sexual assaults, including those of the alleged victim and the emotional attachment of the alleged assailant.

These conditions do not exist in any other type of crime. For example, suppose a woman is robbed at gunpoint as she enters her car in a deserted section of a dark shopping mall parking lot. The assailant flees with the victim's purse, and she goes to the nearest pay phone to call the police. When the police arrive, the victim gives the police a description of the suspect and lists the items that were stolen. Barring any ulterior motive on the part of the victim, the assigned investigator can generally assume that the robbery did in fact occur. The number of false reports in such situations is small and they rarely require the commitment of significant manpower.

Rape, on the other hand, whether real or fabricated, generally involves emotional issues that increase the likelihood that a false allegation will be made. The two basic types of false allegations involve either known suspects or unknown strangers. As we will see, the victim may be involved in an emotional battle with the suspect if he is known to her, while in stranger cases the victim may use the report of rape to conceal a banned behavior or to gain attention.

Reasons for False Reports

As Commanding Officer of the Manhattan Special Victims Squad, I always held to a particular standard with my detectives and their cases: "If you can't tell me why she is lying, then she isn't." This mandate required my detectives to investigate the circumstances and to back up their conclusions with solid evidence before they could accuse the victim of a false allegation or reclassify the crime.

False Acquaintance and Domestic Allegations

Because these false allegations are against known suspects and the victims expect those suspects to be arrested, these types of false allegations are particularly insidious. The alleged victim is attempting to have someone arrested for a crime that he did not commit and which could result in his incarceration. Clearly, investigators must do everything possible to ensure that they do not become a party to this subterfuge. A complete and thorough investigation can provide the information and evidence necessary to make an informed decision in this regard. Although most municipalities mandate an arrest in domestic cases, that does not preclude the police from conducting a thorough investigation, provided, of course, that the victim is no longer in jeopardy of being victimized again and there is time to conduct an investigation.

As discussed in Chapter 6, the motivational aspects of all acquaintance and domestic cases should be investigated thoroughly. Just as we may try to determine the motivations of a suspect, we should also examine potential motivations of the victim. Several questions must be asked, and the answers to these questions can give investigators a point of reference from which to proceed objectively:

- Has the victim previously reported false sex crimes?
- Has the victim been rejected by the accused?
- Does the victim possess an abnormal attachment to the accused?
- Does the victim have psychological problems?
- Is there potential for financial gain?

- Is there an ongoing domestic dispute that can be bolstered by an accusation of rape?
- Are the circumstances surrounding the alleged sex crime difficult to accept as true?

A positive response to any of these questions will have to be investigated thoroughly to determine whether or not the rape actually occurred. In those cases when rape did occur, circumstances such as these can provide powerful ammunition for the defense, and good investigators know that they must be prepared for defense attorneys' arguments. When rape has not occurred, answers to these questions can provide the basis for further investigation and a logical understanding of what actually happened.

False Stranger Allegations

False stranger allegations are far more common than in domestic and acquaintance situations. In these allegations, the victim uses the reported criminal activity for several reasons:

- The victim may want to conceal some form of activity in which she has been engaged. She may be a teenager who has broken a curfew and needs an excuse for being out past the time allotted. She may have associated with people whom her parents or guardians find objectionable and needs an explanation for being where she was. By reporting an assault she can justify her behavior. It may appear that young girls would use this excuse exclusively, but this is not the case. Adult women who wish to hide some form of behavior from others may also use this as a reason to justify their accusations.
- The victim may want to gain attention. This is more common in adults but can occur with alleged teenage victims and even younger children. I have seen it used when a woman has had an argument with her boyfriend or her husband; she feels that by making herself a victim of a serious crime, he will give her the attention she craves. She may also use it to make her boyfriend or husband feel bad for not doing something that she wanted. Or, she may merely want attention because she has emotional problems. She feels that, by becoming a victim, she will gain the attention she craves. Teenagers and young girls generally fall into this category. In these cases, they frequently lack the emotional stability and the maturity to understand the repercussion of their actions.

To Believe the Victim or Not? The False Report Trap

Over the years, I have seen many untrained investigators and police officers fall into the trap of either believing the victim when she is lying or not believing her when she is telling the truth. Let me say this, experienced sex crime investigators generally have a better feeling for these situations but can never be sure without corroborating their suspicions. Mere suspicion is not enough. Investigators must back up those suspicions with evidence that can corroborate their suppositions in order to change a classification or to bring charges for falsely reporting an incident against the alleged victim. At all times, however, the standard must be "If you can't tell me why she is lying, then she isn't." An investigator who thinks that the victim is lying and that the crime did not happen must be able to prove it. Remember, as shown in Chapter 5, most victims will lie about something for any number of reasons. They might feel that they are to blame or that they did something wrong to cause the attack. An experienced sex crime investigator is well aware of this and weighs what the victim says accordingly.

Case History

A young, pretty, 16-year-old Hispanic girl reported that she was raped on a moving train in Manhattan around midnight. Maria's (not her real name) family recently moved to Brooklyn from the Bronx. She left all of her friends behind and frequently went to visit them. The subway ride from the Bronx to Brooklyn took about an hour each way. Maria's parents would typically let her go visit a friend in the Bronx on Saturdays during the daytime, but insisted that she be home by 7:00 P.M. that night. She would have to leave the Bronx by 6:00 P.M. in order to be home on time. If she was not home on time, she was punished and not allowed to visit her friends for weeks.

One Saturday, Maria stayed with her friends in the Bronx all day and then went with them to a party that night. She did not have her parents' permission nor were they aware that she would be late. She then alleged the following: She boarded the train at about 11:00 P.M. in the Bronx. The train route required a trip through the Bronx and into Manhattan before entering Brooklyn. Maria states that she was in the last car of the train and that several other people were in the same car. Those people, however, exited the train at various stops in Manhattan, and she found herself alone in the last car with a male. She states that he attacked her and raped her around midnight as the train moved under the East River from the last stop in Manhattan to the first stop in Brooklyn. He threatened to kill her and she succumbed. Maria did not sustain any physical injuries other than the sexual assault. The alleged suspect then exited the train at the next stop. The victim, however, stayed on the train for two more stops and exited at her normal train station. Upon arriving there, Maria went to a pay phone and called the police.

The police responded, and an immediate search was conducted for the suspect to no avail. The train was held when it reached its final destination to process the car for forensic evidence. Crime scene investigators could not find any evidence that a rape had occurred as described by the victim.

Other problems arose, of course. Anyone familiar with the New York City subway system knows that many people who work shifts ride the train around midnight, and frequently the trains are full (although it was later discovered that the last car in that particular train is frequently empty). Maria alleges that they were alone in the last car of the train. A medical examination indicated vaginal penetration and that semen was present, but no physical signs that force was used were observed. Perhaps Maria had engaged in sexual activity earlier in the day and wanted to seek medical attention to prevent pregnancy or perhaps she needed to divert attention from her failure to be home on time and the punishment she would surely receive from her parents. It seemed as though too many questions were raised, and Maria seemed to fall into a category that is typical of those who make false rape allegations.

Maria was brought in for an interview the next day. She recounted the story of her attack, and her responses to the investigators' questions appeared to be honest and candid. After about 2 hours of going over all of the details, the investigators felt that she was either a very good liar or the attack actually did occur. They had two options: (1) go after the inconsistencies in her story (even valid cases have some inconsistencies) or point out to her that the circumstances as she relayed them were not believable in the hope that by doing so she would tell the truth and admit that the rape did not happen; or (2) believe her story, despite the overwhelming circumstantial evidence that pointed in the other direction.

I sat down with my investigators to discuss what to do. It was important to get at the truth because of the effects that a real attack of this nature would have on the transit system and the riding public. One of my detectives came up with an idea to try to trick the victim into telling us the truth. After a long break, the detectives continued their interview of the victim. They told her all of the problems that they had with her story. She had informed them of the problem she had with her parents and that she was about to get in serious trouble that night. They informed her about the lack of physical evidence and the possibility that she had had voluntary sexual relations with a boy. They also told her about the number of people who normally ride the train at that time of night. She stated that she understood the investigators' concerns, but she still appeared credible when she insisted that she was attacked. One of the detectives then told her that the Transit Authority had placed hidden cameras in each train car and that we had pulled the tape. We would have a copy of it shortly. Her response was "Great! Now you can see what he did. I hope you can see his face in the picture." At that point, we changed our approach and gave the victim every possible consideration. We knew we were dealing with a real victim of a very serious and heinous crime. She had clearly been telling the truth all along, and we did not wish to make her ordeal any worse than it was.

About 2 weeks later, another attack occurred on a moving train in Manhattan. The attack occurred at 5:00 P.M. (the height of rush hour) in a train car that the victim claims was nearly empty. She also claimed that after she was raped the suspect jumped off the train as it moved between two stations. Everyone's first reaction was skepticism, but before a conclusion could be made we needed to take a closer look. It was rush hour and every train heading out of Manhattan is usually full at that time; however, the train that the victim was on was headed southbound and was about to reach the last stop by City Hall, but very few people ride all the way to those last stops. It seemed bizarre that the suspect could jump from a moving car and still survive but we quickly found out that because of some very sharp turns in that area the train must slow down to less than 5 miles per hour. Such a slow speed would easily allow the suspect to jump onto one of the walkways and exit through an emergency shaft.

On a happy note, we arrested the suspect for an unrelated rape that occurred in a Manhattan restaurant/bar. The DNA from the suspect showed that he was responsible for all three cases. He has since been tried and convicted of all three and is spending 25 years in jail.

Discussion

It is imperative that investigators not jump to any conclusions about the victim, but it is also important that they be able to identify cases of false reports as they occur. I have frequently seen investigators inexperienced in dealing with sex crime victims jump to the wrong conclusion too quickly. One inconsistency in the victim's story is used to invalidate everything that she says. They do not take into consideration the victim's psychological condition or the impact that the crime is having upon her.

In Chapter 5, we discussed the fragile nature of the victim and the reasons she may have to hide certain types of behavior. I have found that victims will rarely tell the complete truth about their attack. They are ashamed of some aspects of it or are embarrassed by them, some events are difficult to talk about because of the emotional strain it places on the victims, or some feel guilty or blame themselves for being in situations they knew they should not have been in.

Inexperienced sex crime investigators frequently rely upon the abilities that have served them well over the years when dealing with other types of crimes. They know that inconsistencies and lies are usually indicators that a victim is not telling the truth, usually for some financial or emotional gain. In the instances of sexual assault, however, those assumptions are frequently wrong. If they fail to investigate further, they may find that they have made a serious mistake, particularly if the same assailant strikes again.

Identifying False Allegations

Several red flags will be raised during investigations of suspected false allegations. As before, investigators are warned not to jump to conclusions, and these red flags are merely warnings that something may be amiss. They are not absolutes and their significance is based upon what the investigator can corroborate or refute. Following are some examples of these red flags:

- Factual circumstances do not coincide with the report of the crime (remember, though, that this red flag may be misleading if the victim has failed to be completely candid with investigators for some reason other than falsification).
- The victim is vague about details and is unable to come up with an explanation for not knowing particular facts. This vagueness is usually due to her not fabricating her lie thoroughly enough. These details may be in regard to her attacker, the location of the attack, or the attack itself.
- Statements regarding the victim's prior actions are not consistent with known facts.
- Statements are not consistent with medical evidence.
- The victim may be in trouble for some particular behavior and is hiding that behavior by making a false allegation. Particularly common are false allegations by young women and teenagers.
- In acquaintance cases, the alleged victim is engaged in a dispute in which the victim may be attempting to strike out at her alleged attacker.
- In domestic cases, the alleged victim is involved in a custody battle with her ex-husband. I have seen numerous cases in which women have asked their ex-husbands to visit on the pretext of seeing the children or discussing their relationship. The woman then accuses the man of rape in order to keep custody of the children.

Case History

I was called to the scene of a push-in robbery where the victim was sexually assaulted with a stick. The victim was a deacon in a local church and was well respected and liked by members of the community. He gave the following account to the police who arrived on the scene. It was about 11:00 A.M. when the deacon, a single man in his 40s, went to the supermarket. When he returned home and put his key in his apartment door, two males pushed him into his apartment and attacked him. They demanded money, but he said that he had none. When they could not find any valuables to take, the suspects became frustrated and forced the deacon to take off his pants. They then shoved a 12-inch round stick up his rectum to make him tell them where the valuables were. The deacon stated that he did not have anything of value in the apartment to take, and the suspects left him with the stick wedged in his anus. The victim was transported to the hospital to remove the stick and to be evaluated medically.

There had been a rash of push-in robberies in the neighborhood, but none of them had involved a sexual assault, and none of them had occurred during daylight hours. I arrived on the scene after the victim was removed, and I ordered our Crime Scene Unit to the scene. Before they arrived, however, some significant observations could be made. First, no signs of a struggle were apparent and it did not appear as though the apartment had been searched. Second, the neighbors in the adjoining apartments were home and they did not hear anything unusual. Third, although the deacon was well respected in the neighborhood, he had a number of videotapes with covers depicting homosexual pornography. Fourth, scratch marks on the arm of the couch looked like they had been made by the stick, as residue from the stick could be seen on the spot where the scratches were made.

When we arrived at the hospital, the victim was being treated. We inquired about his medical condition and were informed that the stick was still wedged in his rectum and that x-rays were being taken. The doctor eventually removed the stick but noted that the victim's anus was unusually large. This is a common condition in homosexual men and in those who insert objects into the rectum.

Normally, we would wait to confront the victim with the inconsistencies we had observed, but the nature of the allegation, the stature of the victim, and the time of day combined to make this case more serious than it might otherwise be. It would necessitate a concerted effort by the patrol force to alleviate the fears of the public, and it would require coordination among investigative units handling sex crimes and robberies. We took the victim to a secluded area of the hospital where he could be interviewed in private and confronted him with all of the inconsistencies, but he still remained adamant that he was attacked. We then gave him a deal. We told him that we knew he was lying and that he had pushed the stick up his anus. We even informed him that we were about to get forensic evidence from the couch that would show that he forced the stick up his rectum by sitting on it. We also told him that we would not arrest him if he told us the truth. He then confessed. He told us that he had put the stick up his anus for sexual gratification and that it became wedged there. He could not remove it and he made up the story to cover his actions.

Strategies to Address False Allegations

As outlined in Chapters 6 and 7, the strategies involved in stranger rape cases are significantly different from those that involve known suspects, as in acquaintance and domestic rape cases. Similarly, when dealing with false allegations, the relationship between the alleged victim and the assailant is important. Because the relationships are different, the strategies employed to address the false accusations are also different.

False Stranger Allegations

An in-depth look at the victim is necessary when a false report is suspected, with an eye toward finding a reason why the alleged victim would make up the allegation. Is she in trouble for some recent behavior or is she trying to cover up that behavior by reporting that she was assaulted? Is she suffering from a mental disorder that affects her ability to reason properly? The presence of such factors, in and by themselves, does not mean that the victim is lying. They do, however, support the possibility that she is not telling the truth and supply the motivation that may lie behind her behavior.

Investigations into stranger cases require an in-depth look at the victim, her actions prior to the attack, the circumstances surrounding the attack, and the conditions that led the victim to report the incident to the police. Physical evidence, medical evidence, and circumstantial evidence are looked at closely. In the process of reviewing this evidence, red flags such as the ones mentioned earlier in this chapter will arise in those situations where false reports are made. Further investigation of those red flags will expose the truth and identify those reports that are false.

If the alleged victim refuses to admit her deceit despite proof being presented to her, it may be difficult to change the classification or ignore her persistent position that she is indeed a victim. You may wish to rethink your analysis of the circumstances or you may try one last strategy. As in the previous case history, make a deal with the would-be victim not to prosecute her if she tells you the truth now. Delays will only compound her crime by forcing the commitment of additional resources. If she then comes clean and tells you that she made it up, you have two choices. You can either stick with your deal or not. Of course, the choice is not necessarily yours to make. I have always had a good working relationship with the District Attorney's Office, and if we made a deal they would abide by it. It is generally recommended to honor deals made with alleged victims. Remember, they never intended to have anyone arrested, and they are frequently confused and misguided.

False Acquaintance and Domestic Allegations

The red flags that appear in stranger cases are appropriate for consideration in acquaintance and domestic cases. As indicated earlier, additional motivational red flags should be considered in acquaintance and domestic situations. You can also offer deals to this so-called victim, but you must consider that she was attempting to have an innocent individual arrested. Such an alleged victims is *not* confused and misguided; she is often shrewd and manipulative, and her objective is to have the police put an innocent person in jail.

Before you offer a deal to a prospective acquaintance or domestic rape victim, however, consider the amount of resources you have committed to the investigation and the amount of investigative effort it took to come to the conclusion that the victim is not telling the truth. I rarely made deals in acquaintance and domestic cases; instead, I would exhaust all of the investigative avenues outlined in Chapter 6, including recorded conversations. Recorded conversations are excellent sources of information. They can be telephone conversations, where one of the parties consents to the recording, or they can be meetings where one of the parties consents. In 41 of the 50 states, law enforcement can legally use consent recordings for criminal prosecutions. In suspected false allegation cases, you may decide to have the alleged victim call or meet the alleged assailant to obtain a statement. In these cases, you will generally hear an adamant denial by the male, who will frequently assert that the victim needs psychological help. Another approach that might be considered is to get the consent of the accused male to record a conversation with the alleged victim. This option may be used if the male is aware of the ongoing investigation or if during interrogation you feel that he is innocent and that it would be fruitful.

Conclusions

Investigating false allegations should be taken very seriously. Sex crimes are very serious, and any allegation should be investigated thoroughly. The objective of every investigation is to uncover the truth. If the truth is that the victim is lying to the police, then appropriate action should be taken. If she is not lying, however, the investigator owes it to her and to potential victims to investigate thoroughly and bring her assailant to justice. I have always held one simple rule when considering that allegations are false, "If you can't tell me why she is lying, then she isn't." This simple rule forces investigators to produce evidence in order to convince their superiors that the crime did not happen. If they cannot come up with a reason, then they should consider the allegation as true and investigate it accordingly.

Lineups

11

Under normal circumstances, lineups can be extremely emotional experiences for victims of crime. Those of us in law enforcement have experienced first hand the memory problems that plague the victims of crime. The fear and the shock experienced by a victim of violent crime can overshadow the victim's ability to make a reliable identification of the assailant. Frequently, the victim's memory tends to focus on that fear and shock, creating difficulties when it comes time to give accurate descriptions and to make identifications.

We have all heard of a gunpoint robbery victim who, when asked to describe his attacker, stated that he could not do so. All he could describe was the big gun that the perpetrator had pointed in his face. The victim blocked out every other aspect of the crime because he focused on the gun in his face and nothing else. He feared for his life and nothing else mattered at the time. He did not take the time to inventory the assailant's features or his clothing; instead, he concentrated all of his efforts on his survival and nothing else mattered.

People in these situations are victims; they are not trained investigators or police officers who, despite the dangers confronting us on a daily basis, are expected to overcome our fears and make detailed observations and identifications. Our experiences in these types of situations have generally hardened us to the shock factor. We are therefore able to provide the information needed and perform our duties despite the dangerous circumstances we find ourselves in.

Investigators should also consider that many victims are not what one would call streetwise. If they were, they would probably be able to avoid the situations in which they found themselves. Instead, they are generally nice people who are also unaware of the way criminals operate. They are not skeptical of others, and they do not prepare themselves for situations that may place them in jeopardy.

As a young kid growing up in the Washington Heights section of Manhattan, I was always keenly aware of my surroundings and the dangers that existed in certain areas. I did not go to certain areas, and I was always cautious when I was alone and in secluded neighborhoods. I never placed my property where it could be stolen, and I protected myself by always being aware and searching for escape routes in case I needed them. Many victims, however, do not come from that sort of background. They are not prepared to be victims of crime. They are not familiar with the way criminals operate and have not equipped themselves with the skills necessary to counteract the criminal element. Many have never considered what to do in the event of an attack and, if attacked, they are not ready to react in any particular way. Instead, they play it by ear and do what they are told in the hopes that they can avoid injury or even death.

Experience has taught most investigators how to deal with the criminal element of society. Some come equipped with an instinctive knowledge developed as young men and women growing up in certain areas of society. Their survival instincts force them to be aware of and familiar with their surroundings every day. Most, however, have gained such an understanding by dealing with the criminal element on a daily basis in their work. Consequently, investigators do not fear criminals. They know them for what they are — cowards who prey on the weak and can be very weak minded. Just as they can frequently spot members of the police in a crowd, we can spot them. Their demeanor is different and their awareness is far sharper than that of a normal person. It appears as though their heads are on swivels as they continually survey their surroundings to see if they are being watched. Continued observations will also reveal that they make many attempts before attacking a particular victim. An awareness of common criminal characteristics possessed by most suspects soon becomes an integral part of the investigator's knowledge base.

Most stranger rape victims, on the other hand, have not had the experiences that many investigators have had. They are not able to recognize danger as quickly and are frequently unable to thwart attacks before they occur. Investigators cannot expect victims to react the way that they would. On several occasions, I have heard a victim explain the circumstances leading to her attack and wondered why she did not react differently. Judgments of this nature, however, are unfair and should never be expressed to the victim. The victim could not be expected to deal with the criminal element in the same manner in which an investigator would. Their experiences are different and most have never prepared themselves for an attack by a rapist. They simply do not know how to react. They find themselves in a situation where their lives are threatened and all of their instincts are focused on survival.

Rape victims who are attacked by strangers frequently fall into this last category. Studies have shown that women who have been raped by strangers consistently describe the situation in which they found themselves as life threatening. Most have felt as though they would not survive, that they were going to die as a result of the attack. They acquiesce to the demands of their assailants in the hope that, if by submitting, they will be allowed to live.

Helping the Victim to Remember

The life and death struggle that is played out during stranger rape situations wreaks havoc on the identification process. Some victims find that they cannot make any kind of identification at all, while others can still make identifications even though it is difficult for them. I have found that the sex crime victim who can best make an identification of her assailant is one who is angry. She does not fall into the trap of blaming herself (see Chapter 5). She knows that the attack was not her fault, and she focuses on striking back at her attacker. During the attack, she takes careful inventory of the rapist's physical features and remembers every detail about his demeanor, his expressions, and the terminology he used. When it comes time to view a lineup, she has no trouble identifying the suspect. She spots him at once and is confident of her identification.

Those victims who feel guilty and blame themselves for the attack, however, block out everything else except their efforts to survive. They are sometimes terrible witnesses who can become extremely emotionally distraught when trying to remember the details of the attack. The thought of facing their attackers can be unbearable for some.

What can investigators do to help them remember? First, they need to help the victims through their ordeal. The victims need to understand that they are not to blame for what happened. It may be necessary for investigators to speak with relatives or friends of the victim to be sure that they do not imply that the victim was in any way at fault for what occurred. Once the victim has been convinced that she is not to blame, the investigator's focus should shift toward trying to turn the victim into a fighter. Victims who become angry with their attackers will not block out aspects of the attack. Investigators should try to make each element of the attack another reason why the victim should be angry and should try to motivate her to strike back at the attacker. She could not strike back during the attack, but she has the perfect opportunity to do so now. The best way to do this, of course, is to help investigators identify the suspect. By doing so, she can ensure that he is behind bars for a long time, and will not be able to strike at another innocent victim.

You may find that some victims no longer care about what happened to them. Some have come to accept such an attack as an unfortunate incident in their lives, and all they wish to do is to move on. They do not want to be reminded of the attack or the attacker. In those situations, investigators can try to explain the dangers of letting the suspect get away with the rape, and they can point out that the suspect will surely attack again and that the trauma endured by the victim will be experienced by others unless the suspect is arrested and convicted.

Case History

A young woman and her girlfriend who were visiting New York from England decided to go to a crowded Manhattan bar near where they were staying. They talked with several people at the bar, and one of the men in the crowd asked one of the women to go outside to get some fresh air. When they got outside, he pushed her into an alley and raped her. She then went back inside, retrieved her friend, and told her what happened. The attacker had fled the scene, but several of his friends were still at the bar. The two women went to the hospital, and we were called. When we arrived at the hospital, the victim reported the facts to us, but the victim insisted that she did not want to pursue any prosecution of her attacker. She was clearly blaming herself for going to the bar and then going outside with someone she did not know. She told us that she was going back to England in a week and did not want to identify her attacker. We eventually convinced her that she was not to blame and that the person who did this to her was surely going to attack another innocent woman. At that point, she agreed to help us. We went to the bar with the victim's friend and were able to identify the people who were with the suspect. He was arrested the next day, and the victim identified him without any problem. He is now serving time in state prison for rape.

Prepare the Victim to View the Lineup

Crime victims do not know what to expect when viewing a lineup. Some feel that the police have already captured the attacker and that he is definitely in the room. They feel compelled to identify the one who they think most closely resembles the attacker. Others will say that they do not think they can identify their attackers even if they do see them; yet, frequently when one of these women sees her attacker in a lineup, she is able to make a positive identification without reservation.

To prepare the victim, let her know what to expect. Let her know that you understand that this is extremely difficult for her, but that you will guide her through every step. Explain that five or six individuals will be in the lineup room. Each individual will be holding a numbered card. She will be behind a one-way mirror and the people in the lineup cannot see her. You and your partner will be with her in the observation room. In some cases, the suspect's attorney may also be present in the room during the lineup. If the attorney is present, let the victim know that he cannot interfere and that he is only there as an observer. Inform her that she will have as much time as she needs to look at the people in the lineup. If she needs them to come closer to the mirror, this can be arranged. If she needs them to speak certain words, that can also be arranged. In order for a lineup to be fair, you must inform the victim that the assailant may not even be in the lineup. Tell the victim that when she views the lineup you will ask her if she recognizes anyone. Do not ask the victim if the attacker is number three or number four, for example. Let her volunteer if she recognizes anyone.

Expect the Unusual

Investigators should be prepared for the emotional state that confronting her assailant might trigger in the victim. Let her know that she cannot be harmed and that you will ensure that she is safe.

Case History

A young Hispanic teenager was the victim of a vicious rapist. After she had walked home during the early evening hours, she entered her apartment building and was confronted by her attacker as she entered the elevator. He produced a knife and forced her to the top floor. He then forced her to go up the stairwell to the roof. Once on the roof, he appeared to become irrational. He started calling her names like bitch and whore. As he held the knife to her throat, he told her he was going to fuck her and if he didn't like it he was going to throw her off the roof. He then compelled her to perform oral sex on him, followed by anal and vaginal sex. When he was done, he threw her clothes off the roof and stated, "I should kill you now." The victim remained motionless on the roof landing, and the suspect told her not to move. He then fled the scene.

During the investigation, we came up with a suspect who had been seen in the area by several people. He did not live there but was known by several of those who identified him. His criminal record indicated past arrests for sexual misconduct, but none for rape. We interrogated him, and although he was vague and contradictory about why he was in the neighborhood on the night of the attack, we were unable to come up with any ties to the victim. We obtained his DNA, but at that time DNA tests took about 2 months to conduct.

We knew that the victim was emotionally distraught, but, if we had the correct suspect, we could not let a vicious rapist like him go free for 2 months. That left us with one alternative. We would conduct a lineup with the victim, who was emotionally fragile from her harrowing experience. We prepared her as best we could and brought her into the viewing room. When she took a close look at all of the men she began to cry. When she was asked if she recognized anyone, she said she did not and then collapsed in our arms. We walked her back to an interview room, where she continued to cry for about 15 minutes. We knew that something was going on, and as we tried to console her she admitted that she had recognized one of the suspects. When she saw him, she became so emotionally distraught that she could not tell anyone. She remembered the attack in vivid detail. She could not get his face out of her mind. She remembered the fear she felt when she thought she was going to die, and she could not bring herself to confront him when she saw his face in the lineup. Had it not been for the extra time we took to console her and to inquire about what triggered her reaction, we would have been forced to set a vicious rapist free until we were able to identify him through his DNA. Luckily, the identification held, mostly because she was a very credible witness. Her reaction to seeing her assailant is not rare. It gave credence to her identification of him and was proof of what he had done to her emotionally. The suspect was held on a high bail, and when his DNA matched his fate was sealed. He is currently serving a 25-year sentence in state prison.

Conclusion

No set reaction can be expected of victims. Investigators may never know what to expect, but they can count on victims reacting in different ways, as each is a unique individual. Investigators should be cognizant of the emotional trauma that may be triggered when victims confront their attackers for the first time. The best that investigators can do is guide victims through the process and give them all of the support they need. Unlike victims of other crimes, a sex crime victim is burdened by a whole host of disturbing psychological and social baggage, including her own sexual mores and the impact that the attack has had on her. She is also forced to deal with the larger social issues surrounding her attack. Is she going to be blamed by some for being in the wrong place at the wrong time? Did she not see it coming? Could she not have done something to prevent it? Investigators should give victim as much support as possible while guiding her through the investigative process. They should assure the victim that none of the blame lies with her and encourage her to become angry with her assailant. He is the one at fault, and he is the one who should be suffering, not the victim.

Index

A

Acquaintance rape
  case study, 15–17
  deception by victims, 105–106, *See also*
      Deception; False allegations
  delayed reporting, 71
  epidemiological studies, 93
  lack of physical evidence, 107
  prior consensual sexual activity and, 84
  rape on campus, 111–114
  reasons for false allegations, 200–201
  reporting delays, 98
  statistics, 92
  substance use or misuse, 2–6, 96–102, *See*
      also Drug-induced rape
  terminology, 103–104
  unique investigative aspects, 104
  victim as sole witness, 106–107
  victim credibility, 107–111
  victim's prior actions, 106–107
Activists, 198
Age of consent, 17–18
Alcohol-associated rape, 96–98, 101–102,
      See also Drug-induced rape
  case history, 2–5
Anchor points, 192, 193
Anger excitation rapists, 189–190
Anger retaliation rapists, 189
Arrest policies, domestic rape cases, 118–119
Automated fingerprint identification system
      (AFIS), 47

B

Birthmarks, 80
Blackouts, 96
Blaming victims, 127, 129–130
  self-blaming, 69–70, 91–93, 127
Blood, 51–52, *See also* DNA evidence
  rape kit, 51
  sample collection, 55
Buccal swabs, 55–57

Burden of proof, 90–91, 92
Burglary, 128, 190

C

Campus rape, 111–114
Canvassing, 137–139, 188–189
Captive victims, 95
Chat rooms, 102–103
Child victims, 11–12
  delayed reporting, 71
Circumcision, 80
Clothing evidence, 39, 58
CODIS, 170
Community impacts of rape reports, 7,
      123–124, 198
Commuter canvasses, 139
Compassion for victim, 26–27
Computer-generated model, 154
Computer systems, 144
COMSTAT, 192
Condoms, 40, 43, 48
Consent, 17–18
Coordination conference, 160
Coping strategies, 65
Corroboration, 9–11, 199, *See also* Crime
    scene
  lack of, 10–11, 90
  unique aspects of rape investigation,
    24–25
  victim as sole witness, 90, 106–107
Counseling, 66–67
Court order, for blood collection, 55
Courtroom testimony, preparing victim for,
    86
Credibility of victim, 9–10, 90, 107
  need for immediate arrest, 108
  past criminal behavior and, 84
  pursuing DNA indictment and, 172
  strategies for addressing problems,
    108–111
    e-mail and instant messages, 111
    recorded conversations, 108–111

215